JAMES R. JACKSON

© Jacqueline Jackson
Published by Bay Books 1991
National Library of Australia
Card number and ISBN 1-86378-024-6
Printed in Singapore by Toppan Printing Co

JAMES R. JACKSON

Art was his life...

Jacqueline Jackson

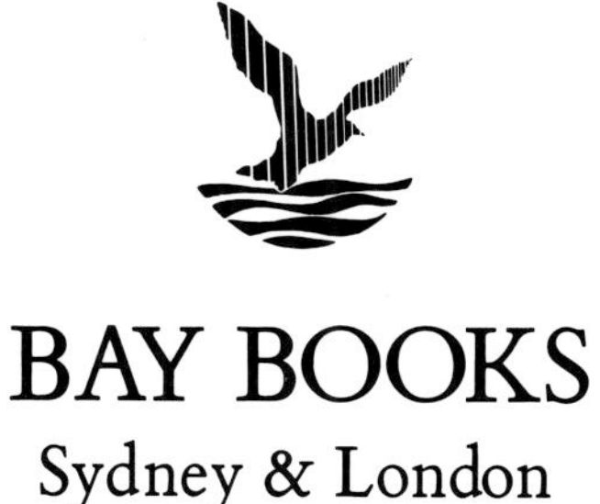

BAY BOOKS

Sydney & London

Contents

Foreword

My research into the life and work of my artist father, James R. Jackson, started some fifteen years after he died, when I decided it was time to record my memories of him and those of the many people who still remembered him. His friends and contacts were most encouraging and said, 'Why don't you write a book about him? It's about time someone did and you're the best person to do it as you know all about him.' Well, I didn't know 'all about him'. He was aged fifty when I was just a toddler and there was this long half-century gap stretching back into the 1880s. There were few records but many paintings.

His first known interview was in 1917, when he was an established artist, and until his latter years he rarely admitted his age. As the recorded year of his birth varied (it was frequently given as 1886 and not 1882) and also the date of his arrival in Australia, tracing his family records was difficult. Fortunately, in his mid-eighties, he had written down memories of his childhood, his early student life in Sydney and recollections of his art training in London and Paris. He also made a tape recording in which he recalled some incidents of his early life and discussed the painting of some of his works. However, as these records were done in his old age, his memories sometimes reflected a time warp. His recollections, combined with months of research, my memories of him and what he told me, form the basis of this book.

This was a long undertaking, which involved interviewing his friends and relatives, reading old newspapers, verifying dates and memories, locating old art catalogues, researching transport and local history and tracing family and church records. Combined with this was the task of locating his pictures, then viewing and dating them before integrating them into the larger picture of his life.

My correspondence has been worldwide and the response from all people, institutions, libraries and art galleries has been most helpful in locating old records and tracing his known major works. I have used newspaper critiques and forewords in his catalogues to describe my father's earlier works.

I would like to thank the following people and institutions for all their help and encouragement. The staff and librarians of all the regional, state and national galleries and libraries. In particular, I wish to thank the National Gallery of Australia, in Canberra, and the state galleries of New South Wales, Victoria, Queensland and South Australia. I am indebted to the National Library of Australia and to the Royal Art Society for their encouragement and access to their records.

I am most grateful for all the assistance given to me by the directors of the following auction houses: Australian Art, Christies, Joels, Lawsons and Sothebys.

All private gallery directors have been most helpful but I would especially like to thank Trevor Bussell, Mike Connell and Tom Silver for their generous support, time and advice.

I give my loving thanks to my husband, Douglas Jamieson, for all his help, including transport throughout the eastern states to view James's paintings; also to my family for explaining some of the mysteries of the computer.

To my encouraging friends, and to all private art lovers, I give my thanks. I hope that you enjoy *James R. Jackson*, as I have had much pleasure in writing it.

Note: Although in his early years my father was known as 'James', from the early 1920s he was popularly known as 'Jimmy' and this is reflected in the text.

CHAPTER 1
Family and Youth

My father, artist James Ranalph Jackson, was born in New Zealand on 3 July 1882. His parents, George and Mary Jackson, had settled in the North Island after they arrived from England in 1874. Their sea voyage via the Cape of Good Hope and Melbourne was rough and tragic — both their young children died on board ship and were buried at sea within days of each other.

George was a surveyor but his father and four uncles were all silversmiths who, as members of the Goldsmiths Company, held the Freedom of the City of London. They were descended from a long line of Jackson craftsmen — including Samuel, Walter, Joseph, George and James — who were all renowned silversmiths or watchcase makers of the eighteenth and nineteenth centuries.

George and Mary had nine more children and settled at Bunnythorpe, near Palmerston. James, who was born in the middle of this large and happy family, remembered that the children helped with family duties from a young age and that outings were few. When outings did occur, so much time was taken to pack baskets, organise the young ones and the horse carriage, that there was little of the day left to enjoy.

In February 1890 Mary delivered her eleventh child but died following his birth. She was the first person buried in the Bunnythorpe Cemetery. George was devastated — he was in a new land half a world away from relatives, a widower with a large young family including a newborn baby. He managed for a few months with the help of the older children and friends, but then decided to leave New Zealand and to take his family to Sydney.

So it was, at the age of nearly eight, that James first saw and fell in love with Sydney Harbour. The beauty of the undeveloped headlands of Port Jackson and the city's busy waterfront activities, involving both steam and sailing ships, had a great impact on the young boy. In this period, and well into the twentieth century, sail was still used by many of the cargo carriers of wool, wheat and timber.

The family lived in a little street, just off Bourke Street, in Darlinghurst. This was possibly narrow Berwick Lane, which still retains some old stone terrace houses. George found it a struggle to keep his large family together but was greatly helped by the older girls. The Depression of the 1890s and the bank crisis of 1893 affected his income and added to his difficulties.

James recalled that they and everyone in the little street were very poor. His schoolfriends were too thin and frequently had nothing to eat as there was little employment. When the father of a family did get a job, there was great joy in the street. Each household contributed some food or a farthing, so that the man could buy some meat and have a decent meal to give him the strength to work properly. Employment was usually shovel work, shifting sand from the sandhills at Moore Park. During the summer the children went barefoot but endured the hot pavements as they ran down the hill to swim in Figtree Baths in Woolloomooloo Bay.

Fortunately, the family was befriended and helped by the local Baptist minister, the Reverend W. R. Hiddleston, who was based at the impressive tabernacle in nearby Burton Street. He had a great influence on the children, especially on James, whom he looked after for several years from 1896.

James's inherited artistic inclination developed early and he was always drawing with pencils or coloured chalks on any surface he could find. He recalled drawing a lamp post for a small drawing competition at school: 'It was one of the old-fashioned hexagon-shaped with crossbars, and the lamplighter came around, and he pulled on the light with a hook and turned on the light at about 5.20 p.m. and they were rather graceful in shape. It was the first study I made and I found it very difficult to draw the perspective of a hexagon-shaped lantern from underneath. However, I must have succeeded somewhat in making it look like a lamp post.'

He only had a basic education, which enabled him to read widely all his life but promoted little interest in mathematics or bookkeeping. Leaving school at an early age, he was very fortunate to be employed by and later apprenticed to a decorating firm based in the city. This firm painted houses, did interior decorations and also designed and painted stained glass for the then very popular leadlight coloured glass used in windows and doors.

James's early jobs were cleaning up, then house painting. As he was agile on ladders, he started with gutters then graduated to the walls and later to interior wall decoration. He recalled getting into strife with his boss and nearly losing his job because of his fondness for drawing pictures, usually of sailing ships, on the house walls before he repainted them. Before wallpaper became popular, he was employed decorating wall borders by hand-painting; he recalls being particularly pleased with his work in one old building in Macquarie Street. After several years he was transferred to the stained glass section, where he learnt about design and how to paint lettering and pictures for the leadlight glass. Here he experimented with pigments and developed his drawing, colour sense and fine craftsmanship.

Early in 1896 his father George, who never remarried, returned to England to settle his father's estate and James, who was under fourteen and employed by the decorating firm, was left in the guardianship of their friend the Reverend Hiddleston. He lived with the Reverend, who transferred from Darlinghurst to the North Sydney parish, near the School of Arts in Mount Street, which was used as a church. James described the Reverend and his family as 'very strict'.

Before he was sixteen, James was encouraged by his boss to show some of his drawings to artist Frank Mahony, who was also a tutor at the Royal Art Society School. James remembered that it took him a few days to get enough courage to see Mahony. 'I selected some of my best drawings and went up to see Mahony. He was a big man who looked me over, then saw my drawings and said that I could start as a student in the Antique class.' In those days the Antique class was the drawing school, which met on Monday and Friday nights, where the students learnt by drawing from plaster casts and still life.

Frank Mahony had a great influence on his early training in drawing. James found the night classes very tiring after work and it was always an effort to arrive on time, but he worked hard. He would take his drawings of fruit, plaster casts and other objects home and show them to the Reverend and his family.

After nine months he graduated to the 'Life Drawing from the Human Figure' classes, which met four nights a week and cost a guinea per quarter. However, he thought that the Reverend would not approve of him drawing nude figures as they were called in the life classes, so he hid these drawings. One day the Reverend said, 'James my boy, is it true that you draw naked women?' James felt very

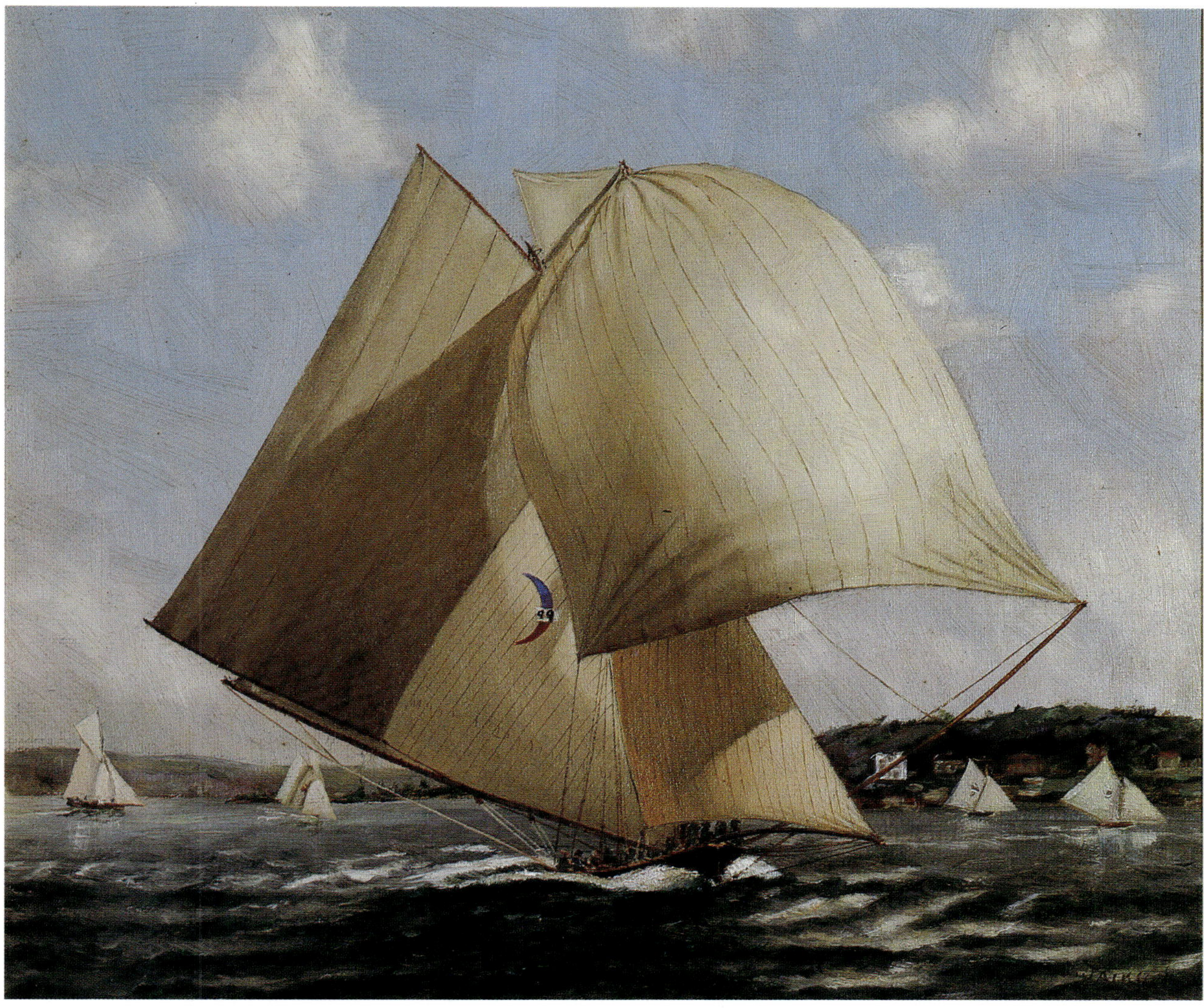

1 **JAMES'S CREWING BOAT** 1901 23 x 30 cm
Private Collection

embarrassed and, although he thought he understood what was asked, he had never heard the expression 'naked women' — in the class the models were always referred to as nudes — and so said 'No'. These nudes created major problems with his art training, which was interrupted until he was old enough to move from the Reverend's care.

During his late teens and early twenties he continued only intermittently with his art training, and briefly attended the J. S. Watkins Art School. He became involved with sailing and crewed for Saturday sailing races of the flying 18-footers. When not racing, he would explore Sydney Harbour in his small sailing dinghy which he kept at one of the numerous boatsheds which dotted the foreshore. He became very fond of Middle Harbour and of fishing. This love of sail and water, started in childhood, continued throughout his life and was reflected in his numerous pictures of sailing boats and of Sydney Harbour.

Two of his earliest known paintings, dated 1901, have been located. Both paintings are of 18-footers; one is of the boat he crewed in, with number '99' on the big blue and red crescent-shaped emblem on its main. He kept a large photo of '99' in full sail and gave the paintings to one of his crewing mates, whose family has kept them ever since. His signature was simply 'J. Jackson' and the style unlike his later work. The pictures are meticulous in detail drawing and depict the boat in full sail on a green-blue harbour.

James was always talking about his crewing exploits, the excitement, and how the 18-footers owned the harbour. He told of the crew overcrowding — up to eighteen lads on top of each other — to hold her up when in full sail, and of being ordered overboard and left to swim in the middle of the harbour when the boat had to be lightened on the homeward run with a favourable wind.

The drawing of his boats, whether they be rowing, sail or steam, was always accurate. He later said, 'It is a difficult painting exercise to portray boat reflections and boats which look as though they are really floating'. In his early professional period, he combined his delight in figure subjects and boats by painting many poetic compositions of his models in rowing boats. He especially loved painting two-masted ketches, yawls and schooners which had just returned and were drying their sails. His love of the old trading ships was reflected by his inclusion of them with reefed sails or under way in many of his early pictures of Newcastle and Sydney Harbour. Later he recorded their decaying hulks where they rested in Berry's Bay, Sydney, until the 1930s.

In his early twenties, having finished his six-year apprenticeship with the decorating firm, he decided to make art his career and to train in regular art classes. He hoped to go overseas to study, as had so many aspiring Australian artists, but this required years of saving to finance. James estimated that he would be able to leave work and afford his desired European tuition by his late twenties. He worked during the day designing and painting stained glass, attended art classes four nights a week, painted with the students on Saturdays, and on Sundays painted and drew around the harbour. His determination to achieve in art meant that he had to sacrifice his love of regular crewing with the 18-footers, but he still maintained an active interest in sailing.

During this period his style in oils was developing and he liked the new, fresh, outdoor approach which Tom Roberts, whom he knew, and others had introduced. His very early works of this student period reflect impressionistic qualities. They are thickly painted with masses of colour and experimental lighting effects. The red-browns frequently used by Arthur Streeton are present, but otherwise there is little similarity. James's early Middle Harbour scenes, painted around 1904, have minimal detail in the foreground, the sky is not emphasised by cloud patterns and shows little smog haze. Interest is in the middle distance on wooded sandstone headlands with few houses, or in the clarity of blue harbour water lapping on clean beach sand. This purity and vibrancy of colour is no doubt an accurate recording of the beauty of Port Jackson before pollution muddied it.

During this year, two of the most influential people on James's early life and career left Sydney. Artist, friend and tutor Frank Mahony went to England and the Reverend, who had continued to keep an eye on James, was transferred interstate. When Mahony was saying goodbye, he shook hands and said, 'Jackson, you stick to it, old man, stick to it'. James considered this to be a great compliment as Mahony 'was a most sincere man'.

In the period 1902–07 there was a re-amalgamation of the Royal Art Society with the Society of Artists. Their records show that in August 1905 James R. Jackson won their scholarship and prizes. Following this, his attendance at their annual dinner was noted in the Sydney press on 28 August.

Selection of the winning student was by ballot and James won a six-month full-time art scholarship, as well as first prize in drawing from life and painting from life. This prize money added to his savings enabled him to fulfil his ambition of full-time art study and to go overseas the following year — much earlier than he had hoped.

CHAPTER 2

Student Days in London and Paris

*B*y early 1906 James's style had changed and developed. His signature was now 'James R. Jackson' and his growing maturity and confidence as an artist became evident in his harbour pictures. Foreground detail of gum trees or close sailing boats was introduced, but as yet there was little human activity. His fascination for figures appeared later.

He painted strongly with great tonal contrasts using thick colour masses in a varied palette. Water reflections are broken by streaks of movement and light and his land masses show patterns of shadows from clouds, which were used to balance his compositions. His subjects were pleasing, painted in the fullness of the day and frequently at the Spit, Middle Harbour, which he reached by the newly installed extension of the North Shore electric tram service, or from the city by ferry to the pleasure grounds at Pearl Bay.

In early autumn of that year he tried to enrol in Bernard Hall's art classes in Melbourne but was unable to do so. Although encouraged to stay by Frederick McCubbin, who was the teacher of drawing at the National Gallery School, Melbourne, James decided to fulfil his ambition of having European tuition and continuing his training in London. 'I visited my father and family who had returned to New Zealand, and borrowed a few quid. From Wellington I obtained a cheap passage to England for 15 pounds on a very old tramp sailing ship called the *Matilda*. The tramp's journey was via Cape Horn, then various ports where cargo was collected or exchanged before it reached London.'

Although used to sailing and the excitement of the 18-footers, he described the trip around the Horn by sail as 'terrifying'. It was early winter and he vividly described the gales, the freezing conditions with icy decks and rigging, the enormous seas and having to stay below decks for several days. 'It was very lonely, especially when we did not sight land for twenty days at one time. Off the coast of Brazil, the ship was becalmed, then without warning a raging storm, described by the Skipper as a Chinese typhoon, nearly swamped the ship.' Fortunately the veteran sailing ship eventually reached London and within several days James had presented his work and been accepted as a student at the New English Art School for the pre-Christmas term. His tutor was Sir Frank Brangwyn.

Brangwyn developed James's composition sense, taught him how to use greys and tried to restrain his vibrant use of colour. He encouraged him to paint thickly, using only first-class materials and brushes. Brangwyn would comment on and correct the students' works late in the day. If he added touches, the works were not allowed to be taken home (this may explain why James's works of this period are difficult to locate).

Here James learnt canvas preparation and the correct mixing and application of paint to minimise later cracking, flaking or deterioration. He revised his basic knowledge of paint pigment chemistry and also learnt about the durability of colours, their preparation and the effects of atmosphere, dust and light on artworks. This good foundation and training in material preparation, pigment use and application is evident in all of his earlier works, which still look fresh and have minimal deterioration after many decades.

James stayed with relatives while he was in London. He toured the city but apparently did not visit the wintry countryside. Although he enjoyed the art school and his visits to Frank Mahony, James did

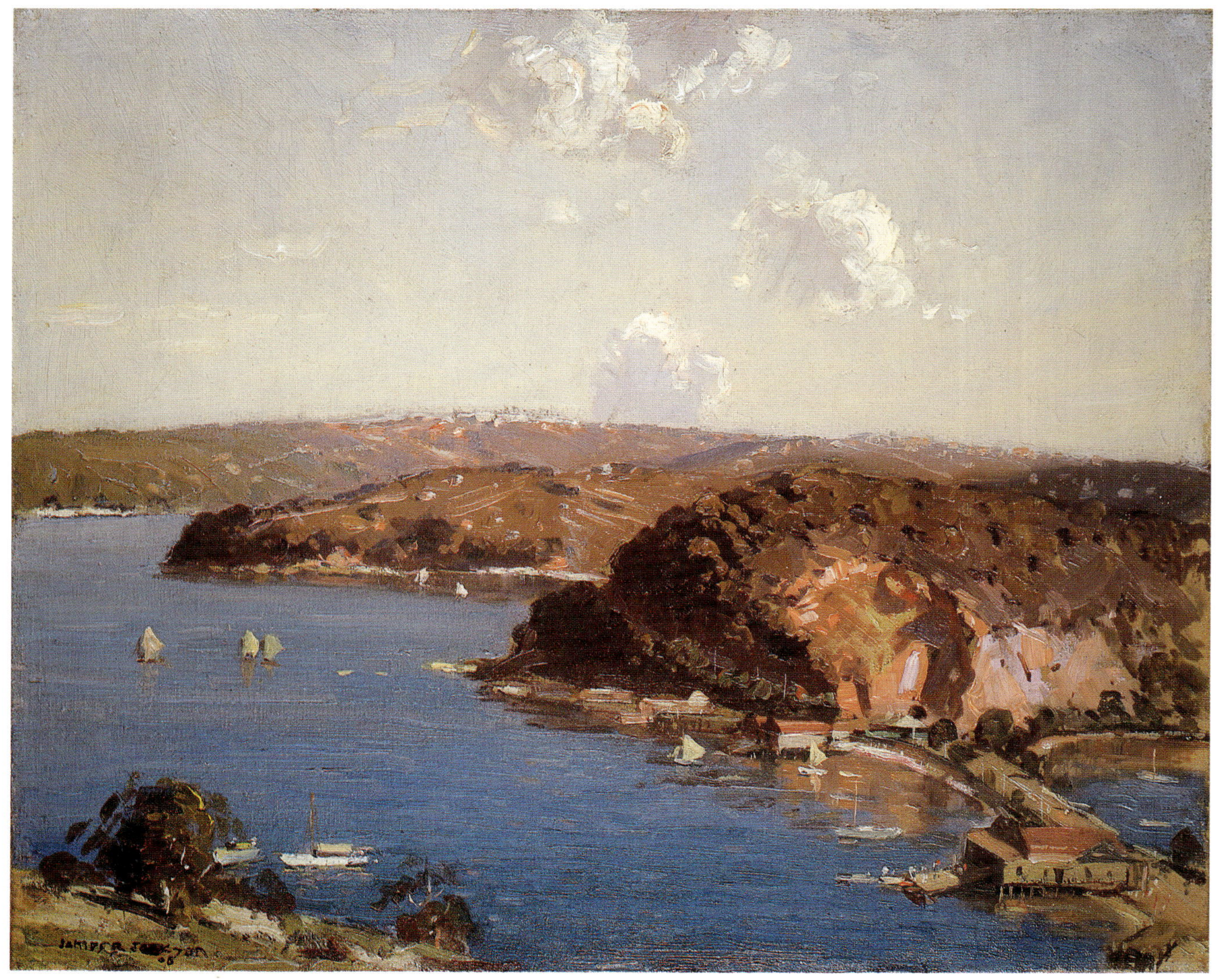

2　**THE SPIT, MIDDLE HARBOUR N.S.W.**　1905 39.5 x 49.5 cm
Private Collection

not like the restrictive English atmosphere, the winter with its snow and slippery streets, or the fogs and poor lighting. The only record of his paintings of this period is one of a cold, grey Thames River with ships against a background of smoggy London.

After six months he enrolled at Colarossi's Art Academy in Paris. He arrived early in the spring and loved it. Here he was free from all his previous constraints and, as living was cheaper, he was able to enjoy this heaven for about a year. He described his introduction to the bohemian lifestyle, which he continued to enjoy for many years, as 'one of the highlights of my life'. He stayed in a Latin Quarter hotel until he was able to rent an atelier and joined the classes at Colarossi's. Here, and at the cafes frequented by art students, he met and was befriended by students of many nationalities.

His cheap atelier was on the fifth floor of an old building in the Rue de la Grande Chaumier, not far from Colarossi's. It was empty of furniture and from its large, high window there was a splendid view of the sky, interrupted by chimney pots of all shapes and sizes. James recorded many incidents in Paris, including the buying and moving of his furniture. 'As was the custom, I bought it for a ''shilling a piece'' from a student who was leaving to return home. It was best to wait for an American student to depart as they usually possessed better furniture. I was very lucky, as such a student was leaving and his furniture included a lovely French bath. I was especially proud of this bath, which hung on a hook on the wall when not in use. I moved my furniture, pictures, and belongings with the help of a rented go-cart and ten students who all wanted to carry the bath as it made plenty of noise as a drum beat for the furniture procession. They suddenly became very tired and thirsty every time they passed a cafe, where I was required to replenish their energy. However, drinks were cheap in the Quarter and after celebrating the safe arrival of the furnishings up five flights of stairs, we returned to our art classes.'

His atelier contents were similar to many others, with a small stove in a corner near his bed, boxes, and a table and chairs. Art materials and canvases were stacked against the walls, which were decorated by his pictures and the French bath. There was enough space for his easel and to pose a model. Soon after he arrived he was initiated by the other students. 'As many students as wanted to, marched two squares of the Latin Quarter, holding a flag which consisted of a shirt with much paint on it. During the march they stopped at four or five cafes for drinks which I paid for. However the cafe owner, who was used to this, would find out how much the student could afford and, if poor, let you off lightly.'

At Colarossi's James absorbed impressionism from his tutors, and his love of light, movement and colour contrasts was encouraged. At exhibitions he saw the impressionistic style of Degas and Manet and was very interested in their wonderful handling of light. He became friendly with E. Phillips Fox, who had recently settled in Paris and whose boating and figure scenes also had great impact on James's representation of water subjects. By using colourful light contrasts, he developed his ability to paint water reflections — many of the early pictures depict simply a boat or a building and its reflections.

His principal tutors were Renard and Gorgia. His old professor taught students from all over the world in at least five languages, aided by his hands and the tone of his voice. James worked hard at his art at Colarossi's and in his atelier, where he painted a variety of models, who were in plentiful

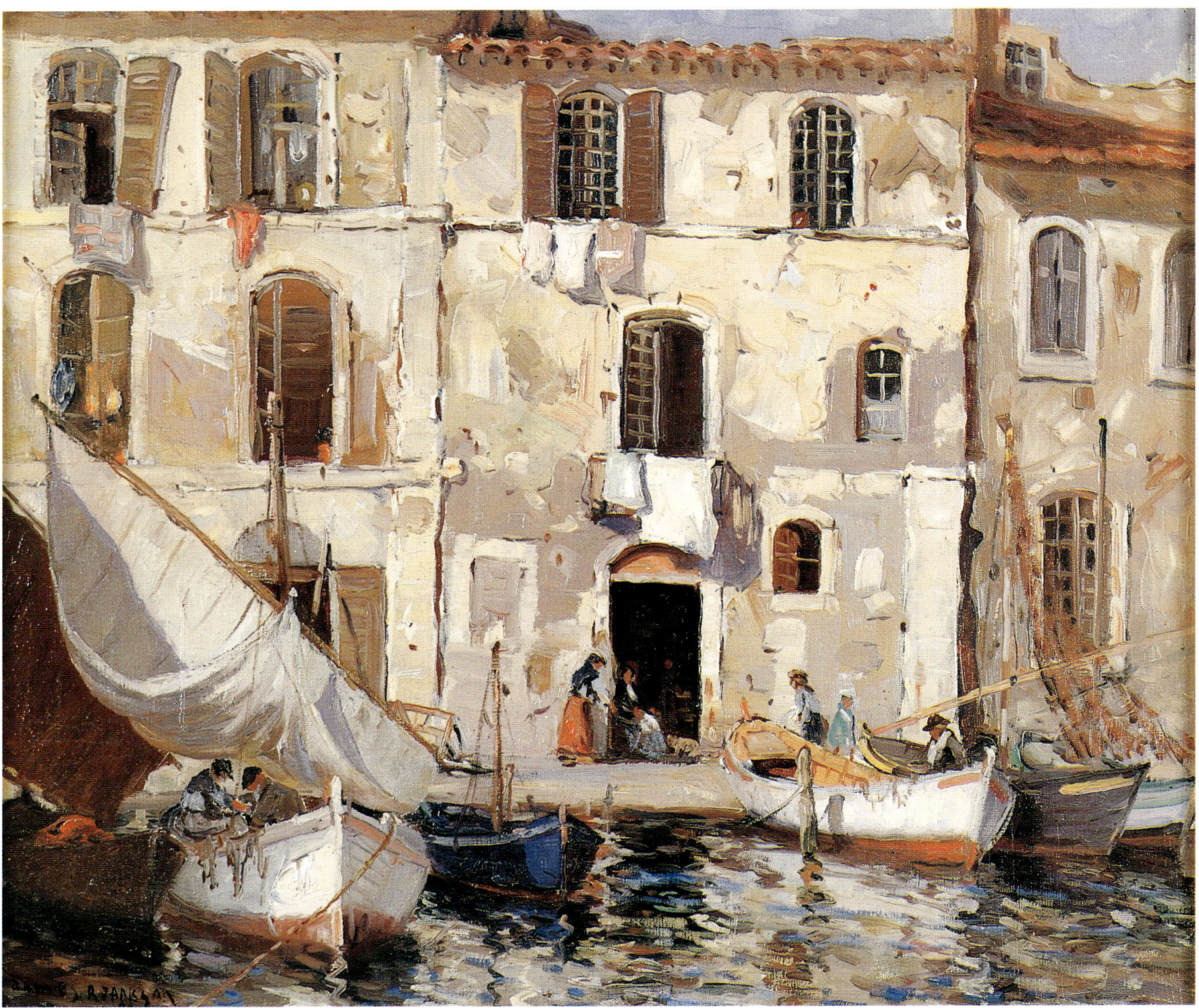

3   **FISHING BOATS, VENICE** 1907 44.5 x 54.5 cm
Private Collection

supply, cheap to employ and used to posing. He already knew several other 'kangaroo' artists and students living in Paris, including Max Meldrum and Frances Payne. With these and the many other friends he made, he experienced a wonderful social life.

One of his favourite stories was of 'a rich American student' whose father was in shipping. 'The boy, who could not draw, had persuaded his father to let him go to Paris to learn to paint ships — but ships were the last thing this boy was thinking of. One day his father notified that he was visiting the following morning to see his son's art work, of which there was none. As I knew all about ships, I was selected to fill the void, so I sat up all night, drawing and painting boats for him. The father was so pleased with his son's progress that he increased his allowance and I dined very well for several months after that.'

James perfected his art of plein-air painting in and around Paris and with other students painted at Fontainebleau, which he described as 'wonderful'. In the long summer holidays of 1907, he toured and recorded many of the beauties of Belgium, France, Spain and northern Italy across to Trieste. In the early winter vacation he returned to Martigues, where many artists worked, as it was warmer and the light for painting brighter. James described this and his meeting with artist Augustus John: 'The light is very brilliant and beautiful. I was working on the banks at Martigues, and there were about forty painters there, all frizzling cold, and a fellow came along well rugged up, who propped at my work and said, ''Oh, that's going well, keep going''. I had no idea who it was until he was introduced to

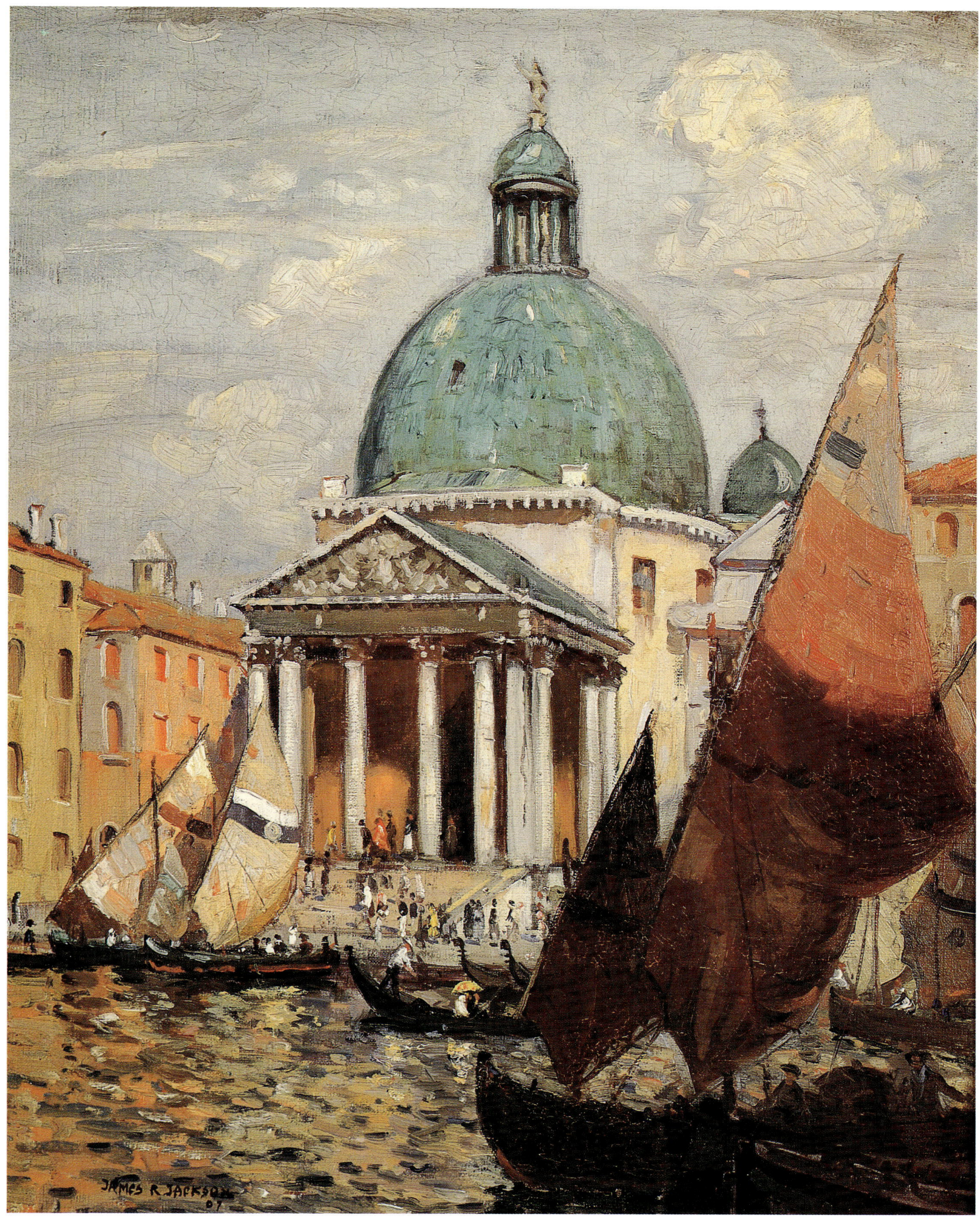

4   S. SIMEONE PICCOLO, VENICE 1907 60 x 49 cm
Private Collection

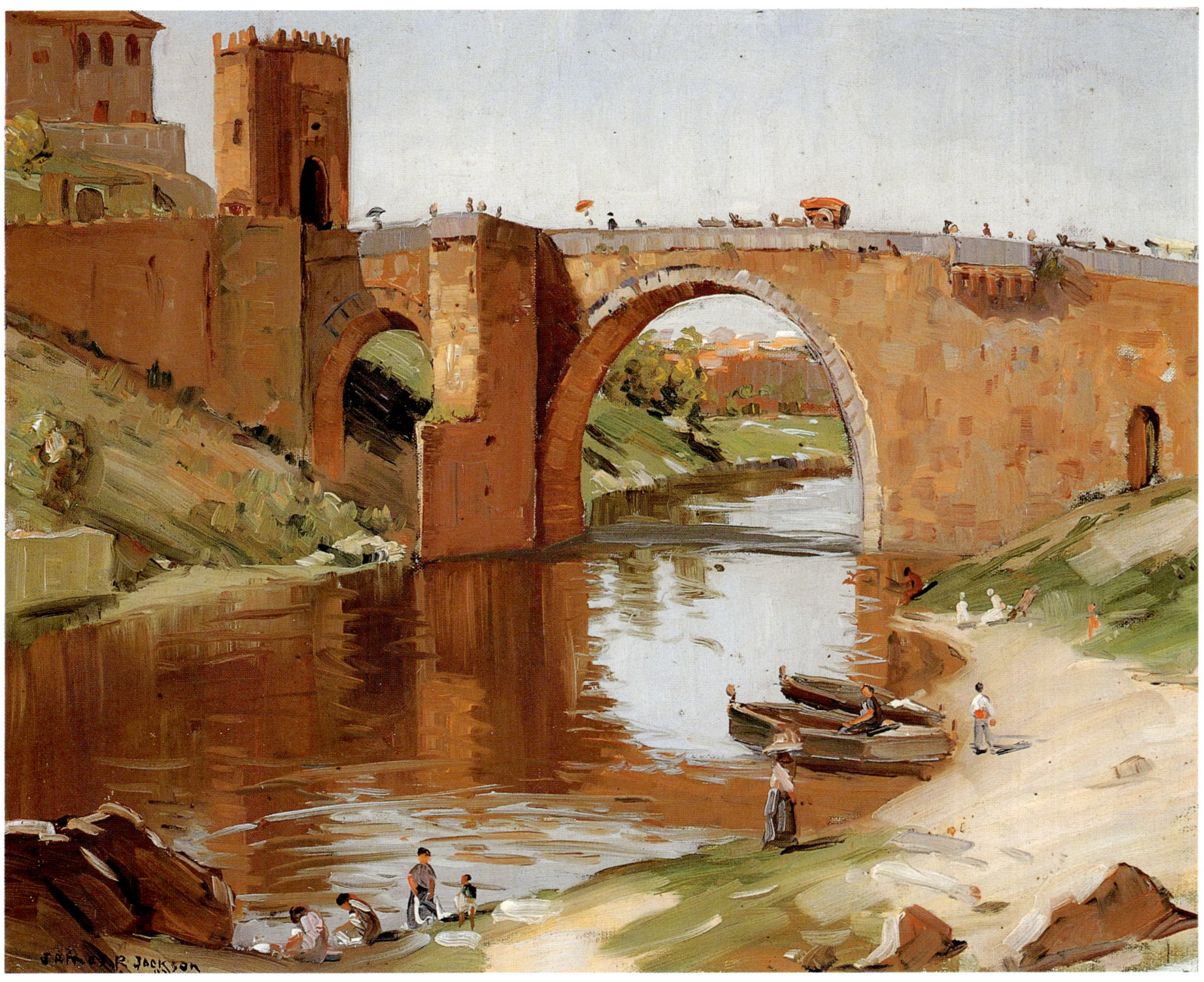

5   **TOLEDO BRIDGE, SPAIN** 1907 39.5 x 49 cm
Private Collection

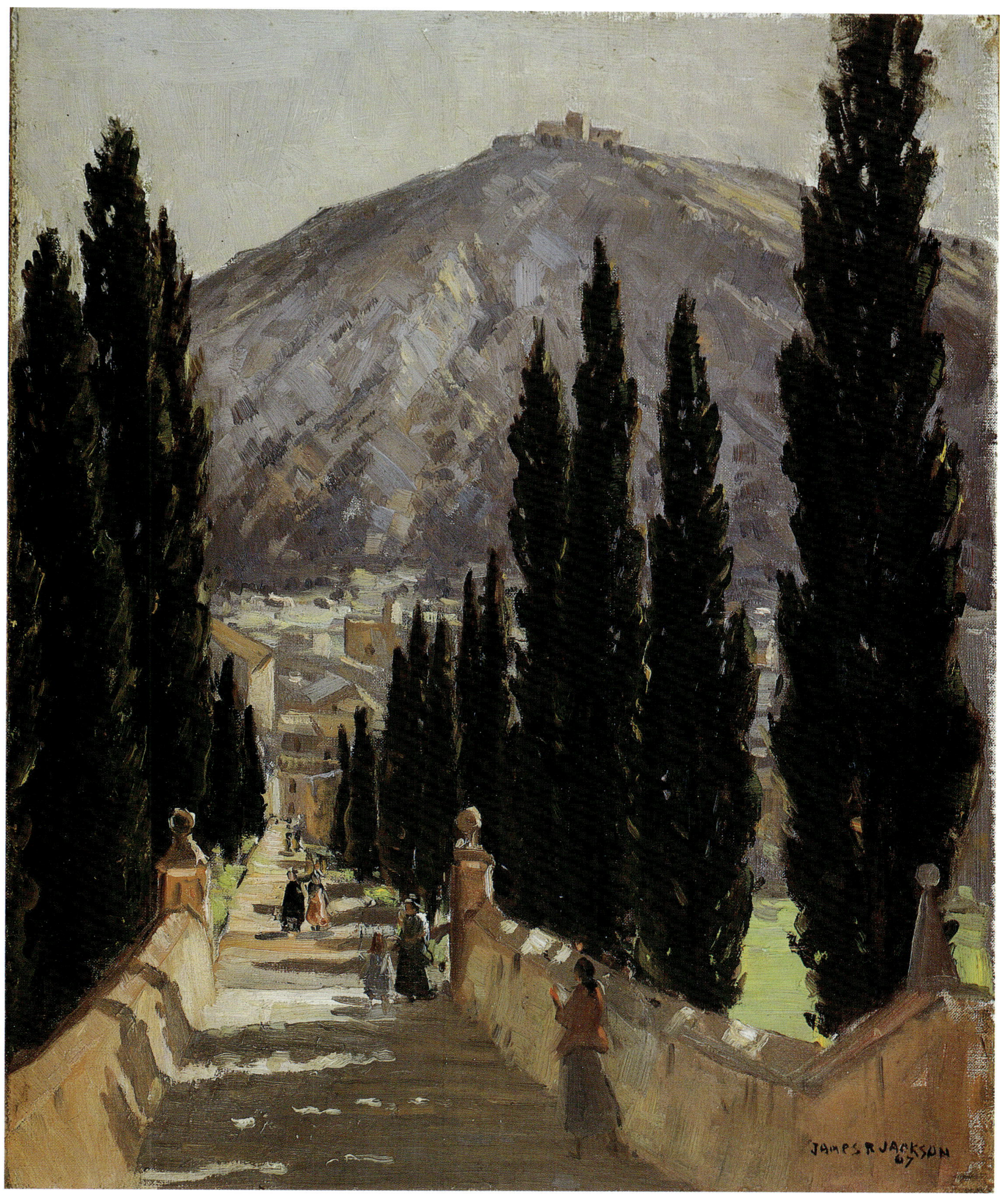

6 **PASSEO POLLENZA, SPAIN** 1907 Oil on canvas on cardboard 45.3 x 37.4 cm
New England Regional Art Museum, N.S.W.

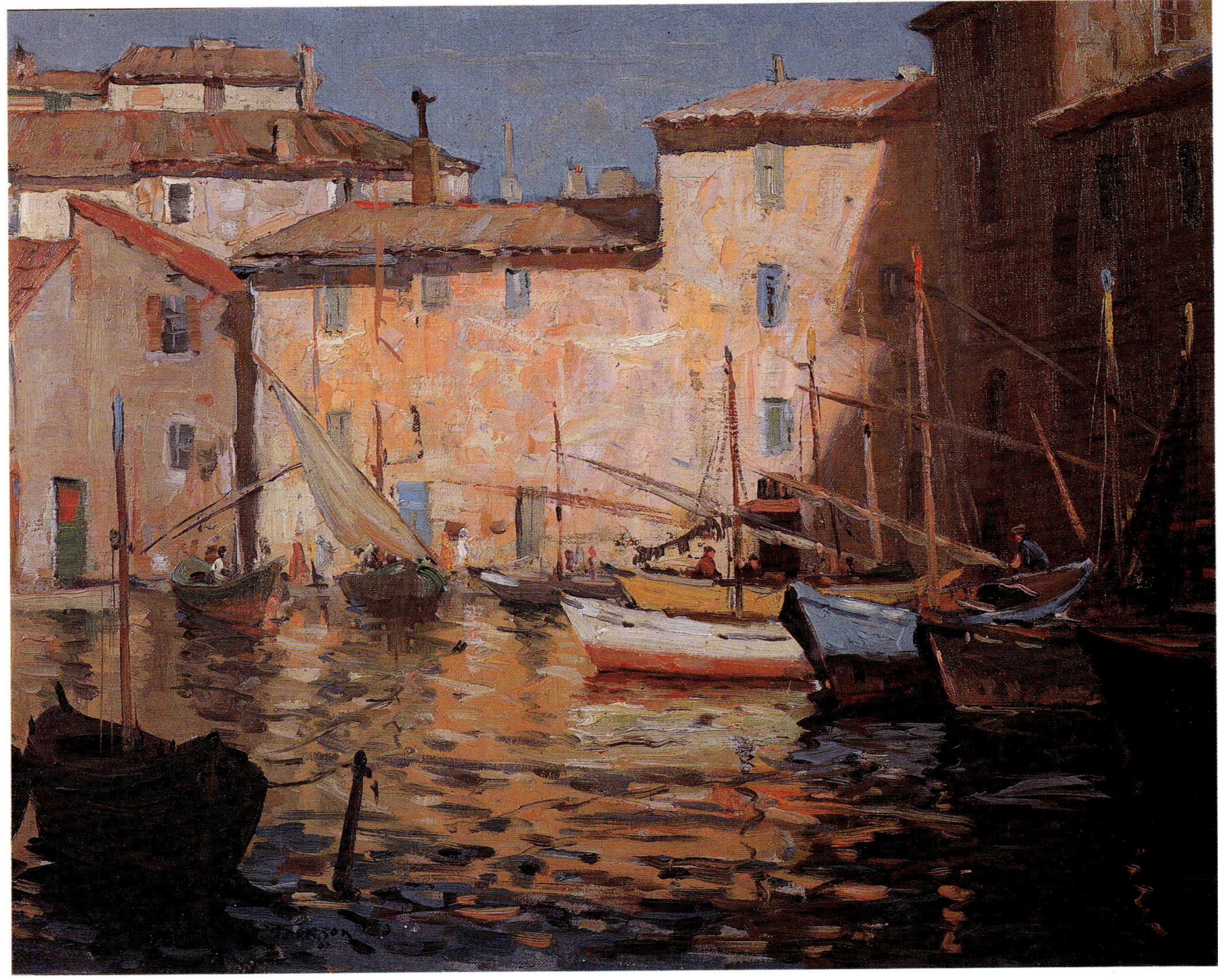

7   **CANAL BRESCON, MARTIGUES, FRANCE** 1907 39.2 x 48.7 cm
From the Collection of the Benalla Art Gallery, Victoria

me at lunch time.' As James was only a few years younger than Augustus John, they became great friends. He frequently went down to John's studio in the south of France and visited him at his London studio before he returned to Australia. They kept in contact and in the 1920s James again spent some time with him in the south of France.

Most of James's European paintings returned with him to Australia and many of them have been located, including several of Venice. He loved this city and must have spent several weeks painting there, as he returned with large paintings of churches, bridges, gondolas and, naturally, the fishing fleets, with their colourful orange sails. These pictures show his developing maturity as an artist — there is quality of paint and technique, with impeccable drawing and brushwork. They are youthfully vibrant, strongly painted — full of colour and light — yet tempered by his training. His palette reflects the local colour but is also reminiscent of the ochres and blues of Australia. He disliked using a green-blue palette and did not enjoy painting emerald-green fields under a blue sky. In fact, it was not until some forty years later that he felt at ease painting the greener grasses of the North Coast of New South Wales.

At the completion of a year in his Paris art classes, James was advised by Renard to paint for the coming Salon. However, his money had nearly run out and there was little hope of him earning much in Paris. He had to leave his studio and plan his return to Sydney, although at that time he was also very tempted to go to the USA with another student.

The voyage to Australia was via Cape Horn and extremely rough again, but this time he was on a steamer.

CHAPTER 3
Early Exhibitions

On his return from overseas James described his financial situation as 'flat broke'. He was fortunate in being able to return to his decorating job, where he worked full-time for about a year. As he was only able to paint at weekends, he recorded local views around Sydney Harbour, including the undeveloped beauty of the upper parts of Middle Harbour, which he reached by rowing boat.

In these early works, his paint was thickly applied to the whole canvas in forceful brushstrokes. The general effect was of patterned colour masses used in a wide tonal range — headlands had strong shadows, while a softness had developed in his close water reflections. In August 1908 he painted many of the ships which welcomed the sixteen white battleships of the visiting American Fleet. Having established a small studio in North Sydney, where he felt at home, he spent most of his income on art materials and frames as he prepared to exhibit some of his pictures.

James R. Jackson made his debut in the Sydney art world at the Royal Art Society's exhibition of August 1908. His six pictures selected for hanging were all painted in Europe, and included three large figure portraits and three smaller landscapes. Of these, two were of bridges over the Seine in Paris, and the other of the old canal in Bruges, Belgium. The *Sydney Morning Herald*'s review of 29 August was very favourable and described in detail the composition and colours of two of his three figure studies called *Harmony in Red* and *Dorothy*. He asked 50 and 80 guineas respectively for these and from 3 to 20 guineas for his European scenes, which were good prices for those days.

Following his election onto the council of the Royal Art Society, he exhibited in their Cabinet exhibitions. In the Annual Exhibition he showed nine pictures and again included several European works. He also introduced some of his recently painted views of Sydney Harbour. The inclusion of figures in his landscapes and harbour pictures became his recognised trademark. These local landscapes were still modestly priced, but he increased his prices for the two large figure portraits to 120 and 150 guineas. These figure studies were among the most highly priced at the exhibition, yet today people tend to buy his harbour pictures and landscapes at much higher prices than his figure studies.

Towards the end of 1909 James was able to give up work and devote himself full-time to his art. He established himself in a larger studio on the north side of the harbour as he preferred painting and looking at the harbour with the sun at his back. He chose an area he knew in Junction Street, North Sydney, where he lived for many years until it was absorbed by the approaches to the Harbour Bridge.

At that time James considered his fame lay in his portraits and figure studies, which he must have sold as he continued to paint and exhibit them at very high prices until the early 1920s. He also believed that the quality of an artist should be judged by his or her ability to draw and paint figures and nudes. At that time it was also fashionable to paint and exhibit them as major works, and to have sculptured figures in the home. However, until the end of the First World War, James rarely exhibited any 'naked women' at an exhibition — his models were usually beautifully dressed. When he did show a nude, the delicately painted contours of her back and neck were twisted to show her facial profile, but only a suggestion of her bosom. The influence of the Reverend on his upbringing and painting subjects was still strong!

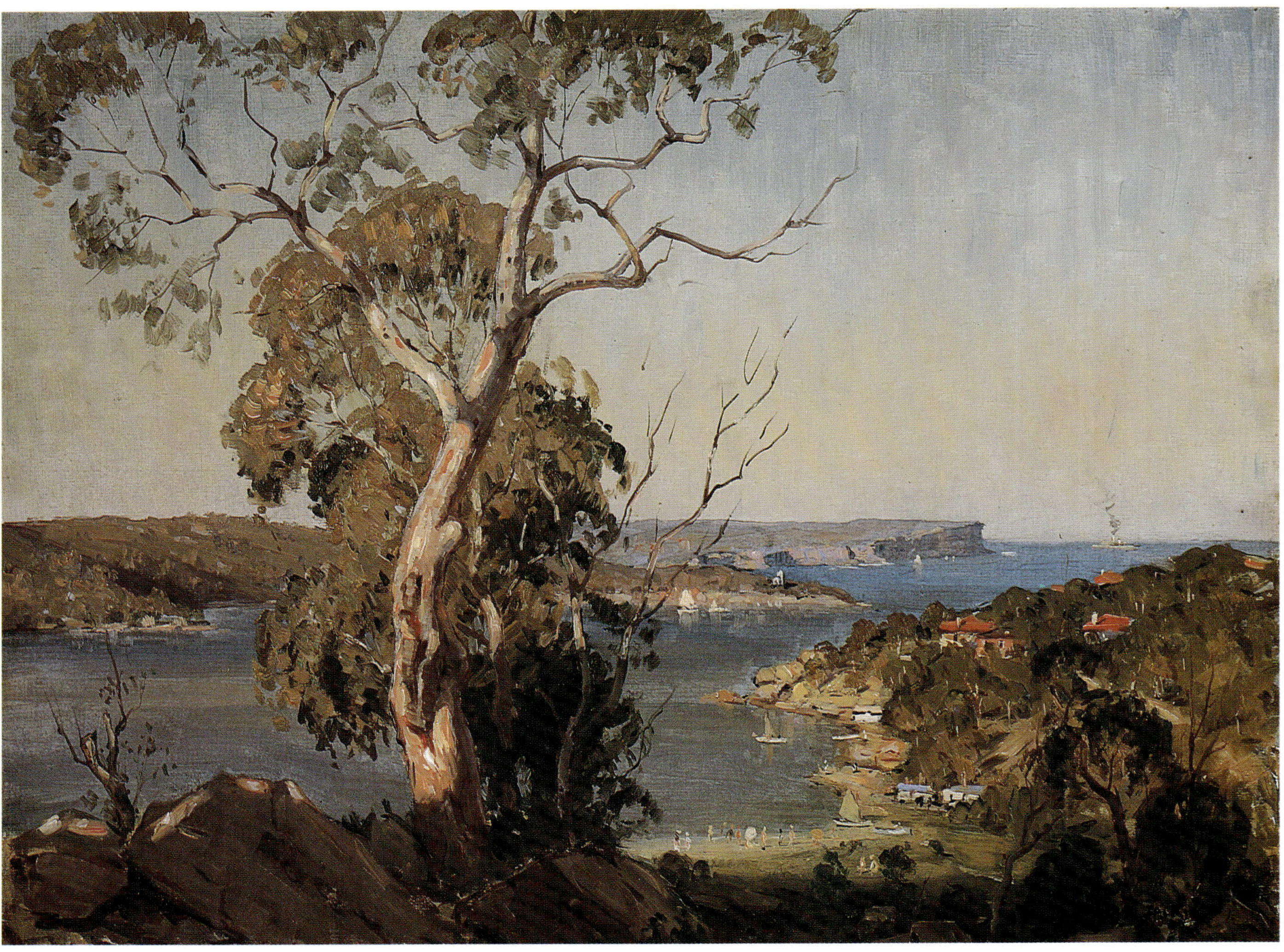

8   CHINAMAN'S BEACH, MIDDLE HARBOUR, N.S.W. 1909 Oil on canvas 51 x 68.5 cm
New England Regional Art Museum, Armidale, N.S.W.

Large vistas of Sydney's wonderful harbour and views of the near South Coast were painted during this period. His well-known *Chinaman's Beach, Middle Harbour,* now in the Howard Hinton collection at Armidale, New South Wales, and his beautiful *Autumn Afternoon, Middle Harbour,* depicting the harbour's shimmering stillness of water on an autumn afternoon, are representative of this period. Both of these harbour scenes show his wonderfully balanced rhythmic sense of composition; his ability to capture a mood, the time of day and the feel of the season; his very Australian sense of colour; and his superb craftsmanship. He used a softer tonal range and perfected his foreground interest with trees and rocks in half shadow, beautifully painted but not distracting from his central focus of interest which, like other of his harbour pictures, was usually people on a beach or in boats near a headland. However, the eye is led by these harmonious headlands to another interest in the distance — a wisp of smoke or a developing cloud.

The Art Gallery of New South Wales bought the first of their Jackson paintings when they purchased *Maidenhood* from the Royal Art Society's exhibition of 1910, where James exhibited ten paintings. *Maidenhood* was a portrait study of a girl in a white dress edged with pink. The review by the art critic of the *Sydney Morning Herald* on 27 August was full of praise: 'The radiant sense of life beneath the flesh tones of the face is all the more remarkable in this really captivating work because the chiffon scarf of palest pink round the neck might have confused the effect had not the painter's talent sustained the harmony of his scheme . . . also [it is] quite remarkable for its poignant sweetness and the admirably vivid colour of the flesh tones. The picture will attract attention in the gallery by reason of its captivating qualities.'

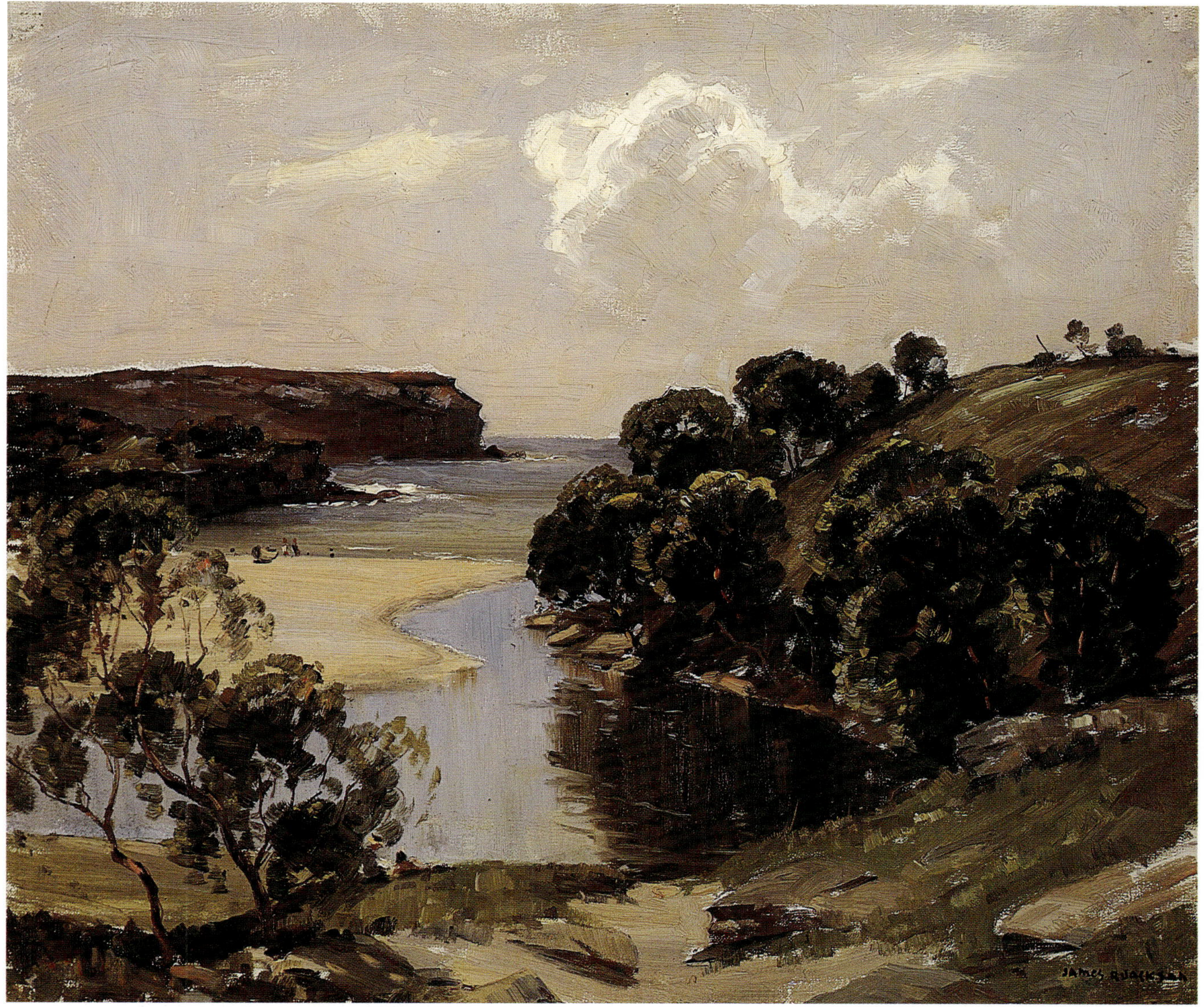

9   **WATTAMOLLA BEACH NATIONAL PARK, N.S.W.** 1909 Oil on canvas 51 x 69 cm
New England Regional Art Museum, Armidale, N.S.W.

With this purchase James felt secure enough to experiment with his art and began to vary his technique and his colour contrasts. By heavily overpainting some interest in his pictures, he created a semitextured effect on the canvas by this impasting. For a short time he experimented with colour effects by altering his palette. In some of his landscapes, painted in 1910, a rosy purple introduced into his middle-distance headlands was contrasted with the orange, pinks and violets of angophoras and with the yellows and pale greens of grass in the foreground. This middle-distance purple may now be considered to look slightly heavy, but the colour could have changed over the past eighty years, especially if he mixed it using some of the old, fugitive crimsons made from cochineal.

Colour alteration is obvious in the reds of the clouds in another landscape also painted in that year, so he possibly unknowingly used an old tube of crimson paint which has since changed colour. Darkening in these clouds is most likely from being hung over a smoky fire. During my research this is the only time in which I have noticed any alteration of pigments in his pictures as he always used permanent colours and was very aware of fugitive colours.

A photo of James in the 1910 Royal Art Society catalogue shows him as a debonair character wearing a hat and an artist's cravat. He had adopted wearing a loose bow tie when in Paris, and photos show that he continued to wear a large artistic tie until the mid-1920s. His self-portrait sketches of this period also portray him in similar style, although the hat he wears is older — most likely it is his painting hat.

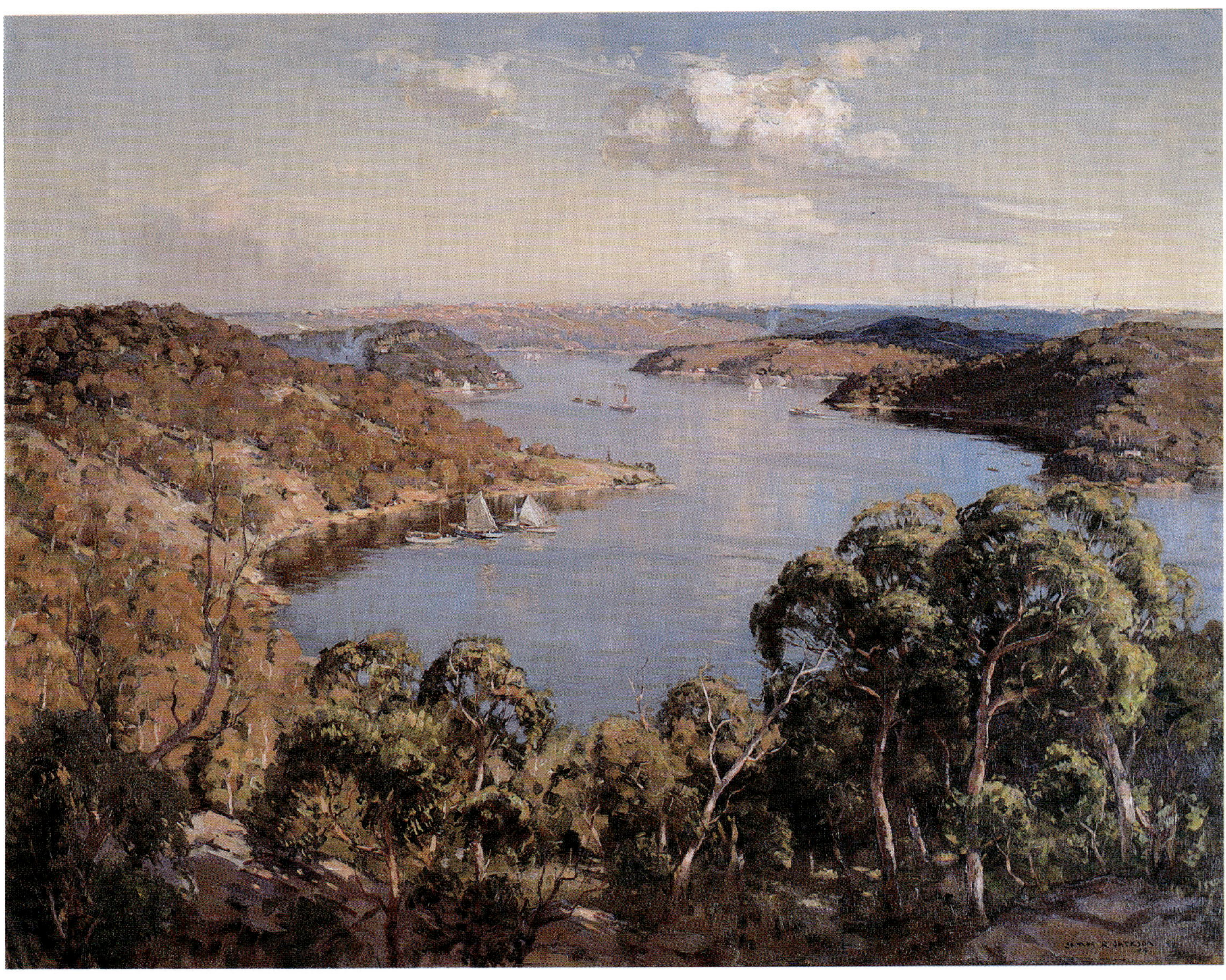

10   **AUTUMN AFTERNOON, MIDDLE HARBOUR, N.S.W.** 1909 105 x 134 cm
Private Collection

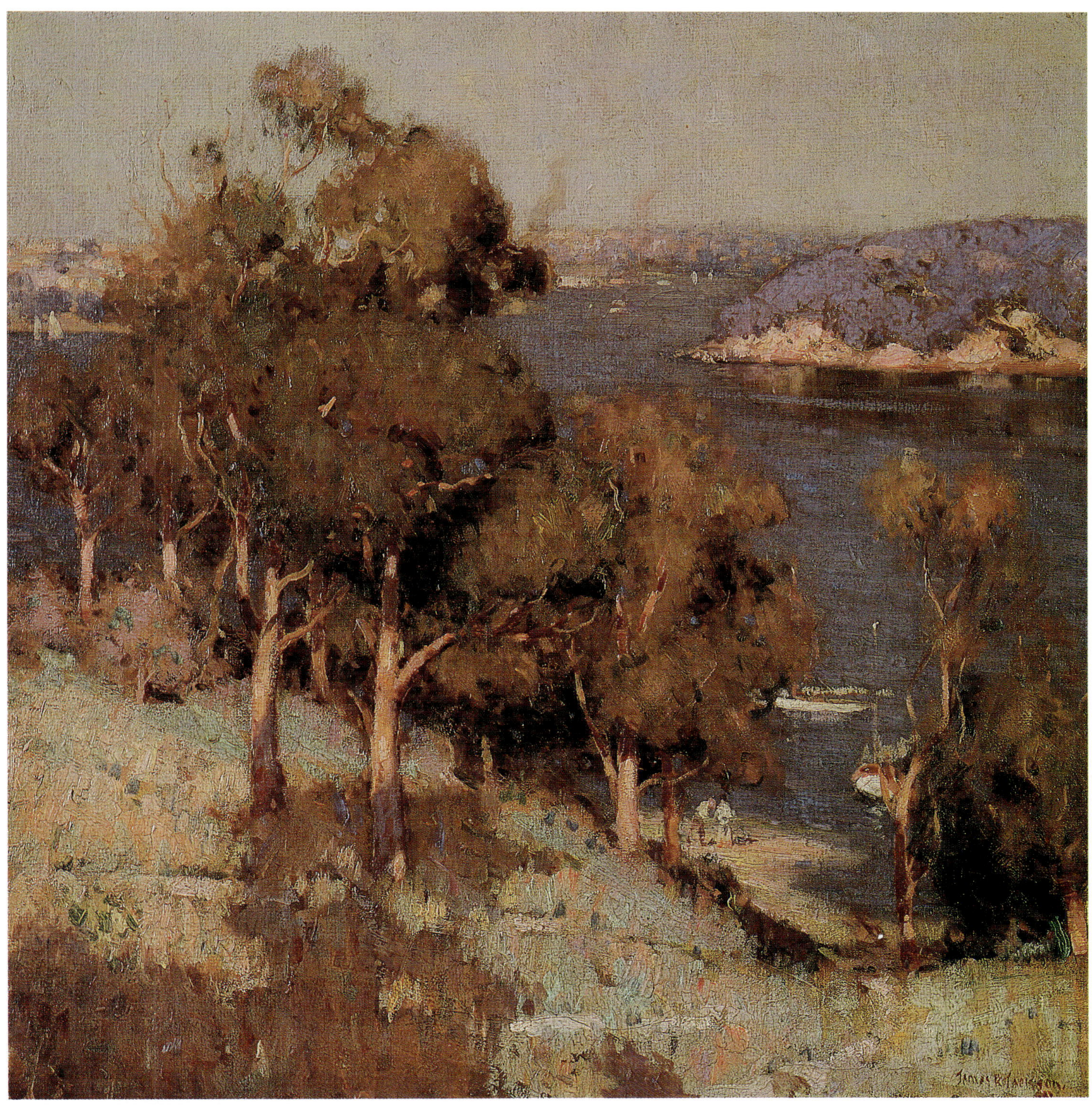

11 BERRY'S BAY, SYDNEY HARBOUR 1910 60 x 60 cm
Private Collection

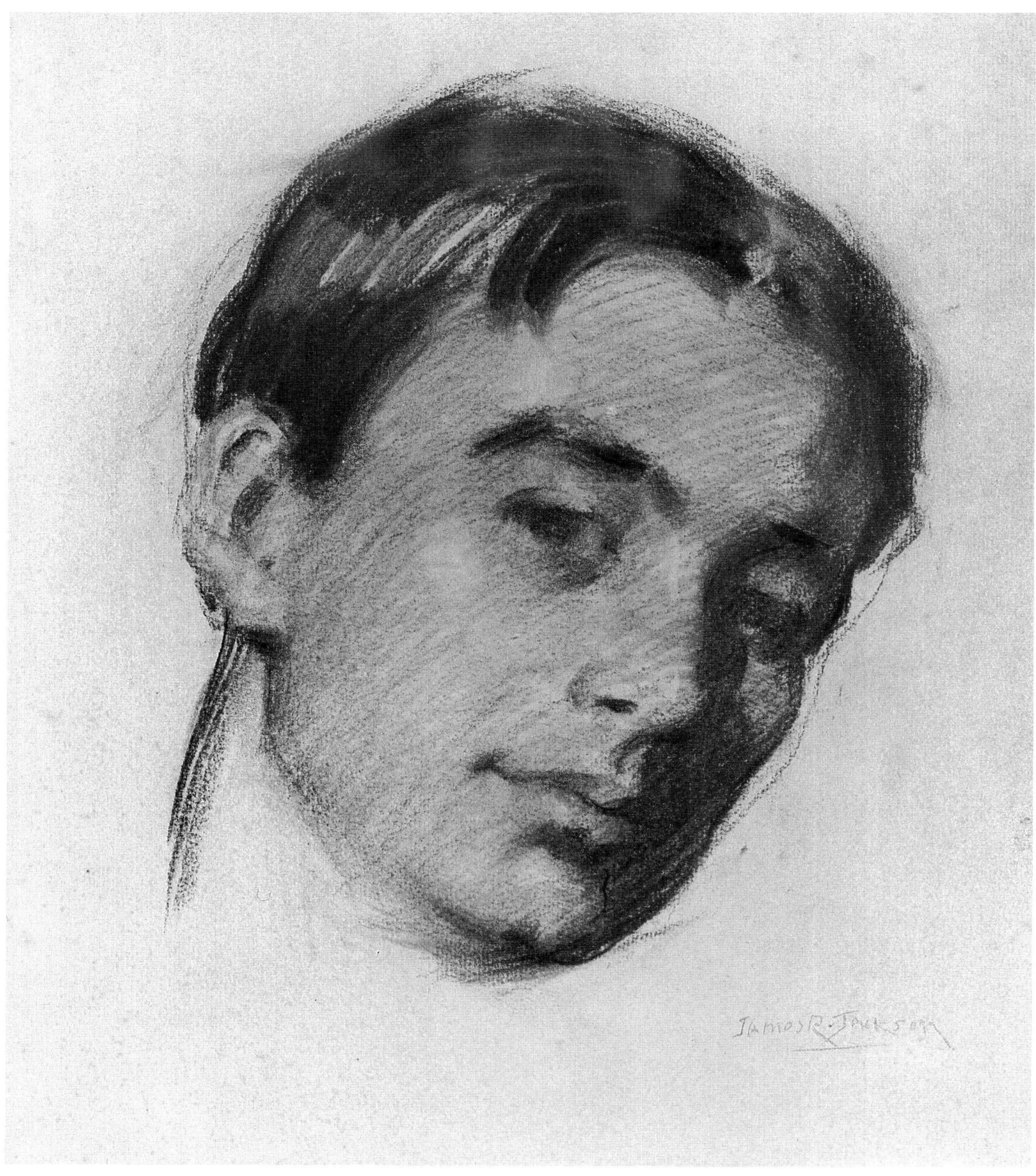

12   CHARCOAL DRAWING OF HIS BROTHER *c* 1910 29 x 26 cm
Private Collection

He always wore a suit with a shirt and tie and unless he was painting outside on 'a hell of a hot day' he painted in his coat. He was never a messy painter and had great control of his paint and brushes. Even when I painted with him decades later, it was most unusual for him to get paint on his clothes and then only occasionally on his shirt cuffs. He had a great fear of paint poisoning and was very wary of all his pigments, especially those made from lead or arsenic bases. He would meticulously clean his hands with turps on a clean piece of paint rag and wash them with soap as soon as possible.

In 1911 James was elected onto the hanging committee as well as being on the council of the Royal Art Society. His own selection of paintings at their exhibitions was mostly of the harbour. The main

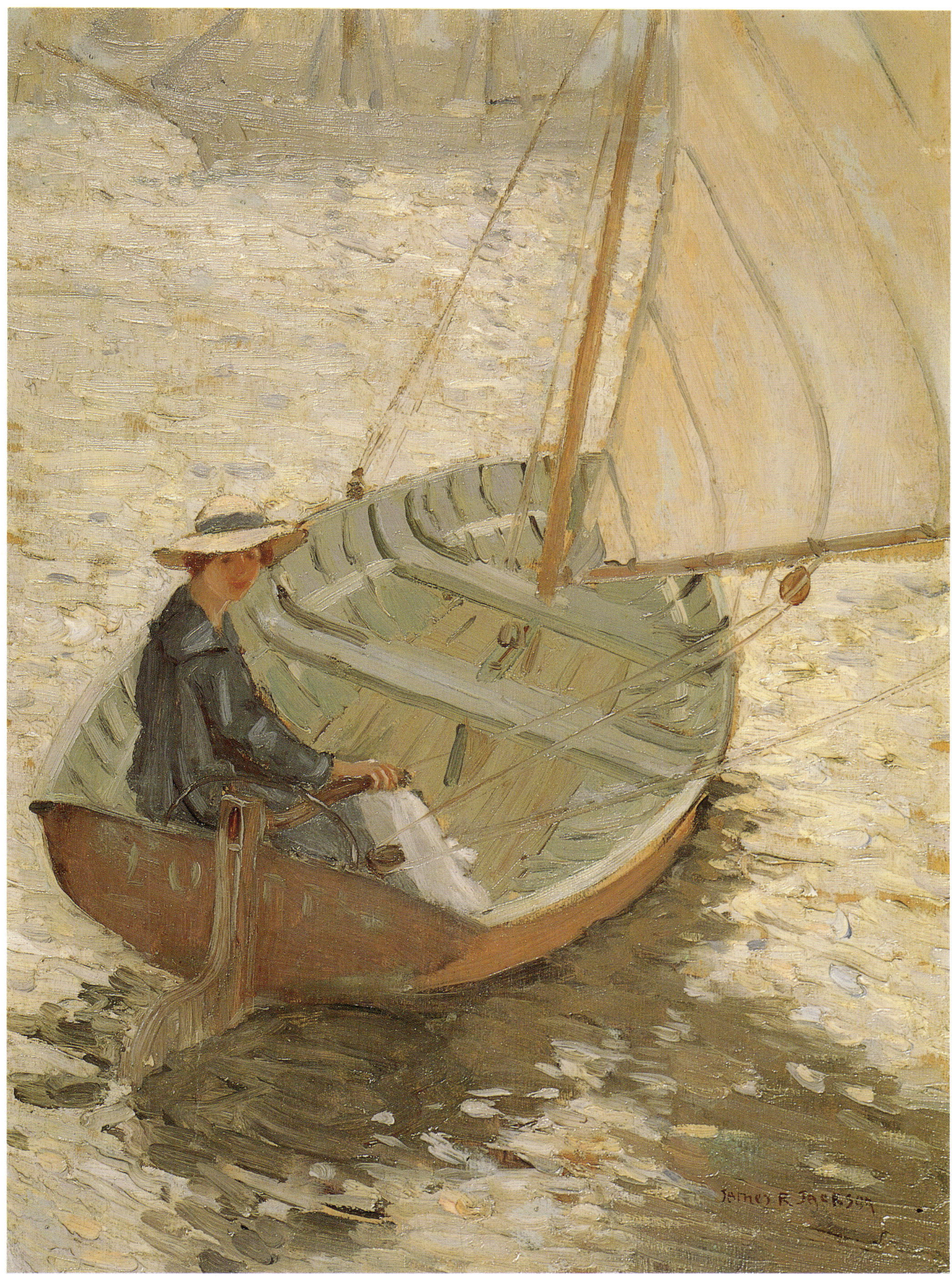

13   **SAILING** *c* 1912 39 x 29 cm
Private Collection

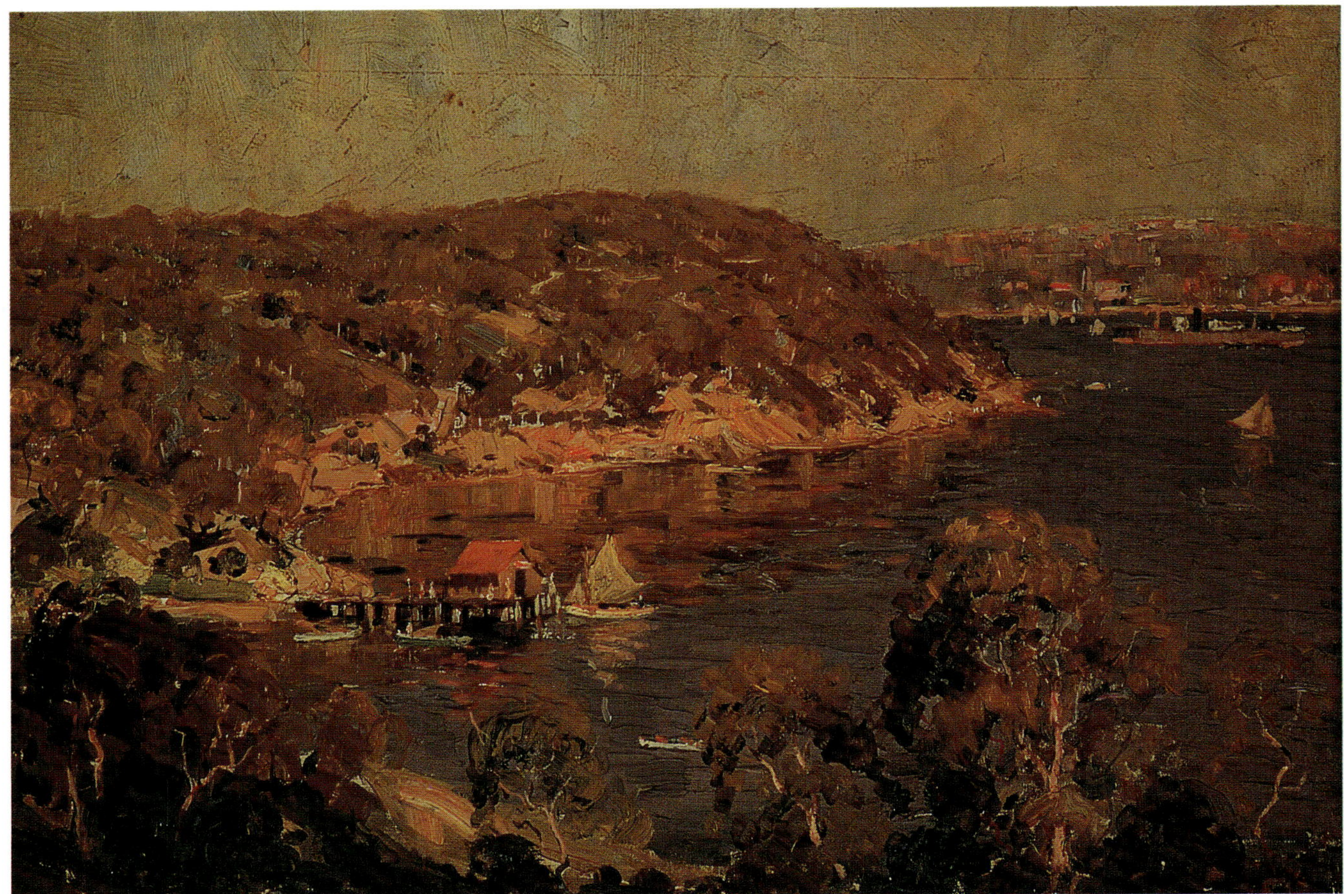

14   BRADLEYS HEAD, SYDNEY HARBOUR *c* 1912 39 x 60 cm
Private Collection

interest was in water activities; and his work on canvas, and occasionally on board, showed a slight change of technique. He still applied his oils thickly, but he painted the foreground water with a multitude of small, colourful brushstrokes reminiscent of his earlier style. He reverted to broad, smoother brushwork in the 1920s. Overpainting was also reduced, the effect required being recorded in one sitting by varying the depth of his paint application. His recent rosy purples were replaced with cooler blues, while his grasses were more ochre in colour.

The following year his exhibits included two black and white drawings and a selection of his oils, including a nocturne and many views of Sydney Harbour. These works were still modestly priced, while he asked 200 guineas for his large figure study of two women in long dresses, titled *The Sisters*.

James painted his models either in the studio or outdoors wearing long, graceful Edwardian-style dresses. Painted outside, they frequently carried colourful parasols and were dappled with dramatic splashes of sunlight, filtered through the trees. Sometimes they rested in boats, surrounded by sparkling colour harmonies in the water. The clinker-type rowing boats were moored near the foreshores of Berry's Bay or Wollstonecraft Bay, which were near his studio. These bays were bushy and beautiful before development and their sunlit, sandstone foreshores and small waterfalls surrounded by stands of secluded casuarinas and eucalypts frequently appeared in his early pictures.

James painted many of these sensitive figure compositions, showing an impressionistic treatment of light patterns on land or water. His development of this subject and setting — figures, boats, water reflections, foreshores and parasols (changed later to round oriental-type cane umbrellas) — continued for over a decade and culminated in 1925 with *The Crevice*. These compositions show the integration of his romantic character and many talents with the impressionist influence on his composition, colour and fascination with light.

The pleasures of camping had been introduced to him by the black and white artists from the *Bulletin*. They had set up a semipermanent camp, which included a bell-type tent, in Balls Head Bay, to the west of his painting sites. Here they would spend a few days painting, drawing, swapping yarns and finding the other chap's buried beer with a divining rod. James would row over to join them and from there sketched some of the western reaches of the harbour. He was very friendly with Lionel Lindsay and with John Flanagan, who left for the USA in 1916 and later became famous as an illustrator.

There was another camp near Dee Why, which Muir Auld and other artists who exhibited with the Royal Art Society frequented. James enjoyed painting from this camp in these early days; then, as the trams were extended further north to Narrabeen by 1913, Sydney's northern beaches area became one of his favourite coastal painting sites. It supplied well-defined headlands, golden beaches, sand-dunes and sheltered lakes for his landscapes, while the fishing was excellent.

In 1913 James commenced his frequent country and interstate painting trips, which he continued many times a year until his late eighties. For a competition, he painted an immense 12 by 6 foot (4 × 2 m) panorama of the site of Canberra before its development. He camped near the foot of the hill from which he painted, and had great problems with his tent and his canvas when the wind came up. He quickly learnt the technique of camping by himself and would 'go bush' for up to several months at a time, exploring for likely subjects and painting in different areas of Australia. He travelled by train and recalled many a freezing night huddled over the railway station fire while waiting for the connecting 'mail' or for the pub to open if he arrived in the wee small hours.

Convenient country hotels, such as 'The Railway', supplied his accommodation for the first night or two then, if the scenery was good, he would set up a camp. Over the years he developed a network of country friends throughout the Eastern states, who were interested in art and with whom he often stayed. He obtained daily lifts to his chosen sites or camped nearby and walked to them. As his oils took several days to dry, he would pin wet pictures up around his room and on the back of the door. When camping, he protected his fresh paint by using drawing pins to separate the faces of canvases, which he hung in pairs in his tent or on a tree. He often sold his smaller works locally, but his large canvases returned to the studio to be touched up, finished and framed. Occasionally, one may still find sand, the odd insect or grass seed which blew onto his paint and was never removed.

Around Sydney, James travelled by tram and train, with the occasional trip with friends. When he found an enjoyable painting site he would return with a light camp and stay for a few days. He painted during the day and fished in the evening. Later he described the brilliance of red Christmas bells and the fragrance of banksia, which grew around the lagoons, and the abundance of wildlife and fish.

In these days of sparse development, there were few people around to disturb him and his only visitors were curious animals. He would pack his small billy with eggs, oatmeal biscuits, fruit and tea and carried this with a rug, his box, a light easel and stool. He relied on his ability to catch fish for the evening meal and the smell of turps and a small mosquito net to protect him from insects. The sea breezes and his fire partially saved him from the evening swarms of sandflies.

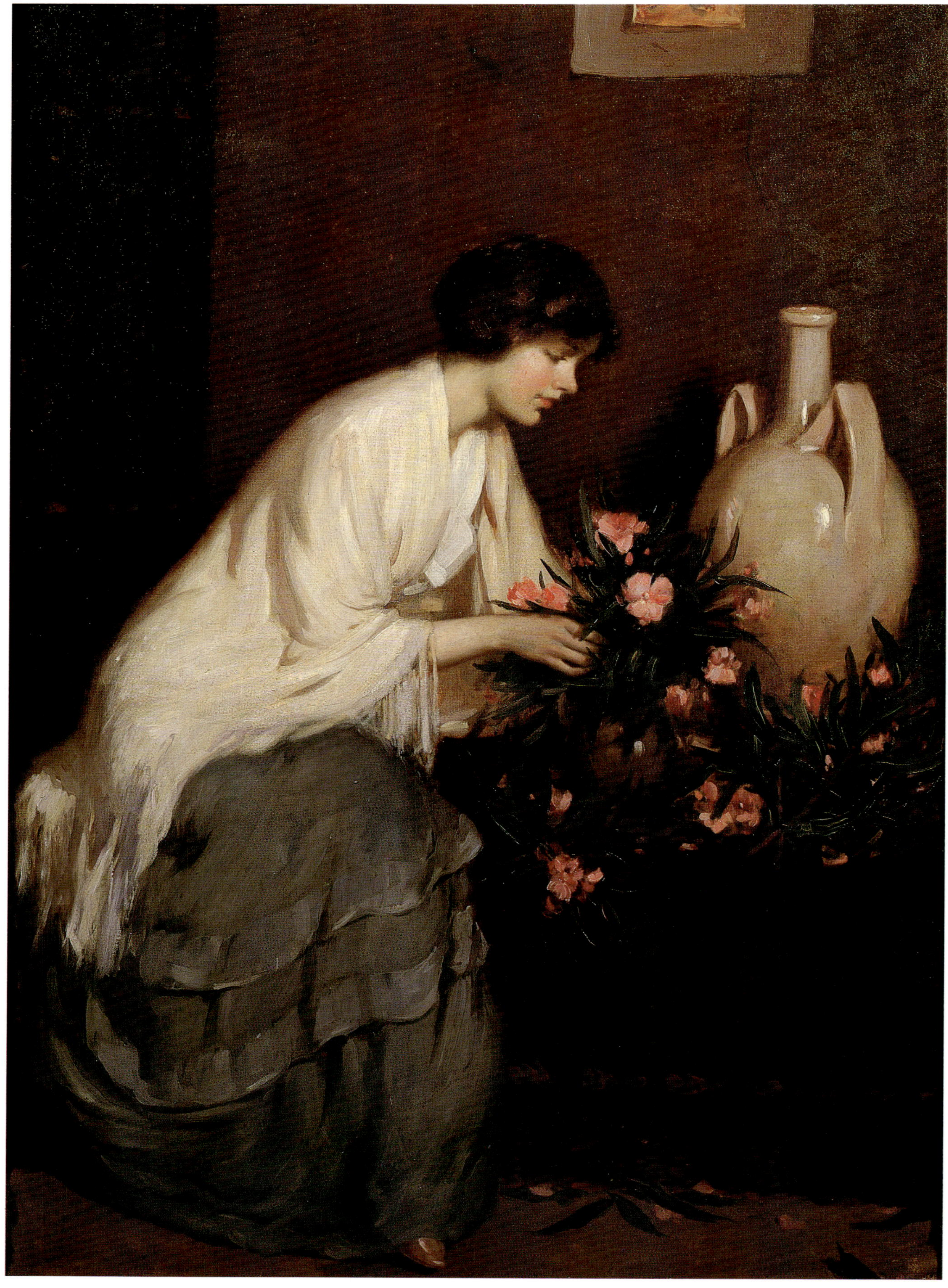

15   **'OLEANDERS'** 1914 Oil on canvas 151 x 113 cm
Purchased 1914
Art Gallery of New South Wales

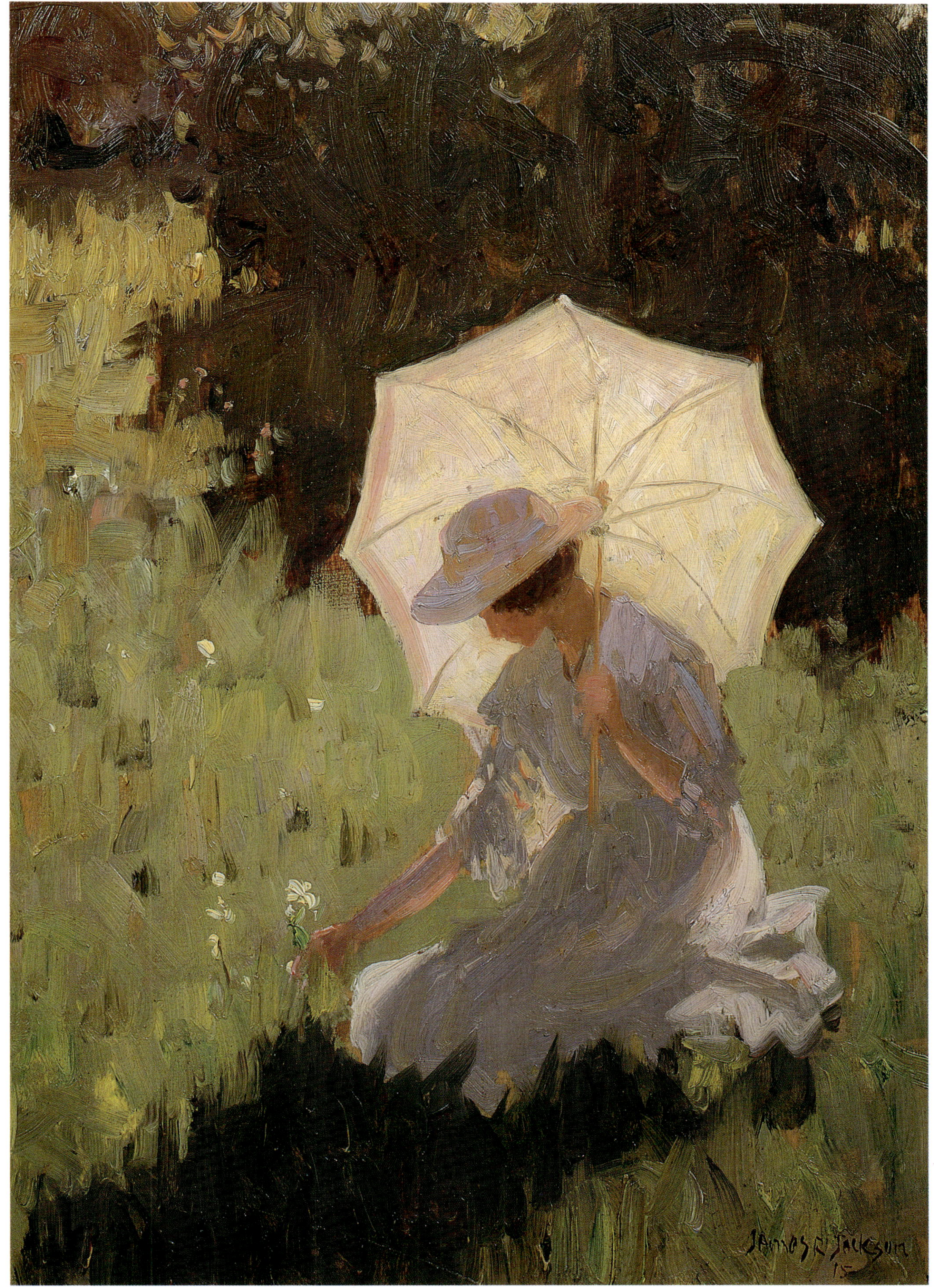

16   **'SPRING'** 1915 Oil on plywood 40.7 x 30.5 cm
Dr & Mrs S. Gillies Bequest 1952
Art Gallery of New South Wales

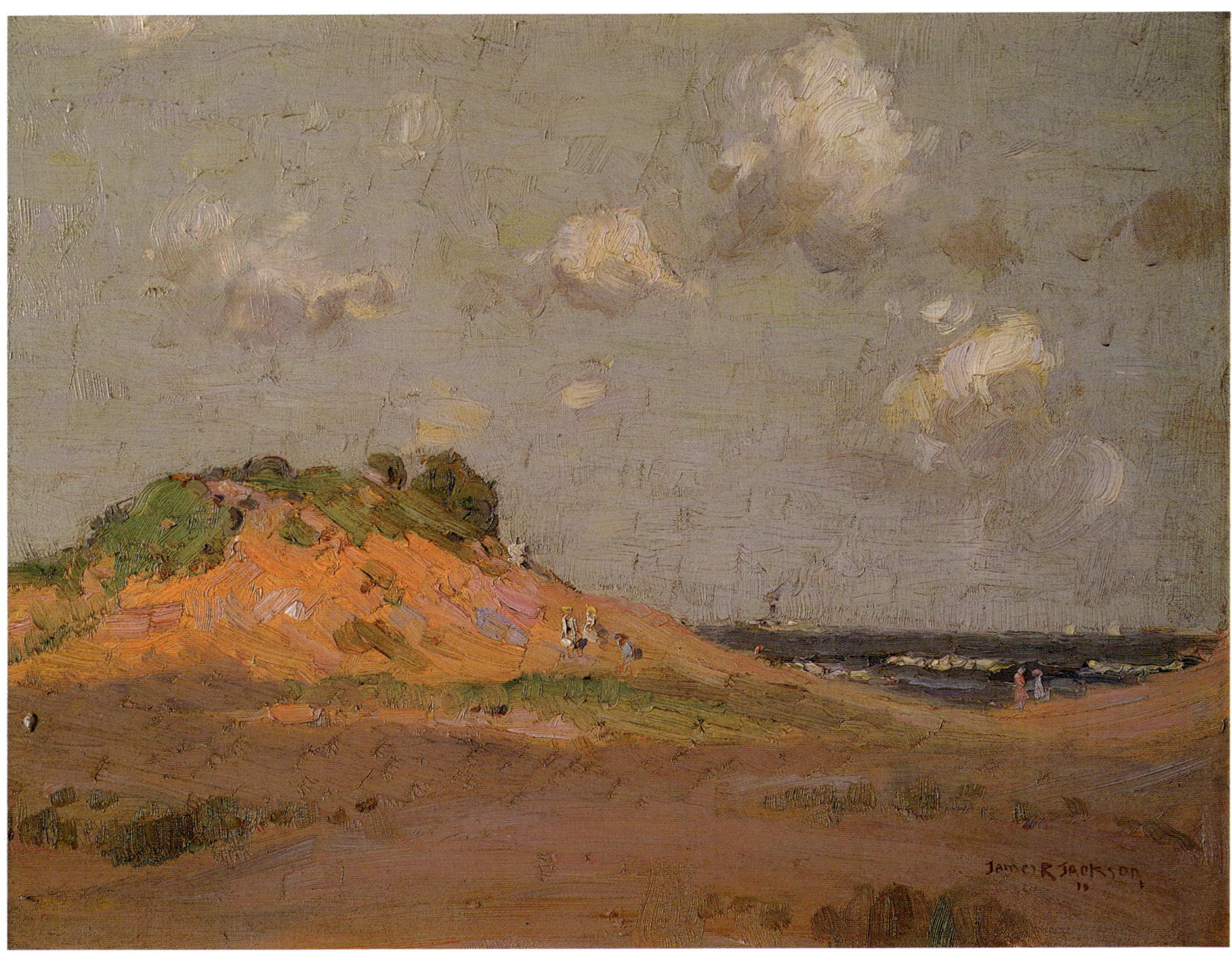

17   **SAND DUNES** 1915 30 x 40 cm
Private Collection

At his studio he was busy teaching and painting his figure studies and a variety of other subjects, including privately commissioned portraits, which he exhibited only occasionally at the Royal Art Society exhibition to demonstrate his skills, as these were not for sale. He advertised as a 'Teacher of Figure and Landscape Painting', holding small classes in his studio or outside teaching sketching of harbour activities at nearby Lavender Bay. His media and signed works included etchings, watercolours and drawings. His exhibited drawings were mostly of heads, done in charcoal or pencil. He was always keen on drawing and continued to practise his skills with the black and white *Bulletin* artists. They drew mostly in hotels and cafes, where they found many characters with faces which were wonderful to record.

James's sales were made at exhibitions and from his studio, where he lived in much the same style as he had in Paris. Later he displayed his works in private galleries such as Gayfield Shaw's Art Salon, the Artist's Gallery and with A. Albers in Sydney.

Newspaper reviews were very complimentary when the Art Gallery of New South Wales bought his figure study *Oleanders* in 1914 for 150 guineas from the Royal Art Society's exhibition. On 14 November, the *Sydney Morning Herald* illustrated *Oleanders* with a large photo and commented: 'This is the principal contribution made by this painter to this year's show and is probably the best work he has painted, possessing as it does, sincerity and charm of style.' In this painting, a seated girl admires the pink blossom of oleanders — in contrast to her lively flesh tones and the textures of the flowers is a large partially-glazed creamy-coloured amphora. James probably carried this antique jar halfway around the world when he returned in 1908. He was very fond of pottery shapes, which he frequently

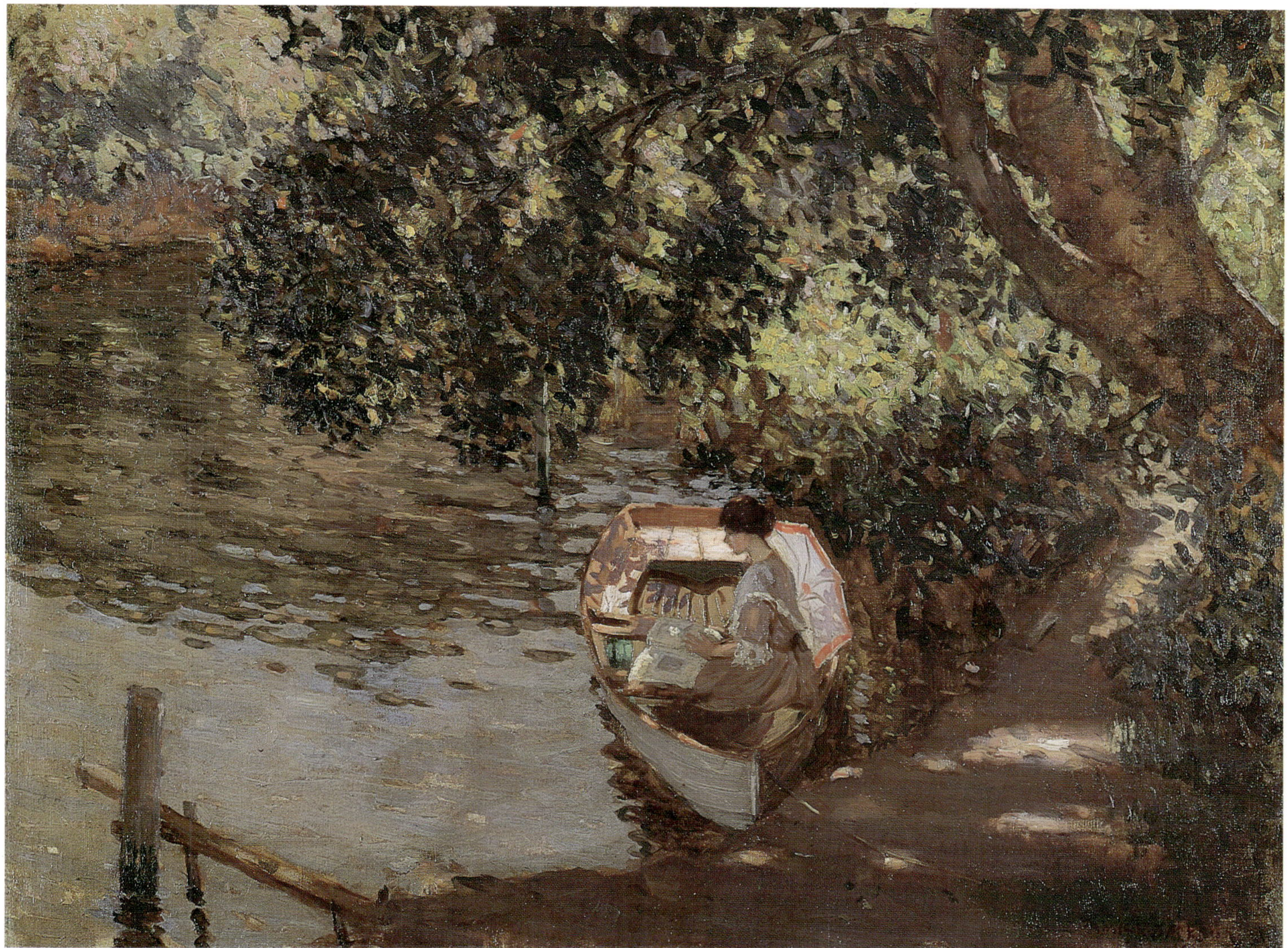

18   **THE DREAMER** 1916 Oil on canvas 74.2 x 101 cm
Purchased 1916   Art Gallery of New South Wales

used as background contrasts in his still lifes and indoor studies. Old Chinese ginger jars, which he found useful to stand brushes in, were one of his favourites, as were large green bottles or coloured glass fishing net floats. During his later trip to Spain in the 1920s, he acquired packing cases full of coralised amphora and plates which had been netted from the sea by local fishermen. These were displayed in his living room and studio.

The Art Gallery of New South Wales acquired his *The Timber Schooner* in 1915, and *The Dreamer* and *The Holiday* the following year. *The Timber Schooner* is a poetic impression of light on the timber-laden schooner and the adjacent hill. *The Holiday* was, again, a picture of ladies bathed in sunlight. The one seated on a stony foreshore is partially shaded by her umbrella, while the other, who rests in a rowing boat, is surrounded by reflections and blue water. In *The Dreamer*, sometimes referred to as *Dreaming*, his model relaxes in her boat under the shade of a large, overhanging tree. This picture would have been painted at Narrabeen Lakes, where he camped at that time, and evokes a mood through the contrast of light and shadow on land and water.

This period was one of his most prolific and his figure studies and harbour pictures were acquired by many other state and regional galleries. In fact, four of his ten exhibited pictures in the 1915 Royal Art Society exhibition are now in major galleries and include his *A Morning in the Studio* and *Lady with Parasol*, both in the Australian National Gallery collection. These are typical early works. *Lady with Parasol* was originally exhibited titled *A Summer Morning* and was very favourably reviewed. It is impressionistic in effect and portrays a girl in part shadow on a bushy path. There is contrast between

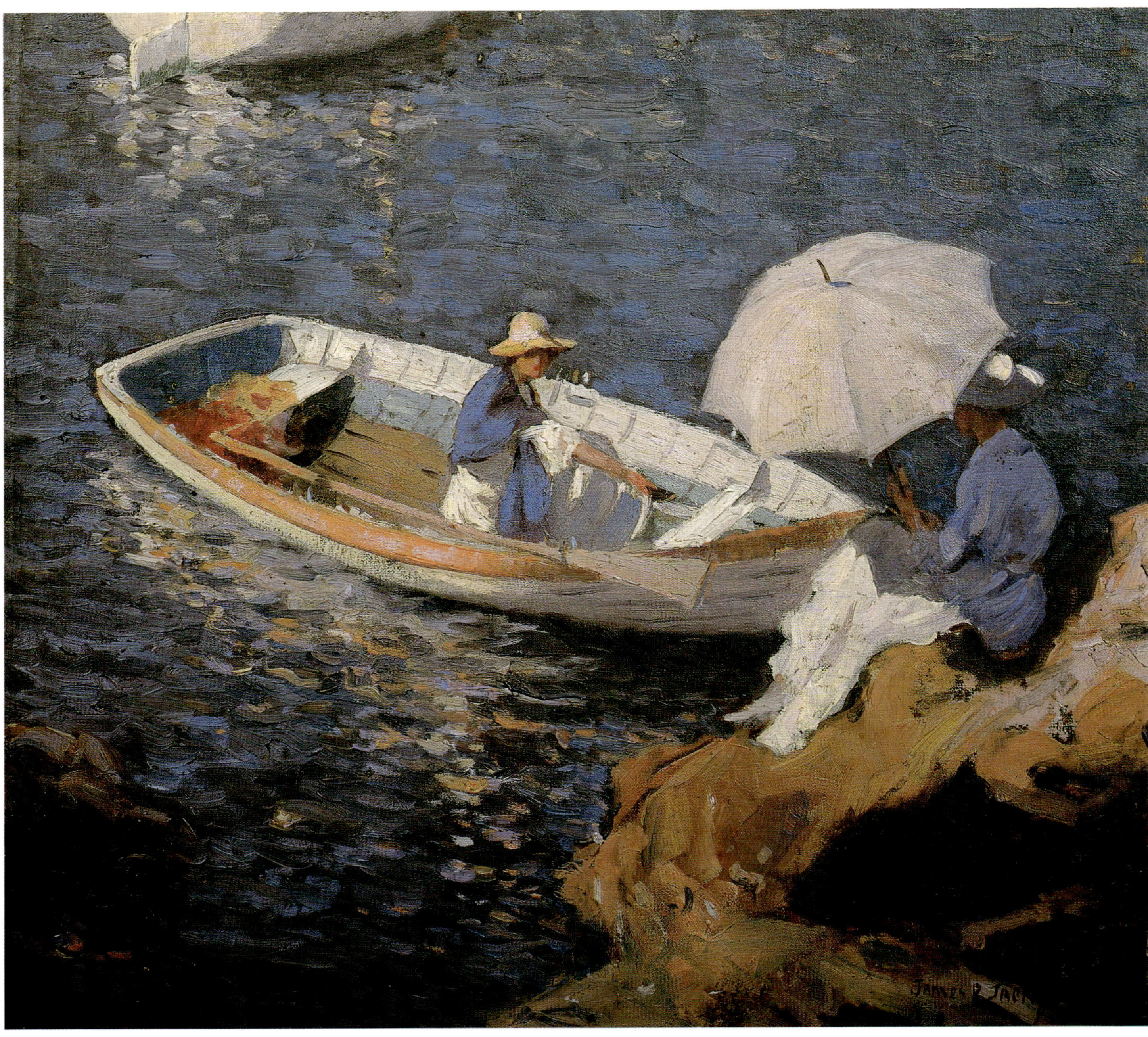

19   **'THE HOLIDAY'** 1916 Oil on cardboard 45.4 x 51.2 cm
Purchased 1916   Art Gallery of New South Wales

the brilliant light which strikes the lower part of her dress and folded parasol, and the dappled light on her upper torso, which is effectively camouflaged into the landscape. The light interest in the lower part of this picture is cleverly balanced by sunshine on the higher saplings, the drawing of which he has deliberately simplified.

James did not enlist in the war as he was emotional and sensitive by nature, and the Reverend's upbringing had produced a dislike for guns. So he was very upset when the first and closest of his three brothers, who joined the army and did not return, was killed at Gallipoli in 1915. He visited New Zealand to see his father, whom he had not seen for years, then on his return painted a studio study of a lady in thoughtful pose, with the unusual title of *1871* — the year his long-deceased mother had married. He exhibited this and a portrait of his brother in army uniform (which was not for sale) in the following year's Royal Art Society exhibition.

In 1916 James exhibited in the Australian Artists' War Fund exhibition, and introduced his work to Victoria when he commenced showing with the Australian Art Association (AAA) in the Athenaeum Gallery, Melbourne. The AAA consisted of a group of prominent artists, including Frederick

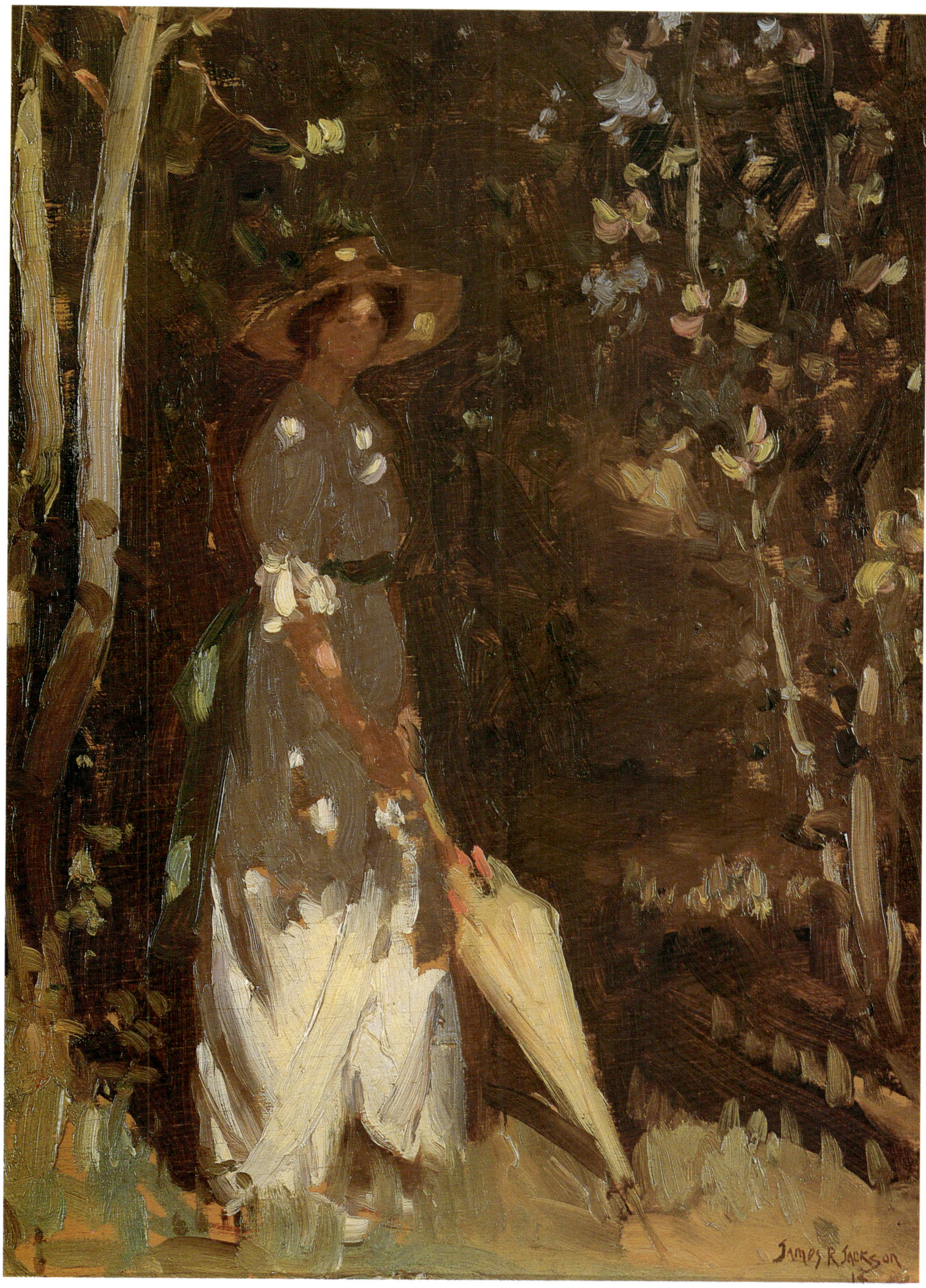

20   **LADY WITH PARASOL** 1914 Oil on plywood 39.4 x 29.5 cm
Reproduced by permission of the Australian National Gallery, Canberra

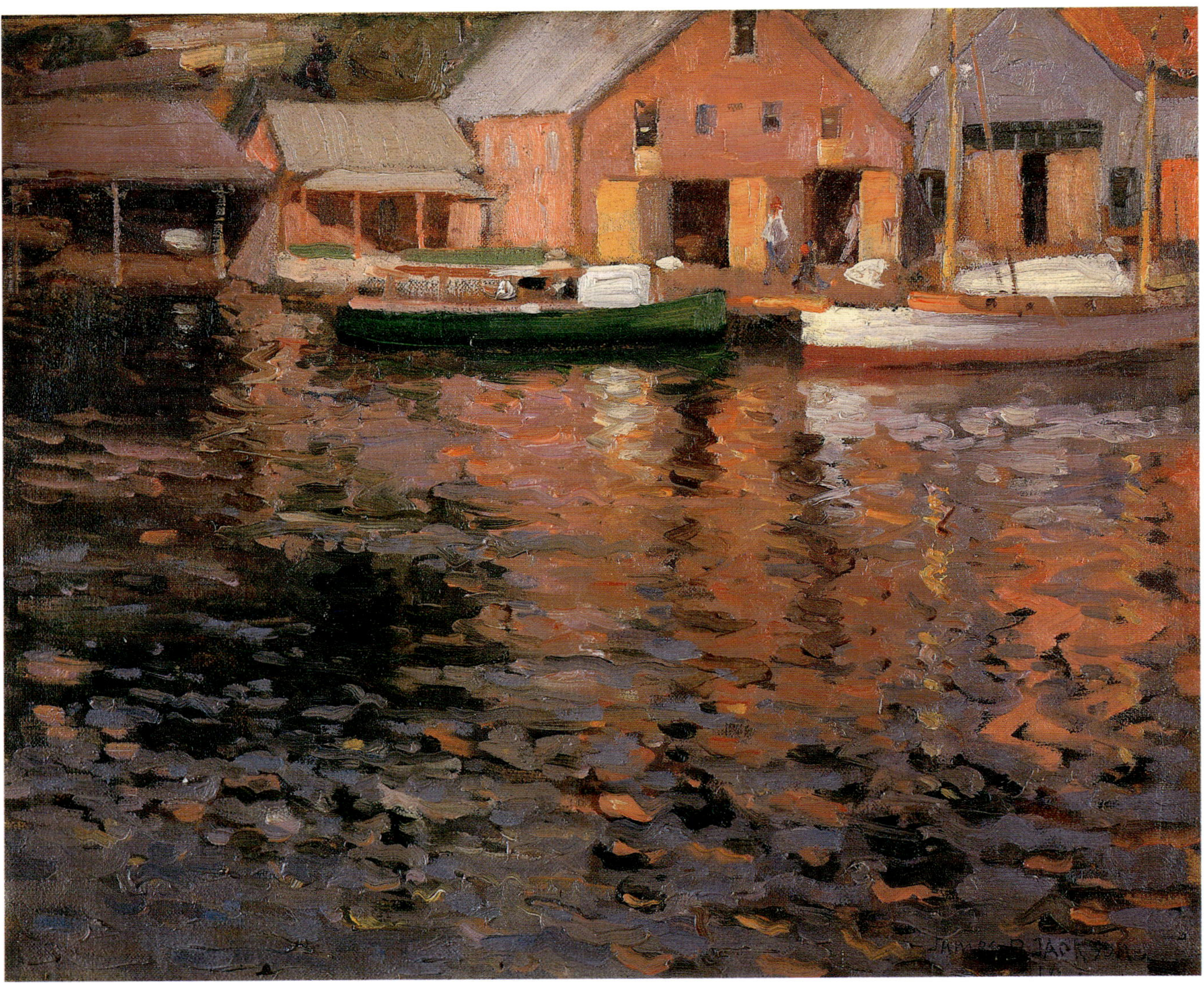

21 **REFLECTIONS** 1916 31 x 38.5 cm
From the collection of the Castlemaine Art Gallery, Victoria

McCubbin, Penleigh Boyd, William McInnes and Will Ashton. M. J. MacNally recorded in the *Telegraph* that in an AAA exhibition 'amongst Jackson's six pictures was one near the door, of a valley in shadow, with two tall poplars in the foreground, their tops bathed in the golden glow of the setting sun. "That is a beautiful picture", said Dame Nellie Melba on her way out, "it is full of music. I must have it." And she bought it.' My father's friend commented that when James heard of this purchase, his smile lit up the whole gallery. He continued to exhibit with the Association, of which he was a member until 1933.

His reception was so good in Melbourne that he visited and painted throughout Victoria many times until in his nineties. At first he stayed and painted landscapes with fellow artists from the AAA including W. B. McInnes, or painted from an artists' camp at Malmsbury. Later he travelled the state, either camping by himself or staying in hotels or with friends. He developed his Melbourne connection with private galleries where, during the following fifty years, he held many successful one-man exhibitions, often staying with the gallery owners, such as the Sedons (Sedon Galleries). Most of his appreciative buyers have retained his works in their homes for several generations, and a large proportion of his paintings hang in Victoria.

CHAPTER 4

Art Instructor at the Royal Art Society

James R. Jackson was appointed art instructor at the Royal Art Society in 1917, where he taught drawing, painting and landscape, and continued in this role until December 1926. He had reached one of the highlights in his career — he was well known, successful and happy. Many of his students became lifelong friends, and some, such as Arthur Murch and Dorathea Toovey, became well-known artists themselves.

James was a very eligible bachelor and he found teaching most enjoyable. His many female students teased, admired and flirted with him. He painted some of them as models — in 1917 he painted Dorathea Toovey in a pale blue dress, standing on a dappled sunlit path in a bushland setting, beneath an orange and cream parasol.

On some weekends he would organise painting camps for his students in the quieter reaches of Middle Harbour or Narrabeen Lakes. The camp sites were reached with much hilarity by rowing boat, with the boys doing the rowing and the girls navigating. His days were spent teaching landscape painting and camp craft. In the evenings he would try to fish, but the girls would deliberately gather nearby or sit in the nearest gum tree and disturb his concentration and solitude by singing. There were long talks and lots of tea-drinking and chorus-singing around the campfire, with the inevitable burnt chops or fish — the girls would not allow him to cook his own dinner.

After a few years, James found the routine of teaching rather restrictive as he was no longer free to disappear into the country whenever the weather beckoned. His prolonged country visits were now limited to the art-term holidays. Years later he made the comment that 'a mature artist should never be a teacher as the students drain you and take too much out of you; also, the repetitious teaching of the rules of painting inhibits the development of individual style'.

Art in Australia (number 3) of 1917 gave him a two-page article with a colour reproduction of *Morning in the Studio*, a figure study, as a representation of his work. This was first exhibited in the 1915 Royal Art Society exhibition and was noted in the art review in the *Telegraph* on 2 October: 'One of the strongest and most uniformly meritorious exhibits on the walls is the group of ten canvases shown by Mr J. R. Jackson, whose picture *A Morning in the Studio* stands out from the ruck by reason of the agreeable harmonies of the color scheme, the graceful pose of the figure, the adequate rendering of the interior and the skill displayed in the representation of textures. A girlish model in a satin dress looking into a mirror on the studio wall is the subject. Perfect finish in the painting of the accessories, refinement in the pose of the figure and impeccable draughtsmanship contribute much to the success of this picture.' This slightly altered work is now in the Australian National Gallery, Canberra.

The young girl used as his model in this picture wore an old-fashioned satin dress which belonged to her mother. He described his painting of the drapery, which he and other art critics considered to be very successful: 'It was painted practically straight through without stopping. Now you have to be in very good form to do that, to make it very satisfactory, do it without touching or messing around with the thing. The head and neck and the arms were painted separately, after having the colour placed around and then wiped away so that it wouldn't embarrass the canvas again.' James also described how he painted figures: 'I like to pose the figure about — it depends how large a picture — but normally

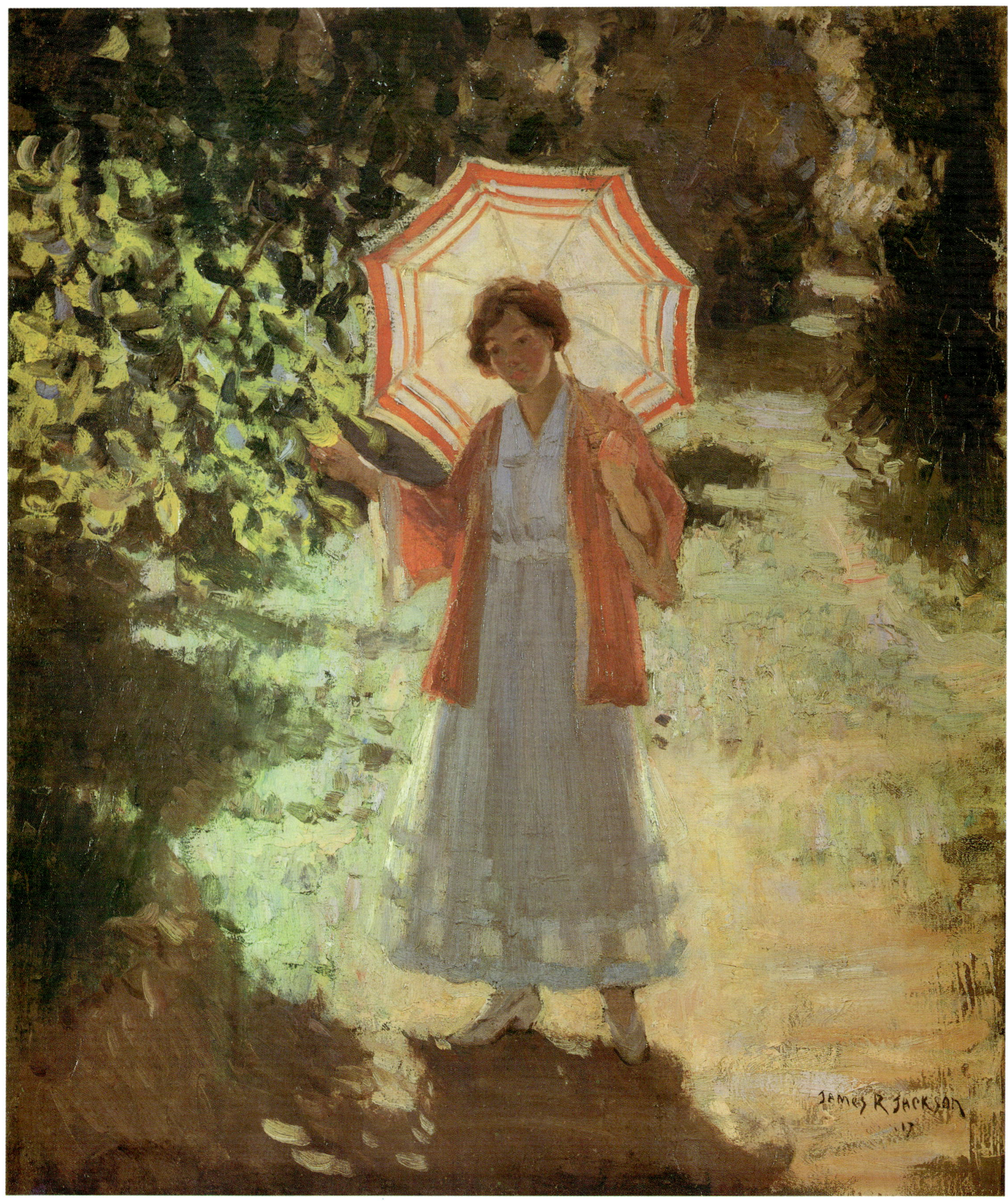

22   **DORA WITH PARASOL** 1917 52 x 45 cm
Private Collection

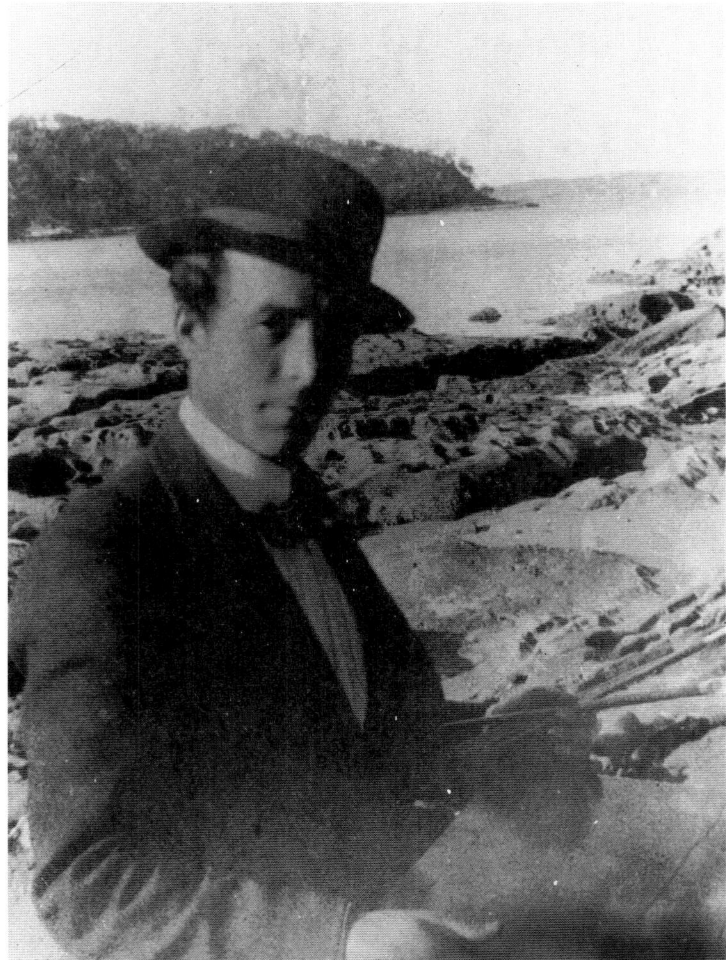

23   James Painting at Taylor Bay, Sydney *c* 1918

indoor would be about 15 feet away so as you can get the true perspective without getting it too near or too close. In approaching the palette, I mix all the colours, the background and the tones of the figure; and first thing, I put down the highest tone on to the canvas, and then that would be — not white — it would be a subdued white because you never go to the full extent of your colour scheme but always have something in retirement so as you can higher or lower the tone.'

In 1918 the Art Gallery of New South Wales held a loan exhibition of works from prominent artists and James displayed five pictures. He also exhibited with the Australian Arts Club, which held its exhibition in Melbourne. The nucleus of this club was formed several years earlier by artists from several art societies, including Elioth Gruner, Hans Heysen, William McInnes, Penleigh Boyd, Will Ashton and James. A Melbourne review commented that James Jackson's landscapes had fine feeling and individuality and also that he had painted in Victoria during a recent visit. This was probably at Malmsbury, a well-known painting area for artists and frequently visited by James, either alone or with other artists.

The following year, at the Australian Arts Club exhibition held in Sydney, James showed a variety of subjects, including beaches of the Central Coast, New South Wales. He liked painting in that area and at Newcastle, where sailing ships used in the export of coal were still to be found until the early 1920s. He painted them in moored line at Ballast Bank, their sails furled, while they waited for a berth to load coal after discharging their ballast. An interesting outcome of this practice is that today much of the suburb of Stockton is built upon ballast from all over the world.

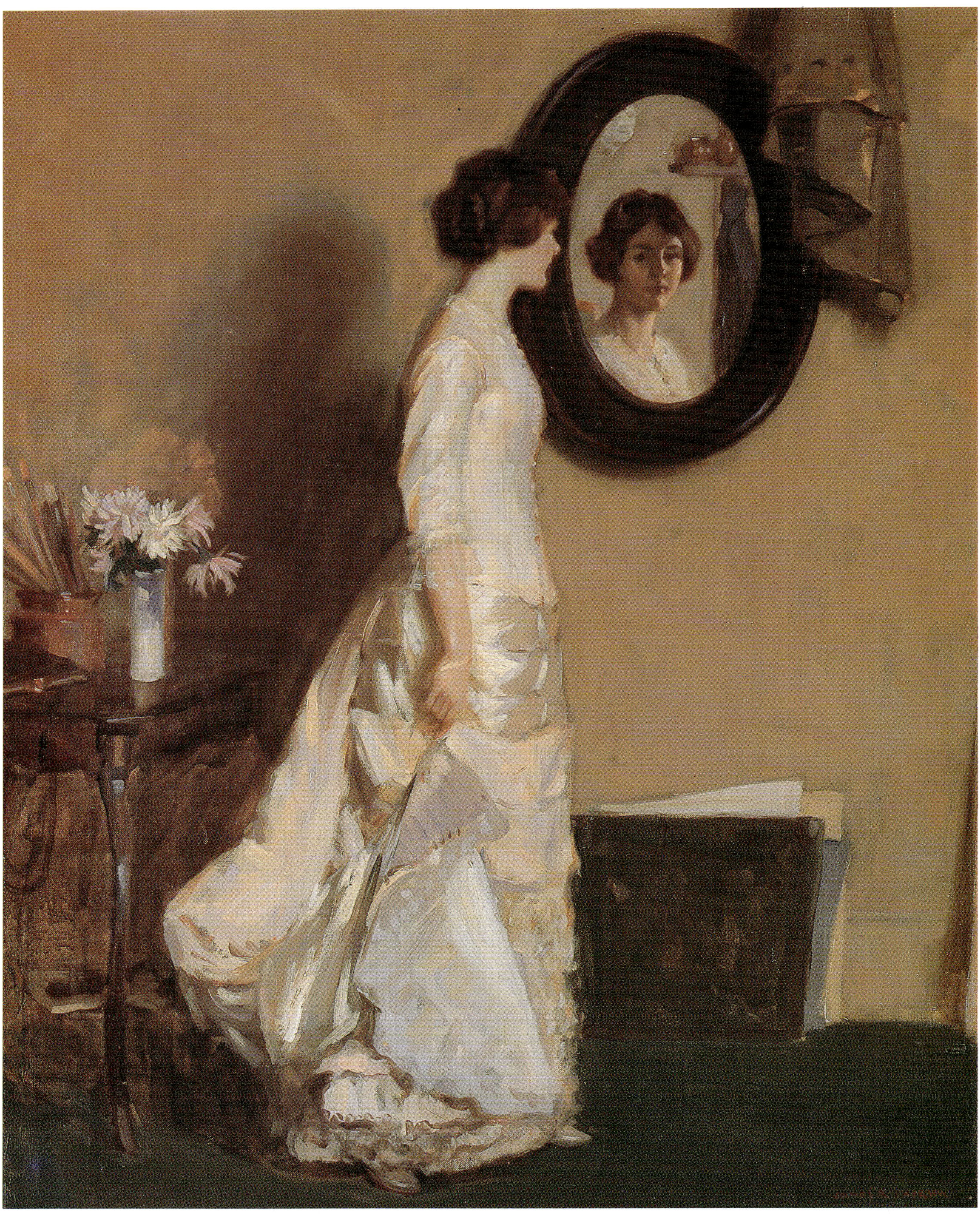

24 **MORNING IN THE STUDIO** 1915 Oil on canvas 81.5 x 66.5 cm
Reproduced by permission of the Australian National Gallery, Canberra

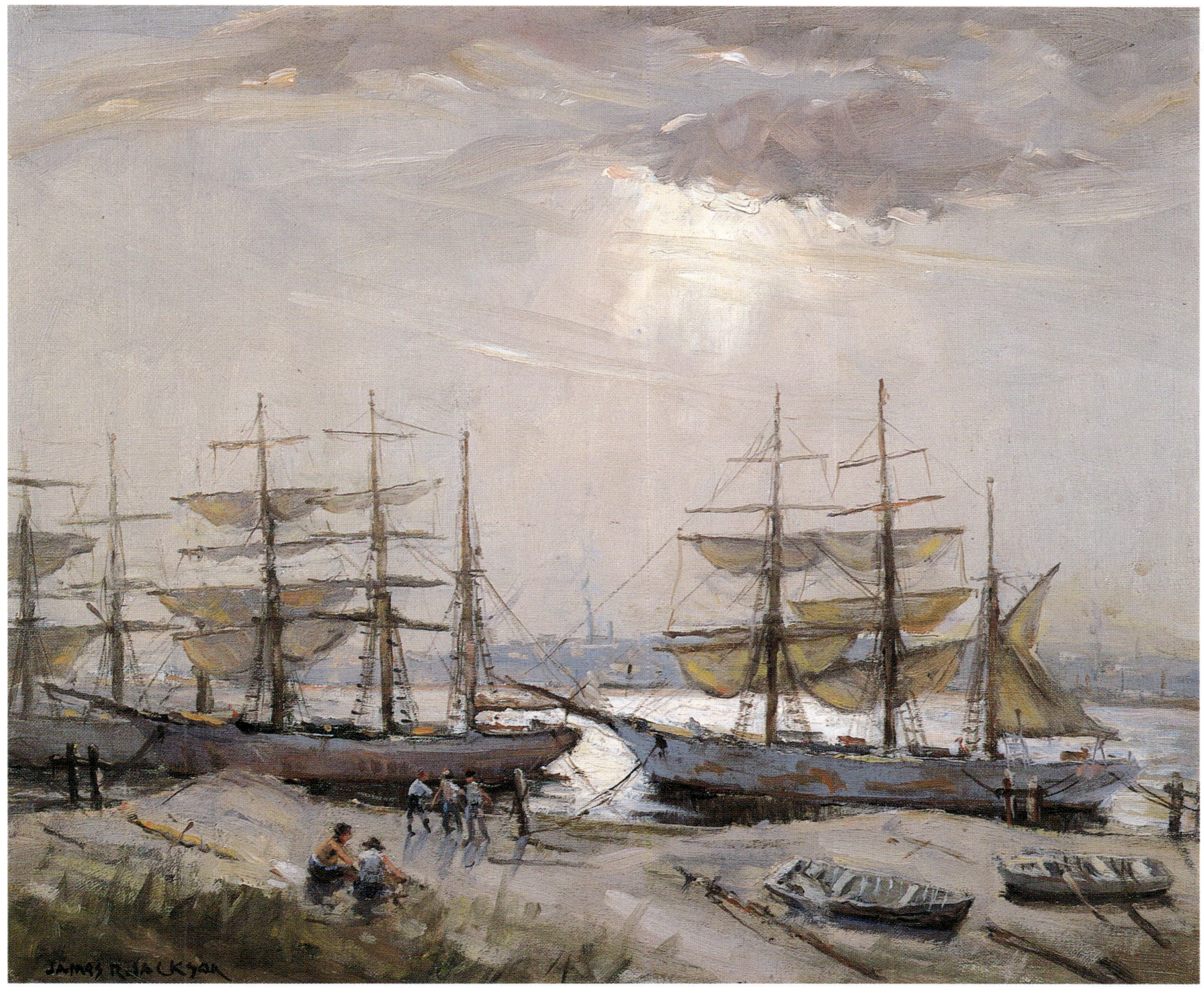

25   **DRYING SAILS, STOCKTON, N.S.W.** *c* 1918 43.6 x 53.8 cm
From the collection of the Benalla Art Gallery, Victoria

For some years there had been little variation in James's brushwork technique. His landscapes tended to be thickly painted and often portrayed close views of the country under blue skies with the occasional fluffy cloud. Skies were painted by many small brushstrokes, frequently applied vertically, in horizontal lines. Now he used freer brushwork, enjoyed the wider country scene and became more interested in cloudy skies.

Although he had painted many landscapes in New South Wales and Victoria he rarely exhibited them with the Royal Art Society exhibitions in Sydney. He tended to sell them privately from his studio, locally where they were painted, or in the Melbourne exhibitions. James felt that although there was a lot of landscape to paint, one had to be selective — often it was some simple subject which attracted him. 'You know very well, when you start, if you like a thing the paint seems to fall off the brush onto the right place and you get so excited about it — you feel instinctively if a thing's going to go right, because you have such enthusiasm about the subject.'

In New South Wales he liked to paint in the Bathurst and Orange districts, which were a comfortable journey by train and had a variety of scenery and colour. He especially liked to paint there in the golden autumn. He captured the light on the changing yellow poplars and contrasted this against the more stable ochres of eucalyptus and sheep hills. He was fascinated by brilliant sunlight and colour variations which he described as 'the essence of a landscape painter's life'. In the evenings he might visit the local pub or fish near his camp by the river using grubs and worms. He often panned for gold in a small

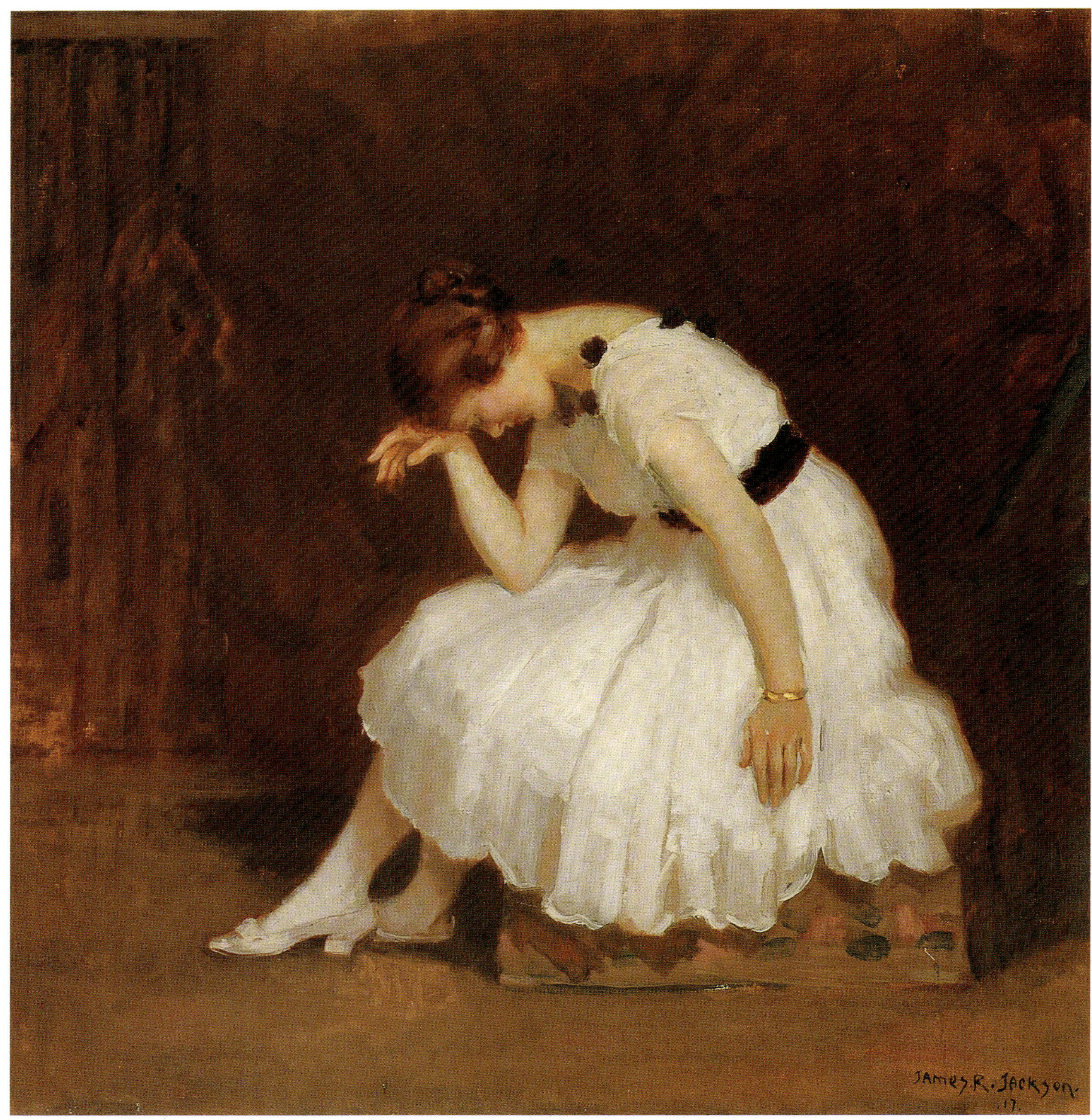

26   AFTER THE REHEARSAL 1917 Oil on canvas 56.4 x 59 cm
Art Gallery of South Australia, Adelaide

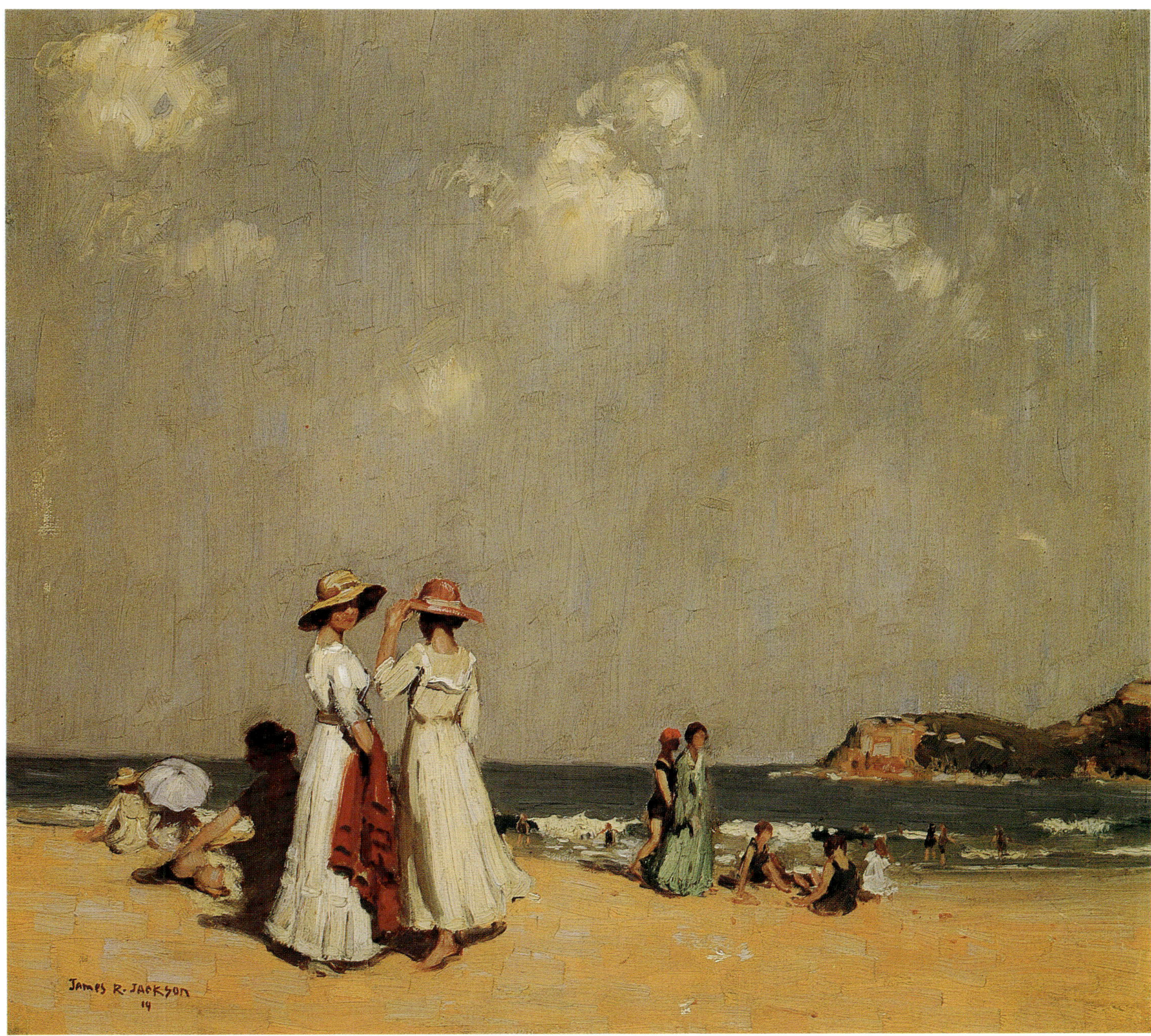

27   PICNIC AT TERRIGAL 1919 40 x 50.3 cm
Private Collection

dish which he always managed to pack. Although he was not very successful at it, he was always happy with any fleeting glint. He used to say, 'the diggers were there first'. This microscopic fortune was kept in a very small glass bottle and as its quantity increased over the years, so did his memories of good camp sites.

His studio in North Sydney, where he had been since 1909, became a mecca for artists and friends. During the teaching terms he held regular evening get-togethers, with a meal of bread, lobster, prawns, fruit and beer. These meetings were enjoyed by his friends, artists, some of his students and writers or conversationalists of the day. They were occasionally visited by Madame Melba, who had bought his works, and was described by James as one of his first patrons. As seating in chairs was limited, his friends would sit around his artist's throne or on the floor, being careful of drawing pins and tacks. His background drapes were used as cushions or to cover any unfinished works, which were not allowed to be seen.

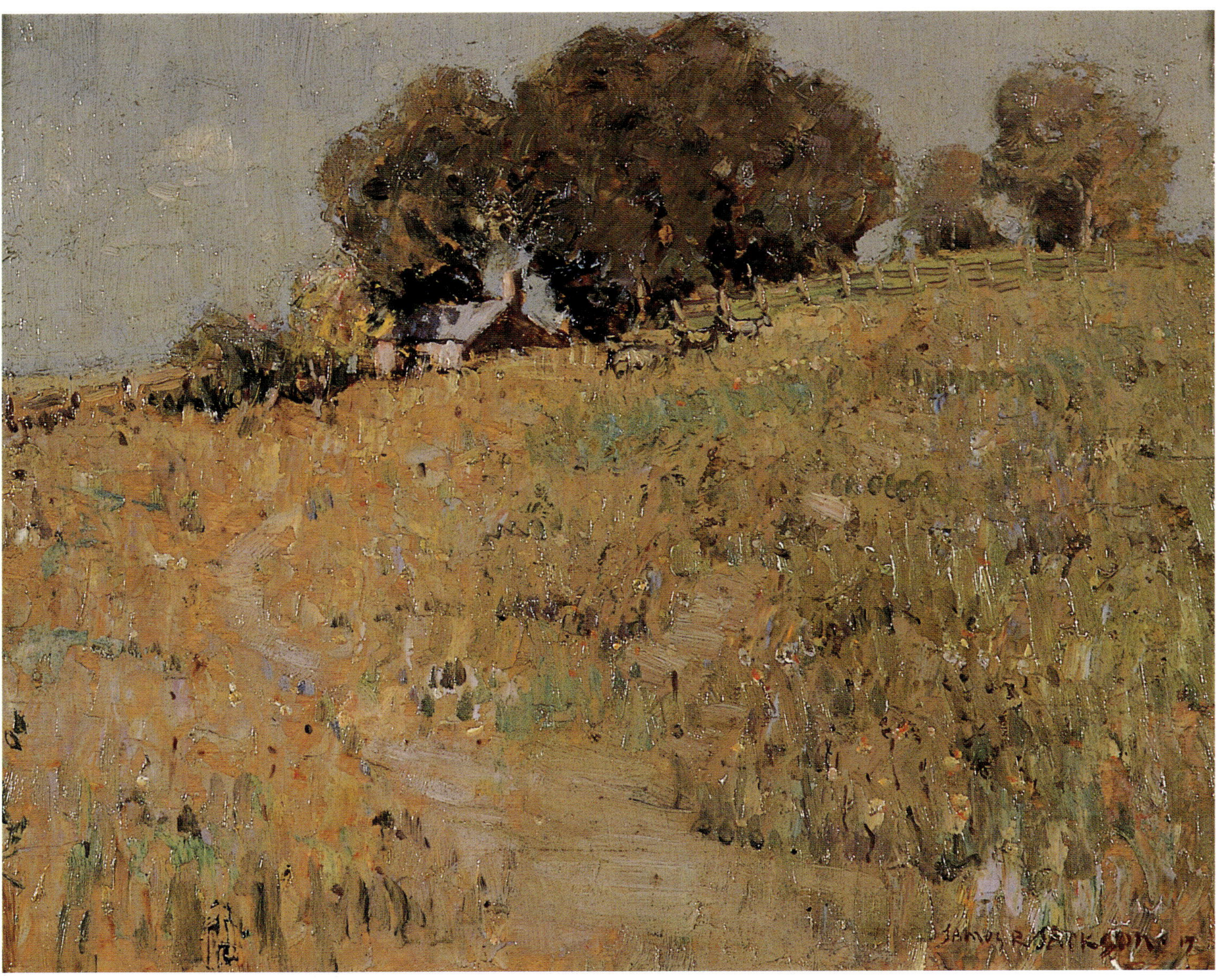

28   **FARM ON THE HILL** 1919 30.5 x 40 cm
Private Collection

Some of his friends with country relatives took him to stay and paint on their properties in various parts of New South Wales. With these new-found friends, and those he had made on his country camping trips, he now enjoyed very comfortable accommodation for his painting expeditions. His hosts appreciated his company as he was a good conversationalist, had travelled widely, loved the Australian countryside, and frequently supplied fresh fish for dinner. He usually gave them one of his smaller pictures of the property, or sold one of his bigger works 'for a fair price'. If it needed finishing, or if framing was a problem, 'Jimmy' — as he was now popularly known — would take it with him to Sydney. Many of his landscapes in the living rooms of country properties in the west from Bourke to Coonabarabran were acquired in this way.

Over these years, Jimmy had gradually increased the price of his harbour and beach scenes as his reputation as a painter of these subjects increased. He now asked up to 40 guineas for larger harbour views and seascapes and 200 guineas for large figure compositions, such as his very moving *Alone*, a picture of a weeping woman painted near the end of the war. His exhibits included more morning or evening effects of the harbour and as he had been selling for over a decade and kept few records, his titles started to be repeated.

Titles become a problem with many artists as the years roll on and Jimmy, with his numerous paintings of Sydney Harbour, tried very hard to vary them by identifying the locality, season and time of day. However, amongst his works are several called *Evening, Sydney Harbour* or *Autumn, Sydney Harbour* and, in his later years, at one stage he appears to have given up his quest for individuality of titles as many are simply called *Sydney Harbour*.

With the war over and the flu epidemic subsiding, the press found time to review the gentler things of life such as art, so that the fortieth Royal Art Society exhibition in 1919 was extensively reviewed by art critics from many papers. The *Sydney Morning Herald* of 23 August reported on Jimmy's *A Romance* as 'the finest figure painting in the galleries . . . the artist's manner is marked by refinement, feeling for colour and confident purpose'. The *Daily Telegraph* of 26 August concentrated on his seascapes and wrote: 'One of the most outstanding of this society's painters . . . Jackson has caught what must be one of the most difficult things in the world to catch and paint — that strange light effect which shows sometimes between showers, or within a few minutes of a coming fall of rain. It is an effect which reminds one of Wordsworth's light that never was on sea or land.'

The *Sydney Mail* article illustrated *A Romance* and his work was favourably commented on in the *Sunday Times* and the *Evening News*. However, the *Sun* was not so flattering in its statements. It commented: 'Mr Jackson's nice pleasant toned landscapes and figure subjects make one envisage a precise temperament with a formula from which nature will not be tempted. Not for him the delight of splashing round in splendid madness, not for him the poet's eye in a wild frenzy rolling. Nowhere does he blunder, nowhere is he moved from his sure—even cocksure—brushwork. Slick painting, pretty painting. Faultily faultless, icily regular, splendidly null, you admire the cleverness and deplore it at the same time.'

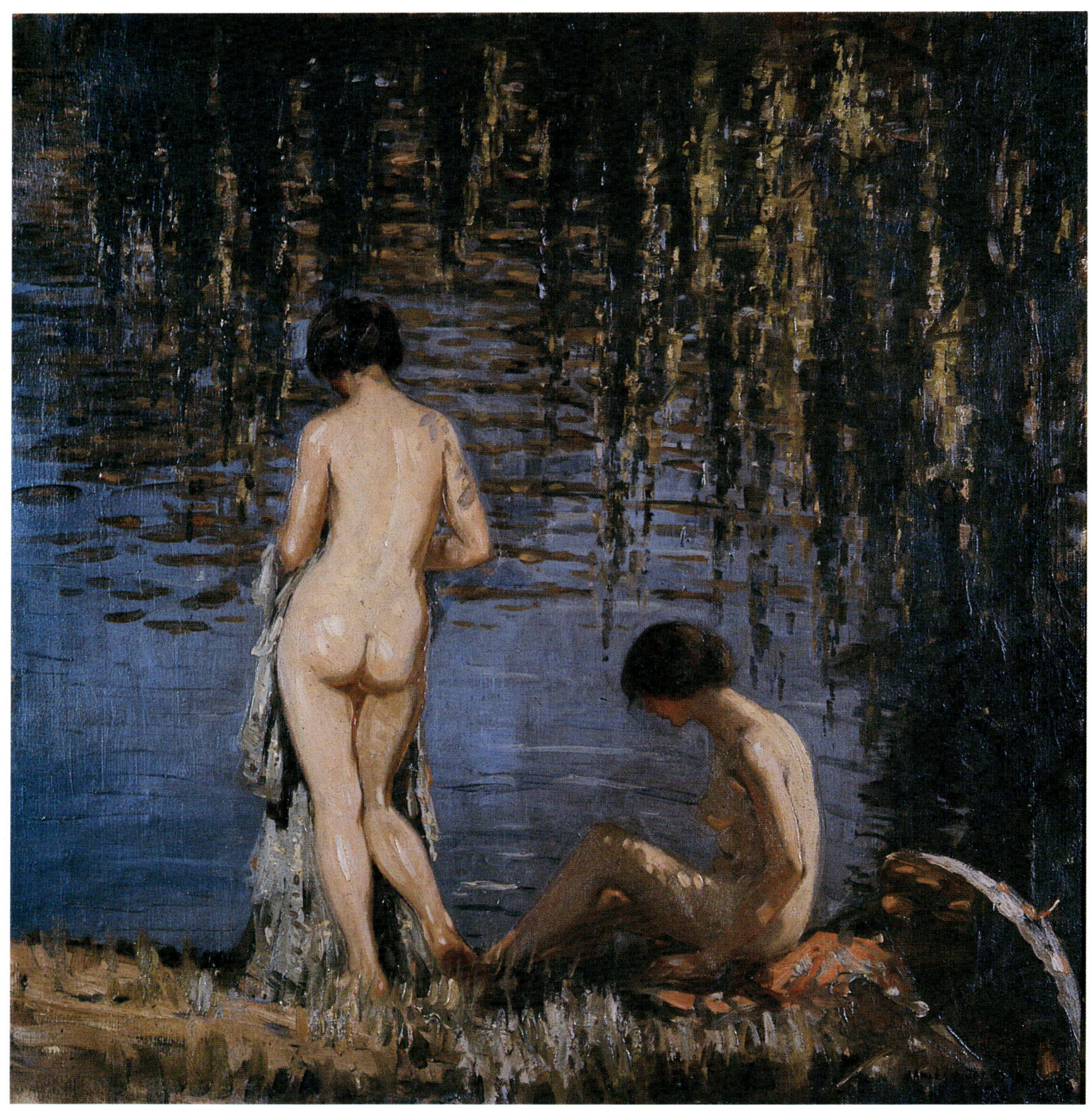

29   THE BATHERS 1920 60 x 60 cm
Private Collection

CHAPTER 5

The Early 1920s

*D*uring the postwar years and the early 1920s, Jimmy altered his style of painting and also his choice of subject matter and composition. Moderate changes in technique and subject occurred in his landscapes and harbour pictures but were most noticeable in his figure studies. His previously exhibited figures of dressed ladies were now replaced by outdoor nudes depicted as water nymphs. They stood in or near a pool of sparkling water and light filtered through the surrounding arbour and their occasional drapes.

These compositions usually portrayed three maidens, one of whom was actually a full-frontal nude. As secluded areas with streams around the main harbour had long disappeared, he painted his models beside pools in the bushy gullies behind Manly. The pictures were mostly large and, being difficult to carry, the detail was usually completed in his studio. As their surroundings had an outside motif, the general lighting effect and the figure was captured outside. He painted and exhibited these Arcadian compositions for only a few years, but continued to paint large studio nudes, which he occasionally exhibited.

Jimmy described how he painted figures outdoors: 'Now, outdoor painting of figures is a very, very difficult proposition , much more so than painting a figure indoors. I think it is owing to the fact of the sunlight and the alteration of shadows, the extreme height of colouring and the lighting of the figure. You have to work very quickly, and the main thing is to keep your drawing and the figure, because the light's changing. To get that scintillation of sunlight — you should have your palette all ready and be able to analyse the values and weights with every colour, so as you get the recession of the figure and the colours correct, otherwise the whole thing never looks as if it was outdoors.'

Changes also occurred in his selection of landscape subjects. For a few years his favourite country scenes altered from trees and pastures to haystacks and barns. He liked to paint these early in the morning to catch the cool light and long shadows. However, as it would have been cold and dewy, perhaps frosty, at this time of the day and as oils take a time to set up, he often captured the effects quickly in watercolour. He had always used watercolour in his sketchbook and during this period he was painting outdoors with watercolour artists M. J. MacNally and Harold Herbert. Jimmy signed and framed some of his watercolours, but the different technique, especially of highlights, did not suit him. He liked oils, where he could use strong, clear brushwork with high tones of thick paint added as final touches.

Jimmy's large harbour pictures now reflected a domination of sky in the composition with the development of stronger cloud patterns. He maintained his main interest in figures and boats in his more intimate harbour views. In these, the near water was alive with a multitude of colourful brushstrokes, while his treatment of a distant bay was more subdued. He also started to paint the harbour against the light, a theme which he developed for many years.

In his studio he continued to paint still life arrangements, contrasting the various textures of man-made objects to those of nature, including flowers and fish. Here he also painted his models and commissioned portraits. These were painted in about five sittings of some two hours each, on a fairly large canvas described by him as 'bishop-sized'. He entered in the newly established Archibald Prize, and in 1922 exhibited two portraits, one being of Hector Lamond, an Assistant Minister in Federal

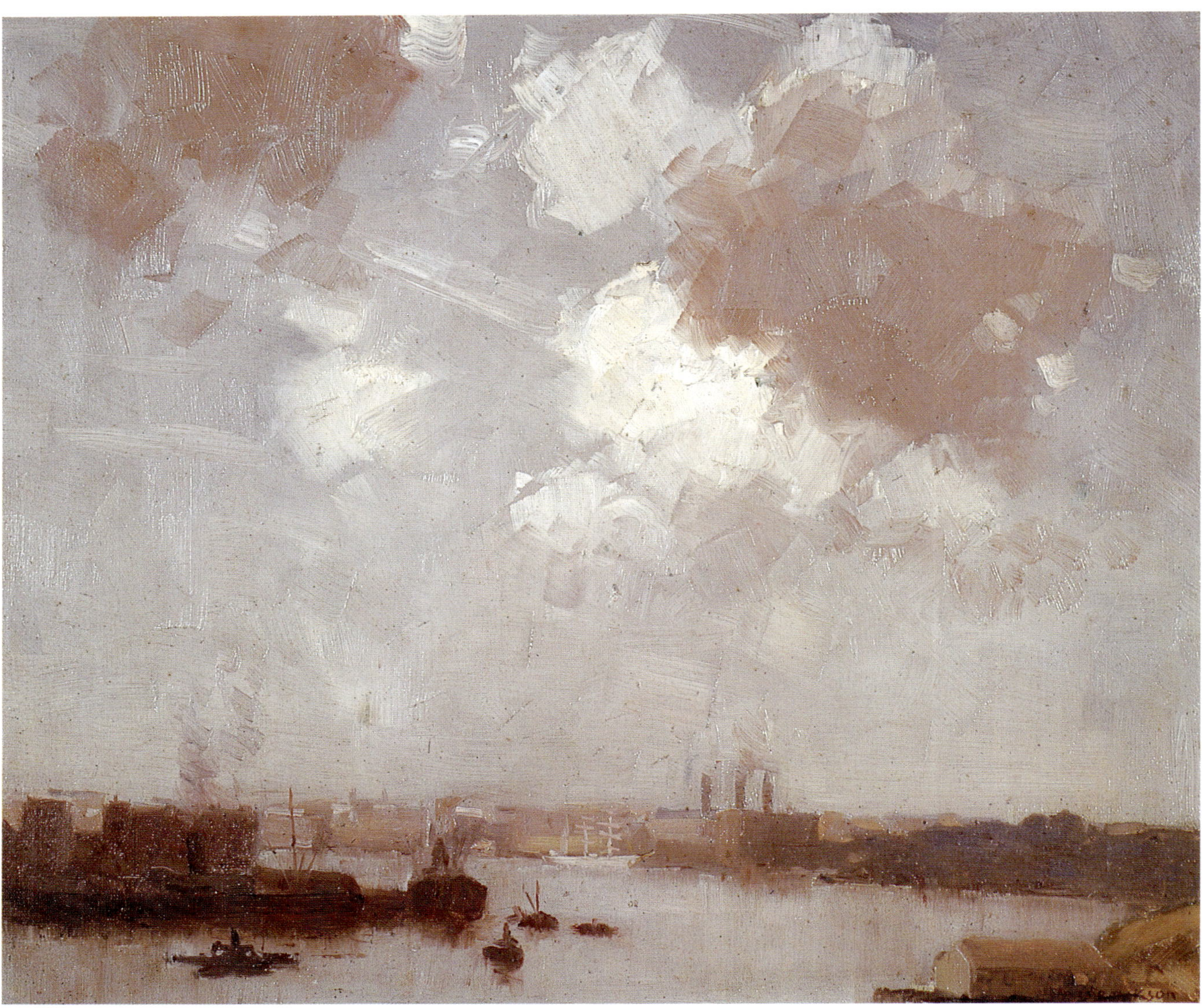

30 **DARLING HARBOUR, SYDNEY** 1919 44 x 54 cm
Private Collection

Parliament. Although Jimmy had always painted portraits, and continued to do so until the mid-1920s, he never entered in this prize again.

To maintain his drawing skills he did quick pencil sketches of the landscape and of people. He had become friendly with Percy Lindsay and with George Finey, who had recently come to Sydney, and joined them doing quick drawings. They did sketchbook studies of people performing everyday activities. Their subjects were found outside, waiting near tram stops or on the ferries; but the best indoor characters were always found in bars or in the cafes where the artists ate.

James painted his landscapes directly outside, and the larger ones — and those which he considered to be important works — were finished in his studio. For the larger works, he usually did preliminary pencil sketches in his notebook. When the subject was composed in his head, he roughed it in on the canvas, sometimes in his studio, but mostly outdoors, where he gained extra inspiration before he painted. He said, 'you lose all spontaneity, colour and light effect if you try to paint landscapes inside'.

Outdoor painting was hard physical work. Jimmy was a slightly built man, not more than 5'5'' (1.65 m), yet he would walk for miles to find a suitable subject, carrying his oil box by a strap over his shoulder, as well as a small folding stool, his easel and a black umbrella for shade. His smaller pictures were carried in the lid of his paintbox so that a common measurement for one side is 18'' (46 cm). These were usually on canvas, although he sometimes painted on plywood. His larger canvases on stretchers were also carried for long distances. As his wet paint needed protection from plants and insects,

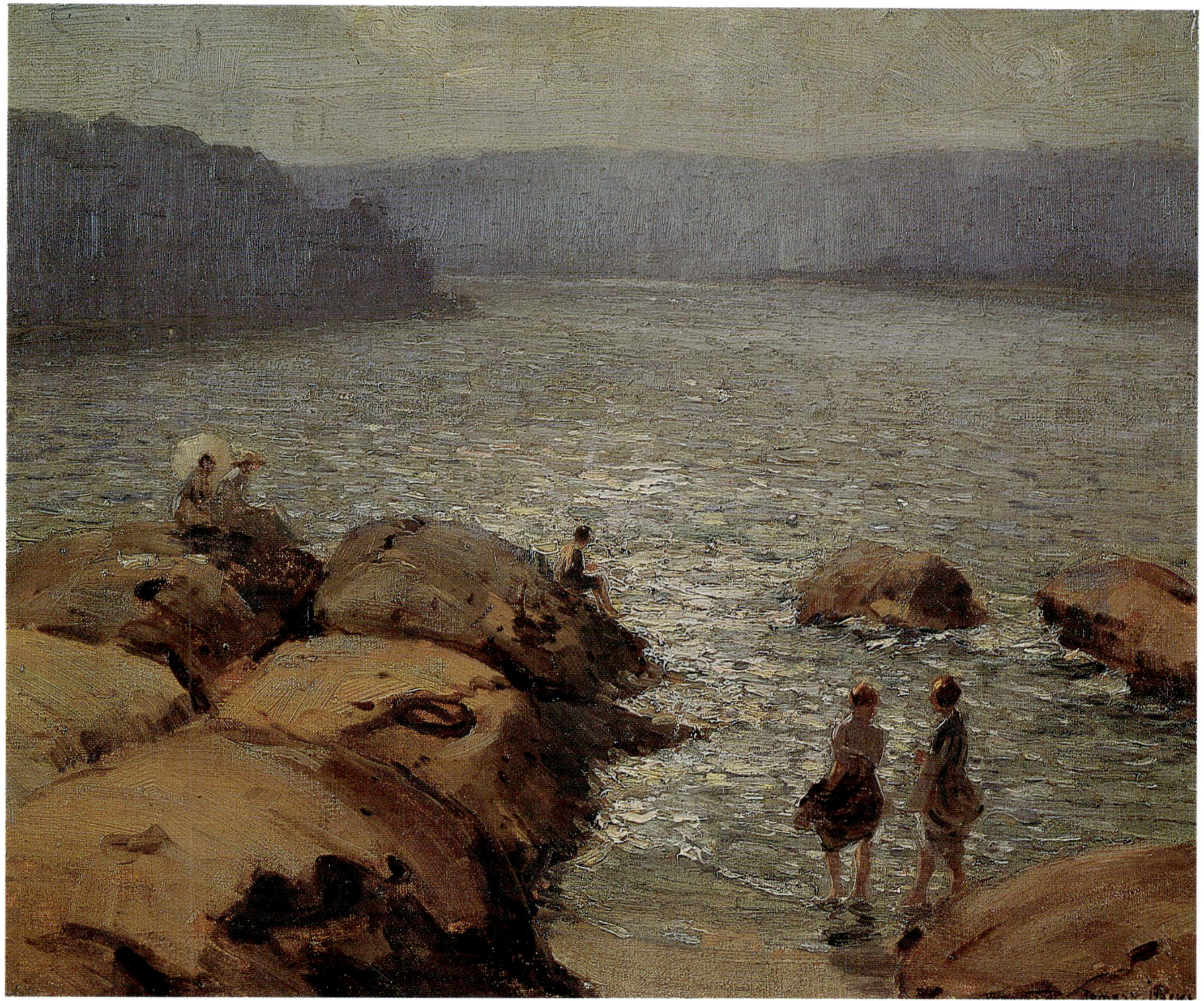

31 **MORNING MIDDLE HARBOUR, SYDNEY** 1920 Oil on canvas on cardboard 45.4 x 56 cm
Purchased 1920
Art Gallery of New South Wales

he used another canvas as a cover and separated the two by double-headed drawing pins. These pin marks may still be seen at the corners and sometimes in the centre of his untouched works.

He always wore his hat and, in those days, leather leggings for protection from snakebite and prickles. In his pockets he carried his cigarettes, a few biscuits, string to steady his umbrella and a small fishing line wound on a piece of cardboard. He continued to paint wearing his dark suit coat as he found the white of his long-sleeved shirts too much of a distracting highlight. Being his own boss, he was able to indulge his love of the outdoor life and the beauty of nature, and this was reflected in his art. A few days of rain were a chance to catch up on the practicalities of living, his studio and framing; but prolonged wet or wind dampened his spirits unless he was 'flat out' preparing for an exhibition.

Autumn remained his favourite painting season because of the milder temperature and relative consistency of the weather. He enjoyed the stillness and colour of an autumn harbour with its ochre headlands defined against the shimmering water and quiet depth of shadow in the bays. He had become friendly with one of his students, Dora Toovey, and he visited and painted from her home in the Bathurst area. This area, already familiar to him, was also his favourite autumn haunt and he continued to paint its surrounding golden landscape until the 1930s.

Many of Jimmy's picture titles include 'Autumn'; if you are a good observer of nature, you can always pick the season captured on his canvas without referring to the name. Winter he disliked: the cold westerlies whipped up the harbour or made the water look unattractively dark, while the country was either too green or the pastures eaten out. As he did not enjoy painting outside in the cold, he used the time preparing for exhibitions, especially the Royal Art Society exhibition which was held in late winter, and in painting portraits and still lifes.

The early 1920s were a busy time in his career, as he held his first one-man exhibition, was represented overseas and had several gallery acquisitions. These included the purchase by the Art Gallery of New South Wales of another of his works, *Morning, Middle Harbour*, from the 1920 Royal Art Society exhibition. This subject, with variations in its composition of figures standing against the light near the natural rock pool at the northern edge of Chinaman's Beach, Middle Harbour, was painted many times by him over the years.

Although Jimmy had exhibited widely and was represented in many galleries and collections, he had never mounted a one-man show. He started preparing for his first one in 1920 and opened the exhibition on 14 February 1921 at Gayfield Shaw's Art Salon, Sydney. His showing of thirty-eight pictures included harbour scenes with titles from *Morning* to *Evening Glow*; also expansive landscapes, intimate haystacks and still lifes. Lionel Lindsay wrote in his long appreciation in the catalogue: 'These landscapes fulfil admirably the dictum of the divine artist. They are the true expression of their maker's mind, of his way of enjoying the beauty of the world. Always out of doors with his painting kit, owning too much artistic courtesy to dictate terms to nature, Jackson awaits the moment when she is propitious to her lovers; when some effect of tone or colour grows magical in the light, some silhouette endowed with pictorial grace. Then he sets it down with all the passion of his mind and hand.' Also: 'Jackson possesses the lyrical impulse, that exultancy in the presence of the beautiful, without which all art expression is in vain. I read it clearly in these charming works, done without any *arriere pensée* of pleasing, but which are so sustained by the painter's instinct for beauty and truth, that they contain those elements which must remain a source of continuous pleasure.'

The art critic of the *Daily Telegraph* said of this exhibition: 'Jackson is, above all things, a painter of Sydney Harbour. His work lies somewhere midway between that of the realists and the romanticists — Jackson does not attempt imaginary flights, but he can catch exactly the feeling that attaches to some far-off blue patch of water, seen across yellow-brown landscape, dim on a hot, moist day. Or the struggling of a pale sunlight through the misty air above the water at dawn; or a long, wooded point, yellow-brown, again, with house-roofs showing, and a line of hills on the other side of the harbour and, between and below, a pale blue sheet of water, all on a hot and hazy midsummer afternoon.'

Jimmy caught the mood of the hour, the atmosphere, the shadow, the reflection and the intimacy of a bay — so much so that by now he was famous as a painter of Sydney Harbour and was mentioned in *Who's Who* in Australia. Throughout his impressions, his use of selective detail was always accurate but never overpowering. His drawings and placement of houses, bridges, wharves and boats form an interesting historical record of the harbour and other development from 1901 until the 1970s. This is especially so in his portrayal of the Spit and Middle Harbour, which he loved to paint. He recorded a beauty which has long since gone.

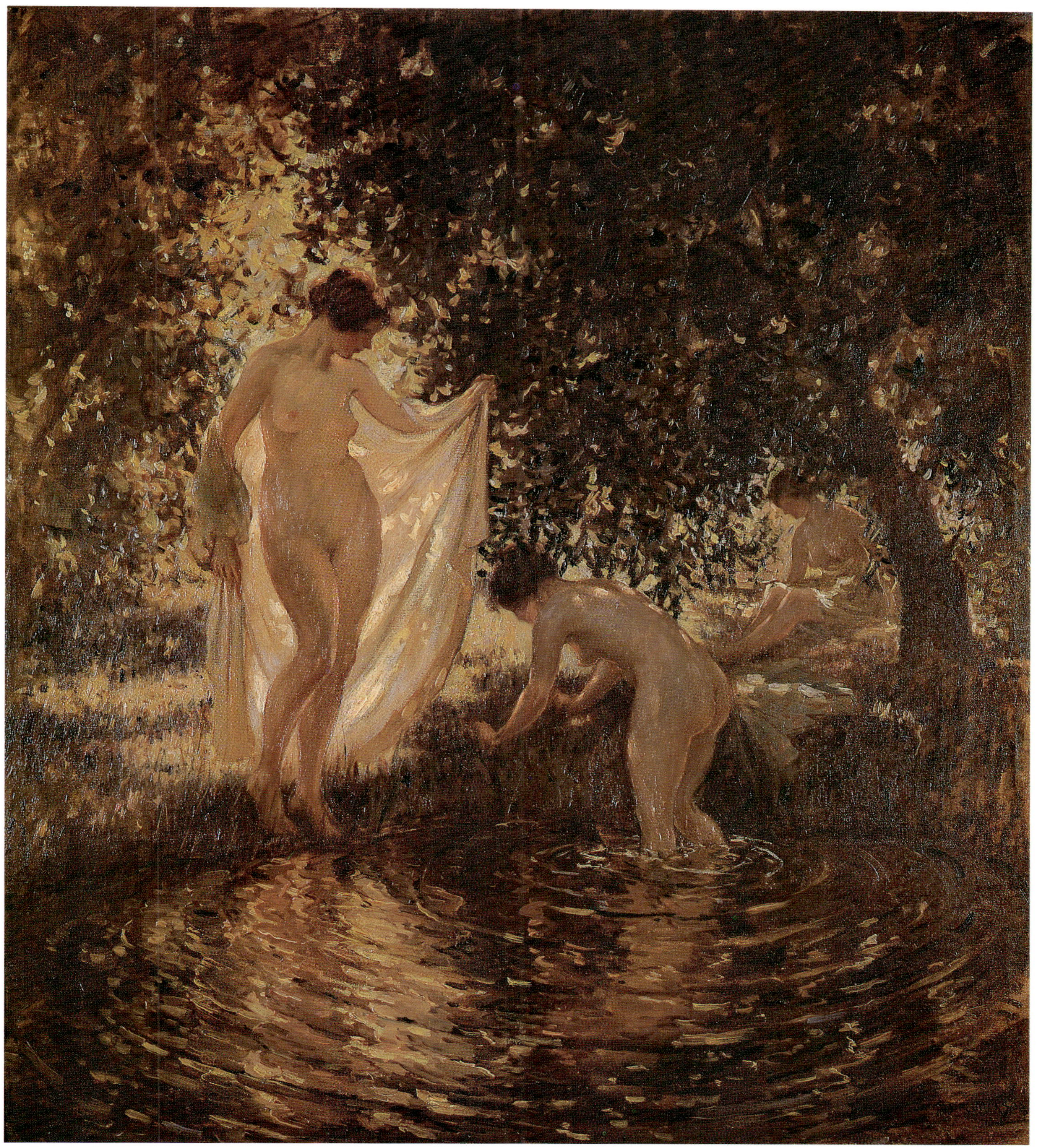

32   **A SYLVAN RETREAT** 1921 112 x 102 cm
Private Collection

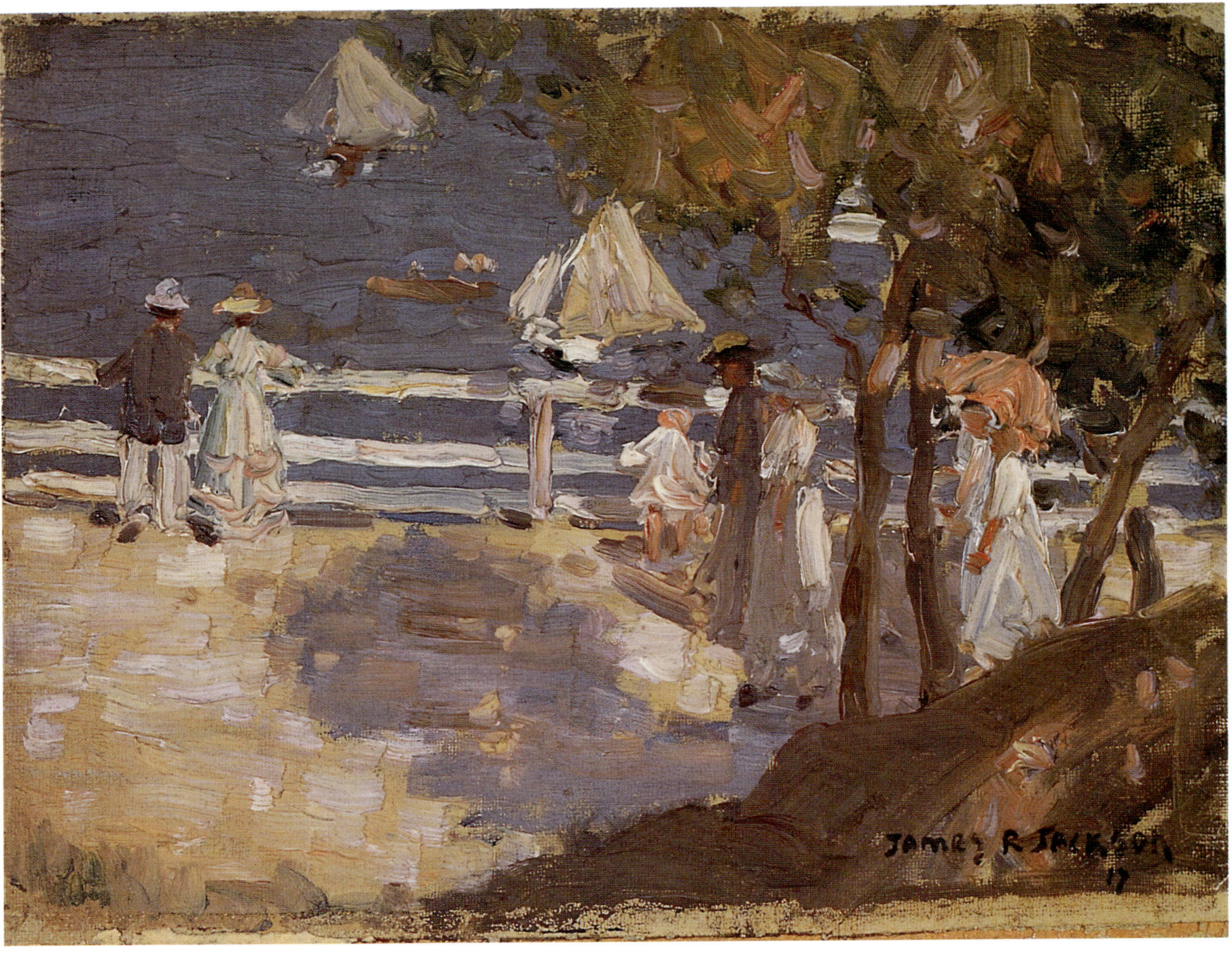

33 PATHWAY TO THE SEA 1917 19 x 25 cm
From the collection of the Tamworth Art Gallery, New South Wales

On 10 August 1921 the *Sydney Mail* gave Jimmy a full-page review titled 'A clever landscape and figure painter'. The article included four photos, one taken of him in typical painting outfit — hat, suit and bow tie — while the other three depicted earlier varieties of his work. They were *Narrabeen Lakes*, a landscape with three figures standing by the shores of the lake; his figure study, *Alone*, painted in 1918; and *Dreaming*, his picture of a girl in a rowing boat in the shade of a tree, bought by the Art Gallery of New South Wales in 1916. They were all pre-1920s works and were probably selected by him as a representative balance of his work. He was by then exhibiting his Arcadian nudes, portraits, still lifes, Sydney Harbour pictures and recent landscapes of the Hawkesbury River area and the Midwest.

Following his 1920 one-man exhibition, he continued to show regularly in Sydney with the Royal Art Society and in private galleries. He exhibited two sketches in November 1921, at a representative exhibition, Colour Notes and Sketches, at Gayfield Shaw's Art Salon. These were *The Moorings* and *The Boatshed*, both priced at 10 guineas.

Very quick, impressionistic sketches had featured in his portfolio for years. Typical examples are his 1919 *Harbour Scene*, painted at Chinaman's Beach, Middle Harbour, and now in the Australian National Gallery, Canberra; and an earlier little gem, *Pathway to the sea*, which is in the Tamworth Art Gallery, New South Wales. These would have taken him an hour or two to put down without alterations, after years of knowledge and practice. Most of these sketches were a simple statement of the moment, capturing a mood, colour or atmospheric effect. They were not retouched or worked on in his studio

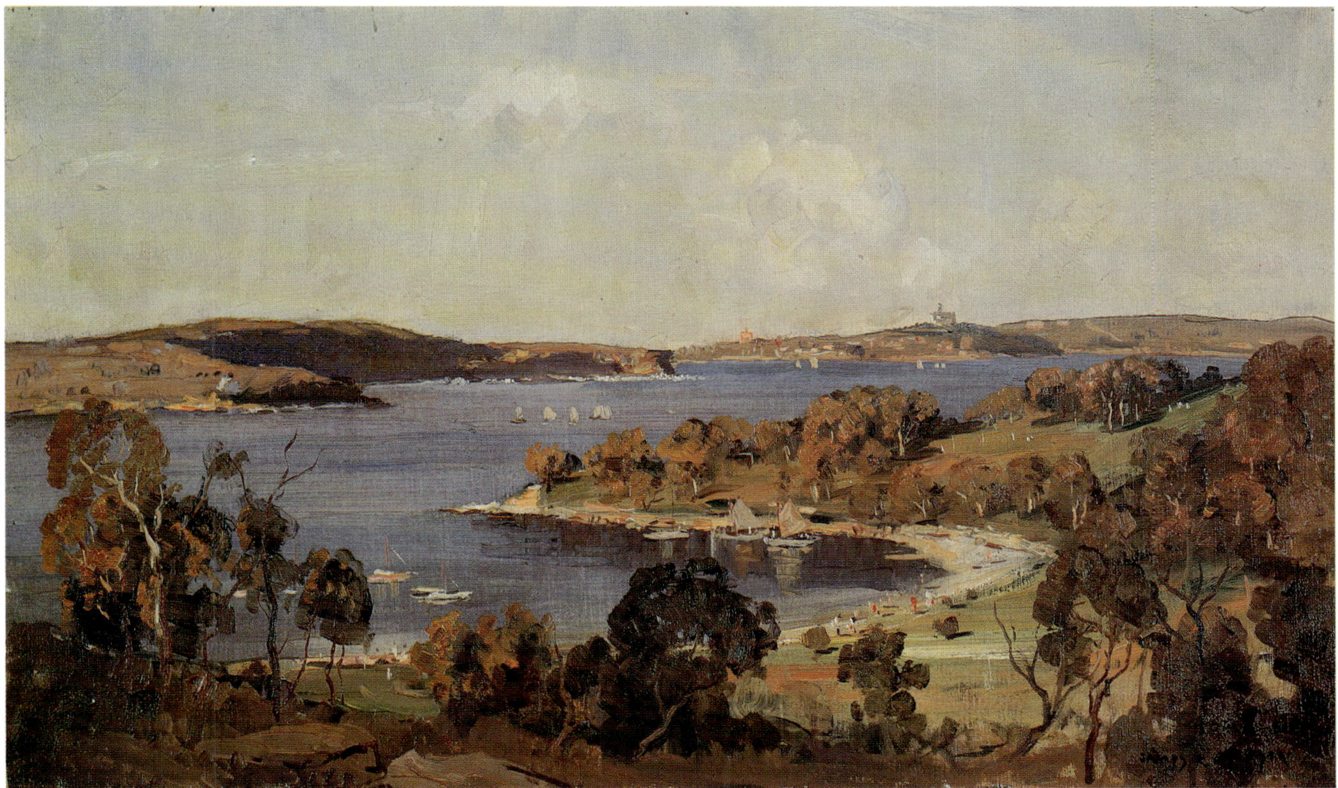

34   ENTRANCE TO MIDDLE HARBOUR, SYDNEY 1922 31 x 61 cm
Private Collection

as were a lot of his larger works. Some formed the basis of larger, stretcher-sized works, which he composed and drew up in the studio then took to the site to do the painting.

Jimmy's first Melbourne one-man show was held in May 1922 at the Decoration Galleries in Collins Street. He had previously been represented in Melbourne at this gallery and also with his annual contribution to the exhibition of the Australian Art Association. His exhibition was titled Oil Paintings of Sydney Harbour and Its Surroundings and consisted of thirty pictures, mainly of New South Wales landscapes and Sydney Harbour. It contained only three previously seen pictures but was not over-enthusiastically reviewed by the art critics of the Melbourne papers. This may have been due to seeing beautiful Sydney Harbour but was more likely due to a lack of sparkle in the actual works. Jimmy's mood and outlook on the day was usually reflected in his work and it is possible that this recent representation in Melbourne showed a lack of sparkle caused by worry. He had just moved from his much loved studio, and this was an enormous, unsettling undertaking. However, the art critic of the *Age* on 3 May commented that he 'deserved a place among the first half dozen of living Australian landscape painters' and mentioned his 'fine and vivid colour sense'.

The Royal Art Society altered its constitution in 1922, the year in which Jimmy turned forty, and Jimmy was elected one of its first eight Fellows. The others were Lawson Balfour, Charles Bryant, Lister Lister, Sir John Longstaff, Margaret Preston, A. Dattilo Rubbo and John S. Watkins. James was a very active member and, with A. Dattilo Rubbo, was the Society's chief instructor at their rooms in lower Pitt Street, Sydney. Jimmy always contributed a wide variety of subjects to interest the viewers of their exhibitions and was now asking as much for his large harbour scenes as for his figure studies. However, he was given only fair press reviews as fashions in art styles were changing. Jimmy had also become what he described as 'paint tired' and needed a change in his routine of teaching. These factors, plus the death of a close sibling and the worry of knowing that he would yet again have to move his studio, depressed him and affected his art even though his sales were still good.

The planning and development of the road approaches for the Sydney Harbour Bridge involved Junction Street, where Jimmy's studio was situated. This type of accommodation was difficult to obtain as he needed a large quiet room with a good southern light. He preferred southern light as it was softer and fairly constant during the day and throughout the year, so that shadows on studio compositions did not change significantly.

As he had saved some money, Jimmy decided to leave North Sydney and build his own home and studio on a narrow, steep waterfront block, just north-west of the punt at the Spit. It was a one-and-a-half storey building with his studio below facing south, and the living area above. Surrounded by angophora gums, it had spectacular views of the Spit and Middle Harbour towards the Heads. He moved into it in 1923.

This was part of the change he needed; here he had his much loved views of the Spit, which he painted many times, and was able to fish from his own beach. The nearby punt took him to tram stops for the North Sydney and Cremorne ferries for views of the city and the main harbour, and he had easy tram access to Manly and the northern beaches.

Two of his Sydney Harbour pictures were exhibited in the Exhibition of Australian Art in London in 1923, which was organised by the Society of Artists, Sydney. These pictures are illustrated in the book of that name. Prior to the London exhibition, he contributed to the fund-raising Gift Exhibition, which was held at Farmers Store, Sydney. Both illustrated pictures glistened with impressions of light on water, contrasting with foreground rocks in *Evening, Sydney Harbour* and with boats and their reflections in *Drying Sails*.

Jimmy had become very fond of painting these intimate glimpses of sail or other harbour activities in the morning or afternoon against the light and exhibited several of them in his 1921 exhibition. These included *Close of Day, Middle Harbour* and *Evening Glow, Sydney Harbour*. They show his mastery of his art. Although painted into the sun, there is no black and white effect as one may have expected. Instead, around the strike of sunlight on the water, there is vibrancy yet control of colour. It abounds in the foreground and the middle distance, while his boats and headlands glow with it. The silhouette of sail or mast in muted colour is spectacular and exemplifies his drawing skills.

The Art Gallery of New South Wales bought his large *Neutral Bay, Sydney Harbour* for 150 guineas in 1923, but the following year exchanged it for his figure study *Dawn*, which was exhibited in that year's Royal Art Society exhibition. *Neutral Bay, Sydney Harbour* was unusual as it was unlike his later paintings of that name, which were usually close views of water framed by gum trees. It showed a very distant view of the harbour with major interest in the then sparsely developed foreground, which led down to and complemented the softness of a quiet harbour.

Dawn is a large picture and was a development of his painting against the light motif, which he had now introduced into his studio portraits. It portrays a semisilhouette of a women — who is standing looking out of a large, highlighted window — greeting the dawn's rosy haze on the harbour as the title conveys. Her cleverly painted, backlit pale blue dress suggests that she has just returned from partying all night. According to Jimmy this was one of his best works: 'I think that was one of my

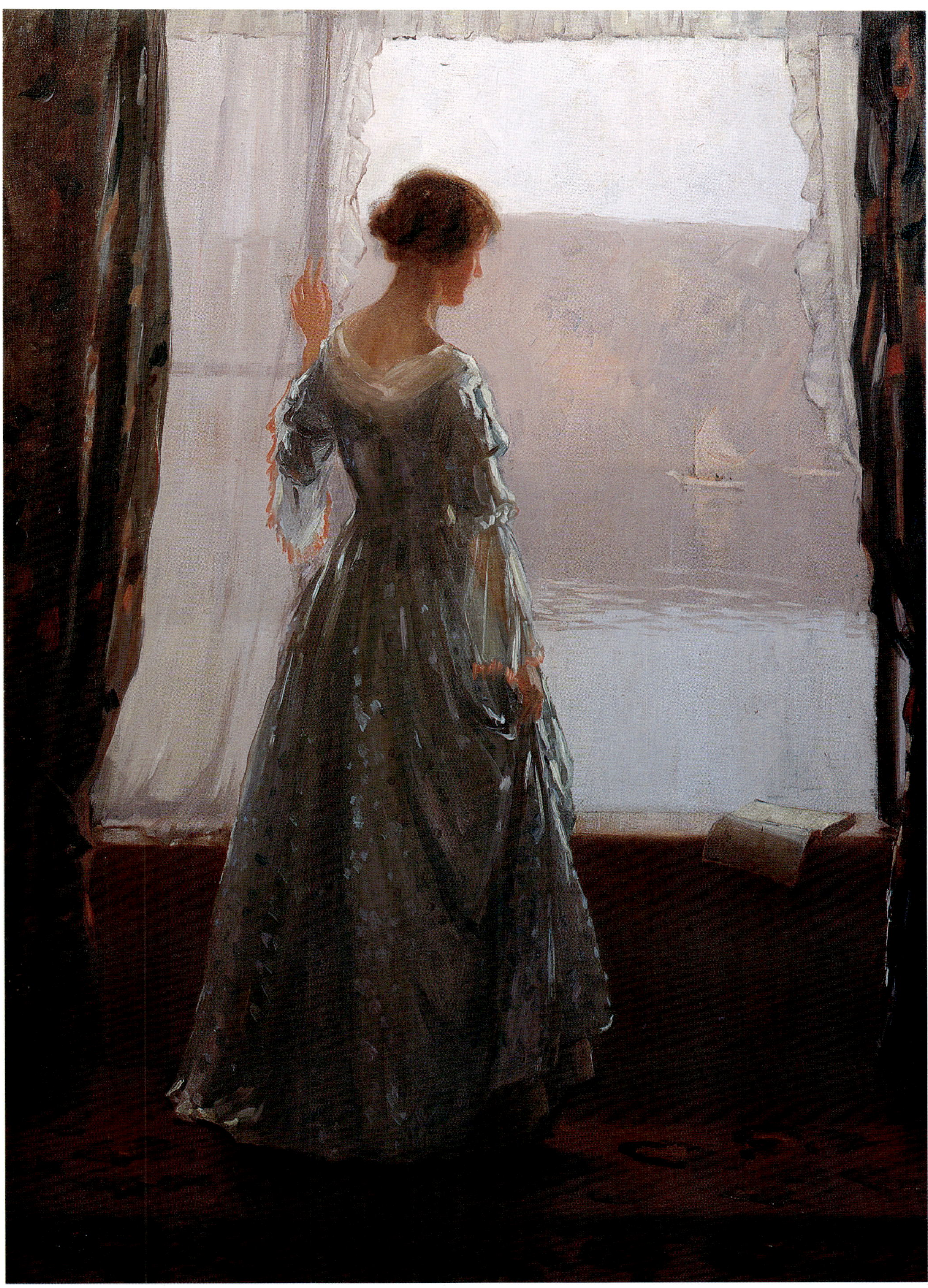

35   **'DAWN'** 1924 Oil on canvas 98.5 x 72.5 cm
Acquired 1924
Art Gallery of New South Wales

finest paintings. I got the idea after a little party — a great old friend of mine had an extremely fine dress with a lovely old taffeta skirt, and she posed for me. I drew the thing in and made a preliminary sketch of it. I painted the head and the hands, and I put different colours temporarily about the dress so as not to embarrass the canvas. I put these colours down and then took them all off with turps. Then I painted the skirt and the blouse and all that in one morning — you have to, because the folds in the skirt alter completely, you've got to be very sure of that. Velasquez, in his *Retreat from Breda*, that wonderful thing in the Prado Gallery, the drapery in that is considered quite a masterpiece — I should say that that was painted directly, straight out, just in the one go or the one painting.'

Jimmy was represented in the Empire Exhibition, held in 1924 at Wembley, England, by *The Holiday*; and, at the beginning of the year, he won the 50 pound Inaugural Manly Art Prize. This was for his major work *Middle Harbour from Manly Heights*, which was one of his last big pictures of the Spit before the connecting new bridge link was opened in February 1925. It is an important picture, both historically and for his stylistic development. The influence and integration of his broadening landscape style is evident in his use of wide and rhythmic land masses, leading the eye up Middle Harbour to distant suburbia — all under a hot, late-summer sky.

Historically, *Middle Harbour from Manly Heights* is important for two reasons. Firstly, it shows the sparsity of pre-bridge housing and road development, and people's dependence on the punt and trams. James shows the horrendously steep grade of Upper Spit Road, which is clearly seen above the enlarged quarry. Enlargement of the quarry, with the destruction of the lower part of the old track, was necessary for the construction of an easier grade for vehicles, which had used the tram grade of Parriwi Road since before the turn of the century. With plans for a connecting bridge, the alteration of the old Upper Spit Road's grade to the more accessible present-day one started in 1922, when this work was probably painted. Jimmy said that the rock was removed by blasting small areas and that men using picks and shovels worked very hard to remove the rubble in wheelbarrows.

Secondly, Jimmy's painting was the first painting purchased by the Manly Art Gallery and Historical Collection and they acquired it in November 1924 for 100 pounds. Following Jimmy's receipt of the art prize, the idea to purchase his painting and others, and to build a gallery to house them (together with local items of historical significance) arose from a letter signed by five prominent citizens to the Mayor of Manly in January 1924. They requested that the Mayor do all in his power to 'retain this beautiful picture for the citizens of Manly. The Council could then agree to become the Trustees of the picture until such time as a public Art Gallery is erected in Manly'. The idea was enthusiastically adopted at a meeting in March and the money to purchase Jimmy's picture was raised by donation. Anyone donating 10 or more guineas was entitled to the honour of having his or her name placed on the Founders' Roll, which was limited to the first fifty subscribers, and Jimmy was one of the first. His picture was shown at the Council Chambers until the Manly Art Gallery was built. In those days, when unfurnished four-bedroom cottages were letting for well under 2 pounds per week, a donation of 10 guineas was a considerable sum.

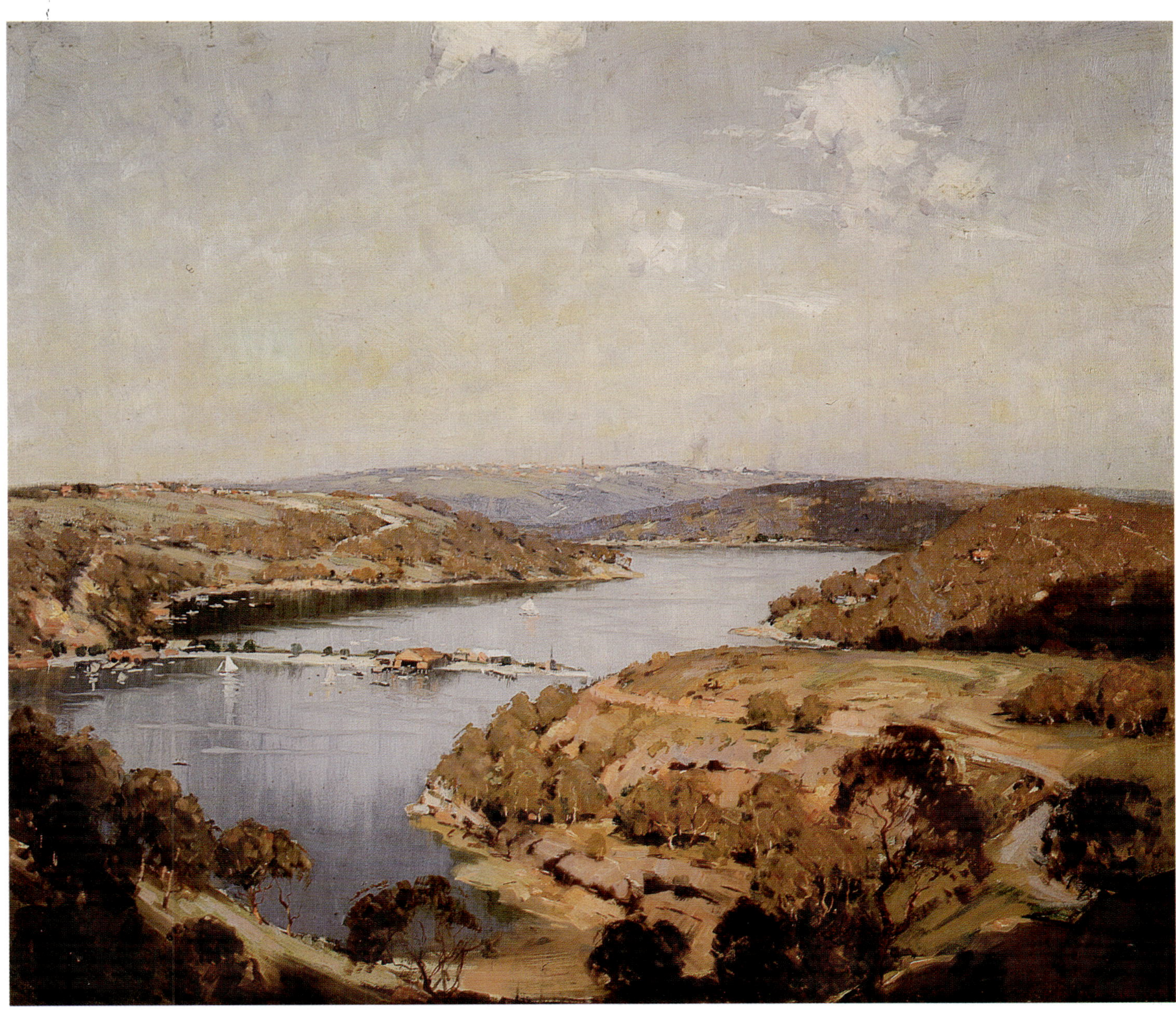

36   MIDDLE HARBOUR FROM MANLY HEIGHTS, N.S.W. 1923 Oil on canvas 77 x 92.3 cm
From the collection of the Manly Art Gallery and Museum

Although James was considered a confirmed bachelor he had in fact fallen in love with his art student Dora Toovey, whom he had been seeing for over a year. Dora hoped to marry him. However, she had become tired of waiting for him to propose and thought a change of scenery was needed to think things out. She arranged a transfer from her position as secretary in the stores office of the Commonwealth Bank in Surry Hills to the country, and announced this news to Jimmy after cooking his now regular weekly baked dinner at the new studio. The old adage 'The way to a man's heart . . .' may have been partly responsible, but more likely the thought of separation forced the issue and finally made him propose. They became engaged early in 1924 and were married at the end of that year.

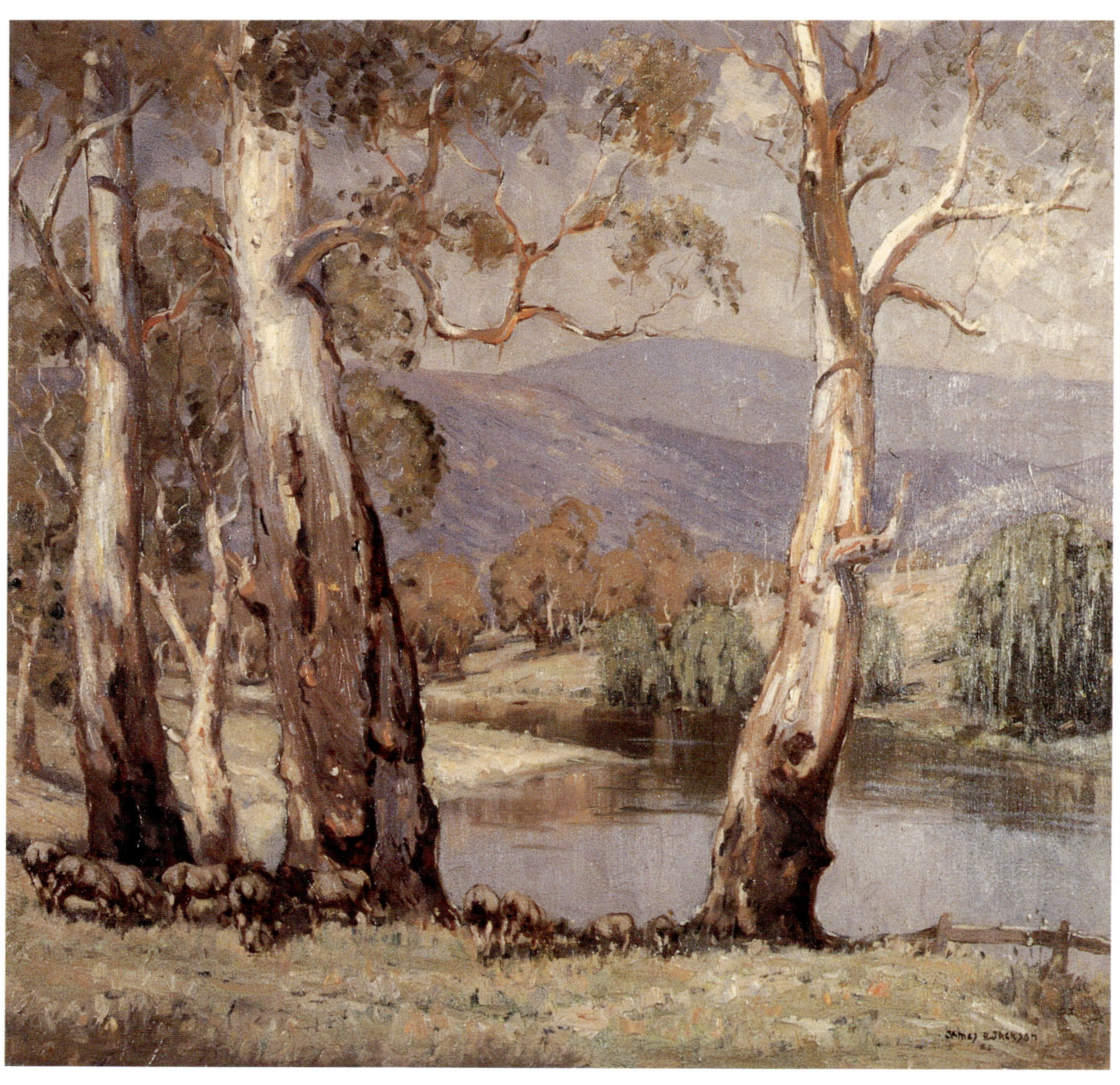

37 SUMMER PASTORAL ACT 1925 61 x 64 cm
Private Collection

CHAPTER 6
Marriage

Jimmy's marriage to Dorathea Toovey in December 1924 in the local church at Seaforth was followed by a reception at his nearby studio. It was attended by the whole of the Royal Art Society and many artists and friends. The church and the studio were decorated with masses of native white flannel flowers and touches of red Christmas bush. As they had little furniture, the overcrowded guests were more than content to sit on the studio floor or admire the view of Middle Harbour while lying on sheets spread out in the garden.

The wedding was arranged for the end of the art school year so that they could enjoy the long summer holidays as their honeymoon. This was spent camping near Tharwa at 'Lanyon' on the banks of the Murrumbidgee River. They travelled to the Australian Capital Territory by train, then by horse-drawn carriage down the steep, winding dirt road to the river.

Dora was sixteen years younger than James. She was descended from early settlers in the Bathurst area on her mother's side and army engineers on her father's. Both her parents were musical, as was Dora, but her main artistic inclination was painting, which she had learnt since 1917 at the Royal Art Society, where Jimmy was one of her tutors. During this time she had worked in the Commonwealth Bank.

As it was summer, they needed only a light camp, so they were able to take enough painting materials to last for several months. Jimmy, as usual, left cheques with the local store to pay for their basic provisions and relied on the mail to drop these off as a weekly delivery. He rarely ordered perishables, which were quickly destroyed by the heat, flies and ants. Their fresh protein was supplied by the fish and rabbits Jimmy caught, which were also often traded for milk.

This was an extremely rosy time for Jimmy and he painted prolifically. His joyful mood and enthusiasm is evident in his colourful, large landscapes, such as the *Valley of Tharwa*, now in the National Gallery of Victoria. This is a fine example of his work, admirably drawn with full brushstrokes, depicting the valley in summer hues. Other canvases portray mountain ranges, such as *Mt. Tennant*, and reflections of the river, such as *Cotter Crossing*. Shaded sheep hide near the dark bases of giant river gums, whose contrasting pale stems tower out of the canvas.

Jimmy studied and painted sheep in small flocks at various times of the day, and made them the main interest in several of his pictures. He drew them going up and down hills, with apparently ungainly but accurately portrayed movements, and captured their interesting shadow patterns. Dairy cows in various lights were also painted as they rested or grazed on flat pastures. Horses rarely appeared in his sketchbook although he enjoyed riding.

After this prolonged holiday, Jimmy returned to the studio with the nucleus of his next exhibition, and resumed his teaching position. In February 1925 the long-awaited first Spit Bridge was opened, giving him an easy walk to city trams. Also in that year the monumental, Egyptian temple-like constructions which guard the narrowing entrance to Middle Harbour were completed. These are the valve houses at the inlet and end of the Spit siphon which conveys Sydney's north-west effluent to the ocean in the east. These landmarks changed Jimmy's view of the Spit, and any of his pictures of this area painted since the mid-1920s show them accurately positioned and drawn.

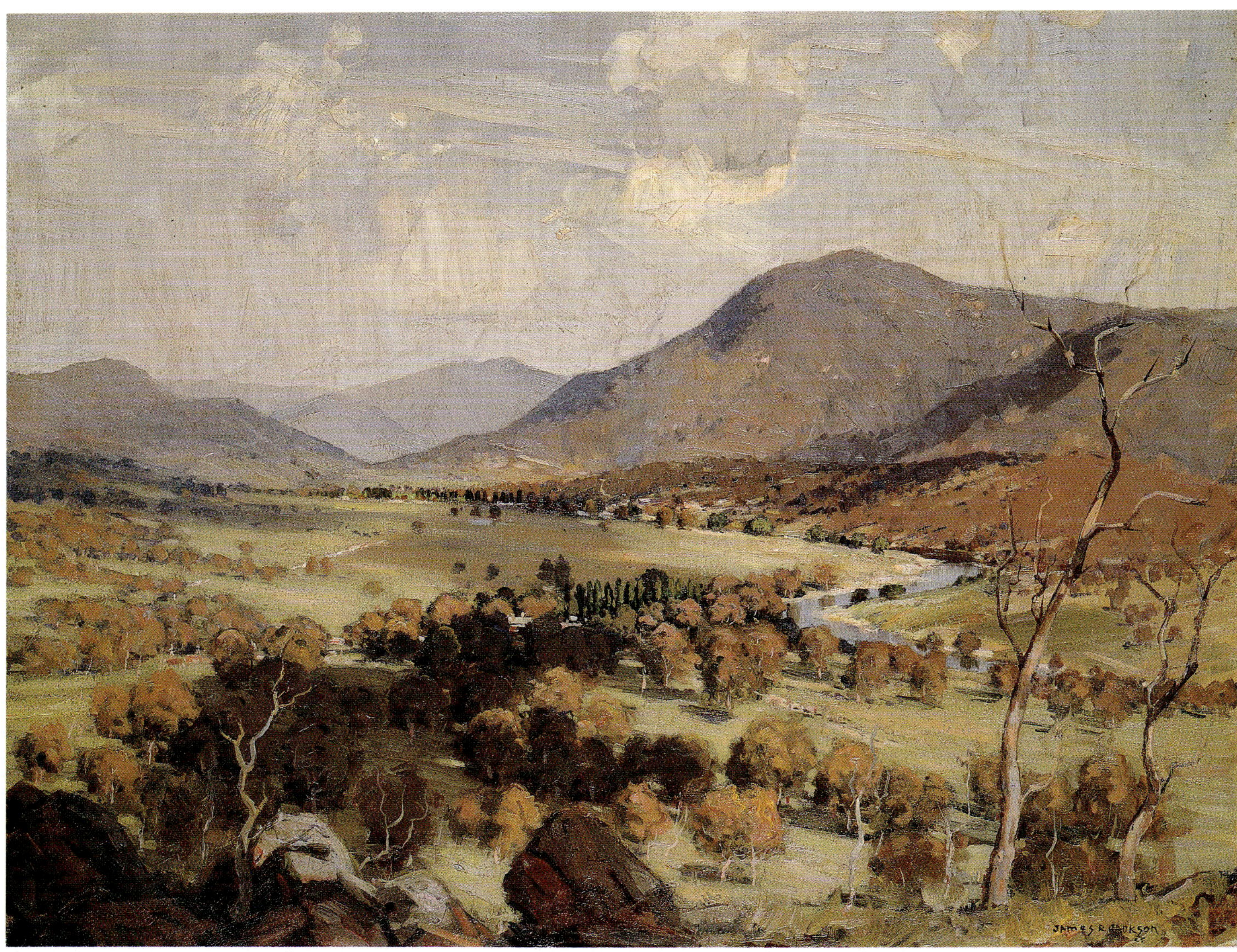

38 THE VALLEY OF THARWA, MURRUMBIDGEE 1925 Oil on canvas 63.5 x 81.8 cm
Felton Bequest 1926   Reproduced by permission of the National Gallery of Victoria, Melbourne

Over the years his paintings recorded a lot of local history: housing and other development in this area; the widening and alteration of Spit Road; filling in for the park and its vegetation; and the disappearance of the wharves, the punt and later the trams. His pictures of the main harbour show similar housing, city and harbour development, as well as the construction of the Sydney Harbour Bridge and, much later, the Opera House.

Jimmy exhibited his Murrumbidgee pictures over several years in both Victoria and New South Wales. In Sydney, he worked hard for his large one-man exhibition of some sixty paintings, which opened in June 1925 at the Anthony Hordern Gallery, Sydney. This showing included a variety of his works and was well received. It included some of his recent landscapes, many of Sydney Harbour, as well as his figure portrait *Morning in the Studio*, painted ten years previously. The *Sydney Morning Herald* review of 24 June observed: 'The artist shows temperament, a ready eye for bright colour, and for the most part a well-equipped technique in the work now on view. His judgment in composition is aptly illustrated in alliance with individuality in handling panoramic effects of colour and distance in his perspectives.'

Jimmy was represented by six works in the loan exhibition held by the National Gallery of Victoria in 1925. During the past decade he had been represented in Melbourne in various exhibitions and with the Australian Art Association while continuing to show at private galleries. He held another one-man show in May 1926 at the New Gallery, Elizabeth Street, Melbourne. This spectrum of his talents at

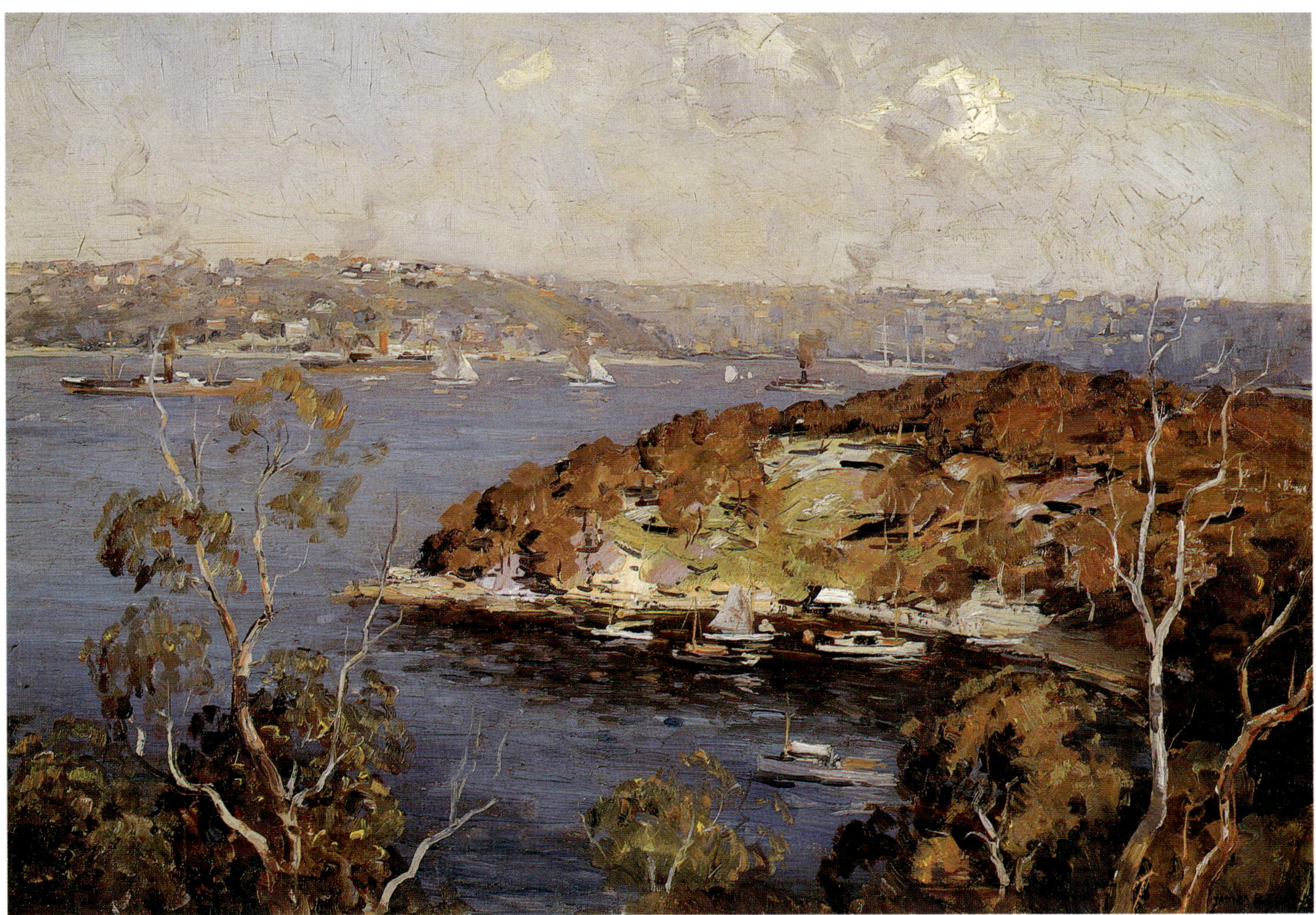

39   TAYLOR'S BAY, SYDNEY HARBOUR 1926 43 x 64 cm
Private Collection

a major showing was most welcome. His display included recent landscapes, outdoor nudes, and still lifes including pottery and flower studies; but the majority were of Port Jackson, seen in a variety of moods with colourful aspects of atmosphere and light. The *Melbourne Herald* on 18 May 1926 headlined it 'Artist's Success': 'few art exhibitions where the exhibitor has been a visitor from another State have met with such success as that attending the display of his own pictures by Mr James R. Jackson of Sydney. It is not often that the Felton Bequest Trustees purchase pictures by Australians to be hung in Melbourne Art Gallery, but this distinction has fallen on Jackson. They have purchased *The Valley of Tharwa*, the picture that attracted the most attention among artists in the collection.'

The art critic of the *Age* on 18 May gave him a lengthy review detailing many landscapes and harbour pictures: 'The gem of painting in the show is entitled *The Bay at Morning* — this little subject is faultless in execution, both in colour and tone . . . Mr Jackson's art is truly his own — entirely personal'. Other pictures mentioned were *Bathing*, *At The Cotter Crossing*, *The Crevice*, and *Antique Pottery*.

By now, Jimmy's style in landscape painting had developed to favour wide expanses of country with patterns of cloud shadows under a large sky. His ongoing interest in capturing light effects was portrayed by highlights on rivers or on hills of windswept dry summer grasses. He contrasted these with the lower tones of shadows from trees, banks or clouds, but his tonal range was not as wide as in his earlier landscapes.

His acute colour sense was tuned to capture the subtle changes of palette in the Australian sheep country — the distant hills and their blue ridges as they folded softly into an atmosphere of heat hazes. Panoramas of this type were popular with him for several decades, but he varied the country scene by capturing many intimate valleys with local interest in sheds or stock resting in the shade of trees. He caught the change in season and the character of the subject in interesting compositions. The previous summer (1925), when camped in the Bathurst area on the Turon River, New South Wales, he had painted the old buildings of the goldmining town of Sofala against a background of close hills. These pictures have strong colour contrasts in the major foreground elements with just a touch of sky above the surroundings.

Broadness of composition was also more apparent in his harbour and coastal pictures, requiring larger canvases. He painted them with a vibrant palette using a wide tonal range. However, while the water was now portrayed with smoother brushwork, his detail, especially of houses and boats, continued to be crisp and clearly drawn in firm brushstrokes of colour. Brilliant light effects on the harbour, painted against the light or in the evening, continued to fascinate him but he had apparently lost interest in portraits and Arcadian compositions. In his studio he worked on his larger pictures and painted flowers, still lifes and nudes. Most of his better harbour pictures were painted in his early period and during his married years.

By this time, the Jacksons had saved enough money to fulfil their ambition of going to Europe to paint. So, during 1926, Jimmy revised his French and both he and Dora had Spanish lessons. After the spring exhibition of the Royal Art Society, in which he sold all eight of his large canvases including *A Western Pastureland* painted at Tharwa, Jimmy announced his forthcoming resignation as teacher at the Royal Art Society, where he had taught for ten years.

James and Dora sailed for southern Europe in December 1926 and greatly enjoyed the Christmas festivities on board ship.

CHAPTER 7

Europe Revisited

Jimmy took Dora to his favourite painting places, first discovered in 1907. The comparison of subjects painted in 1927 to those painted twenty years earlier is fascinating. The composition has improved with more central interest in activities. Jimmy's previous technique of laying colours on thickly has been replaced by a developed use of brushwork and paint to emphasise interesting features or highlights. Backgrounds are accurately but simply treated, at times with small chinks of canvas left as high tones. His draftsmanship is still superb as is his use of colour. He revelled in the Mediterranean colour and design in sails, and in the greens of shutters and doors on old buildings. Light effects have changed, with the emphasis on sparkling splashes of it, particularly on water, being replaced by a more uniform enveloping of light reminiscent of his Australian landscape painting.

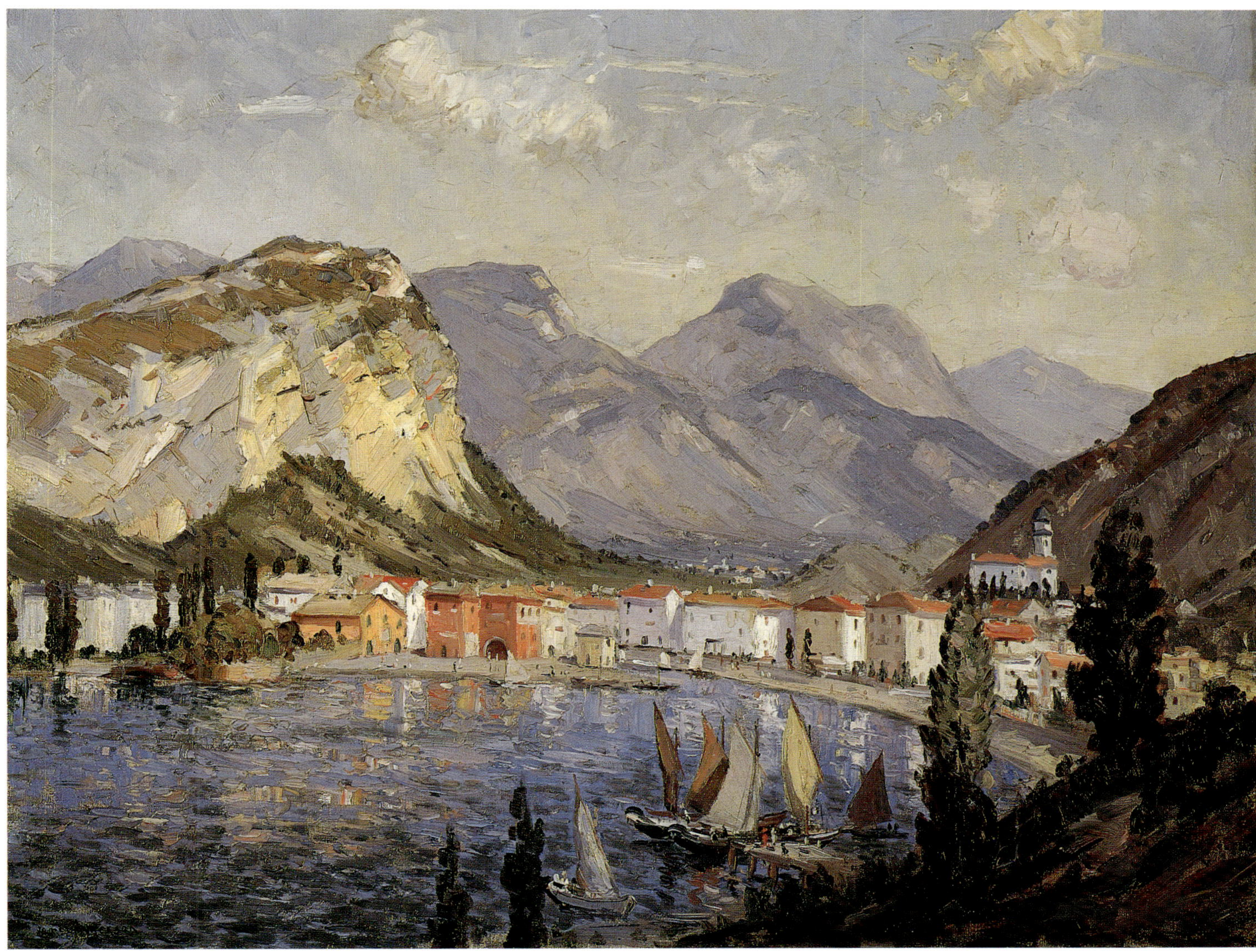

40   **TORBOLE, LAKE GARDA, ITALY** 1927 61 x 83 cm
Private Collection

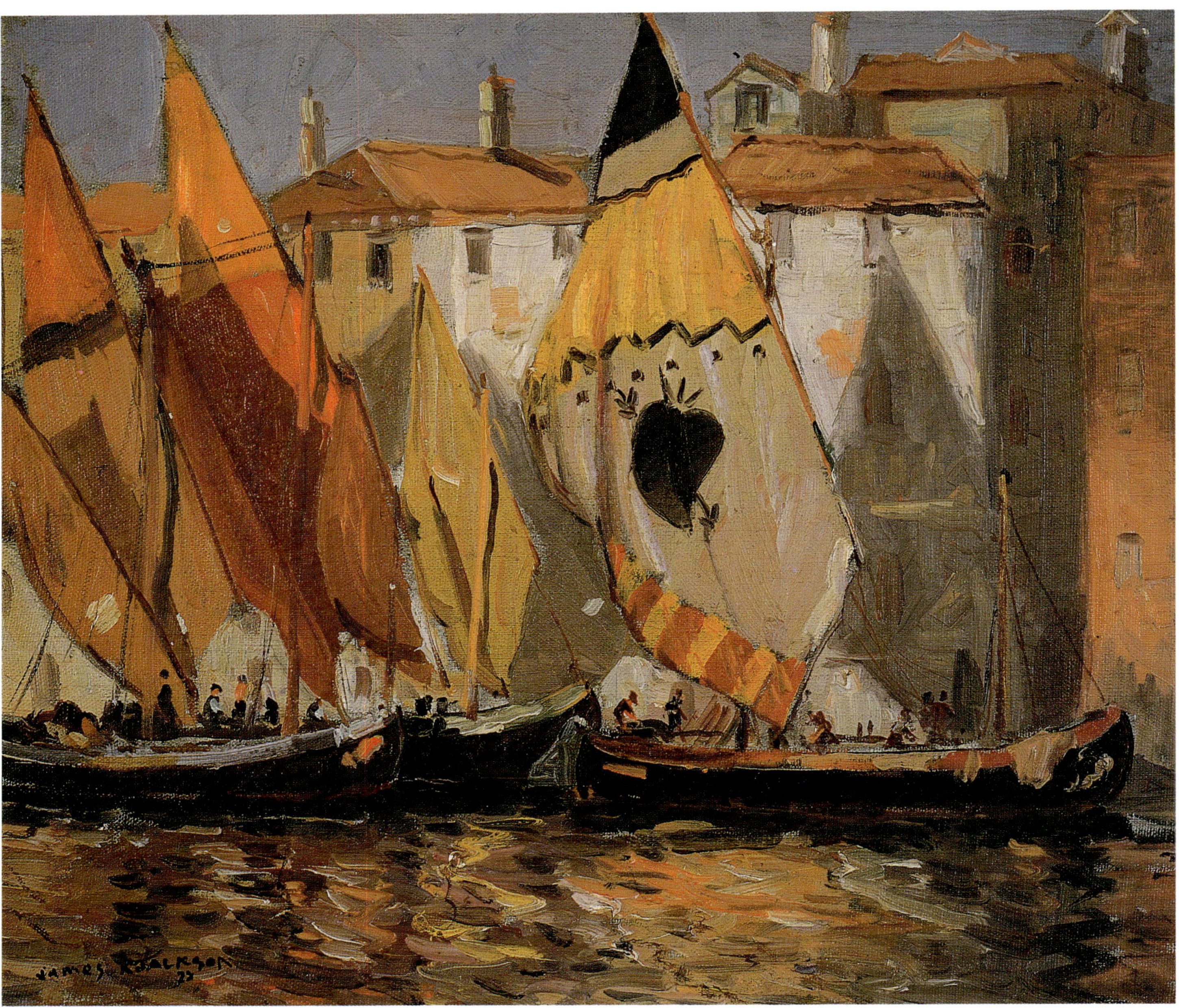

41 VENETIAN FISHING BOATS, ITALY 1927
Private Collection

Arriving at Marseilles at the end of January 1927, the Jacksons travelled through warmer southern France and the Riviera, painting as they went. Jimmy again visited Augustus John at his winter studio, where Dora had art lessons while Jimmy painted.

They stayed in very cheap hotels and their direction of travel and length of stay depended on the weather and the views. Their canvases record many cities and a variety of scenery and activities. Keeping to the warmer seaports, they stayed several weeks in Venice, which they loved. Paintings of the lakes in Italy's northern region, picturesque old towns in Switzerland and a large picture of Mount Blanc record their route to France in the spring.

Paris was alive with excitement and the new season when they arrived there. They visited art galleries and Jimmy's old student haunts around Colarossi's. They painted barges on the Seine and other waterways, old towns and views of the countryside. After several months of painting, their suitcases were full of canvases. To lighten their luggage, they sent their canvases back to Australia during a quick visit to London. Although it was summer and would have been a pleasant painting season, they did not visit or paint in the country but only toured the city, visiting artists and galleries. Their short stay

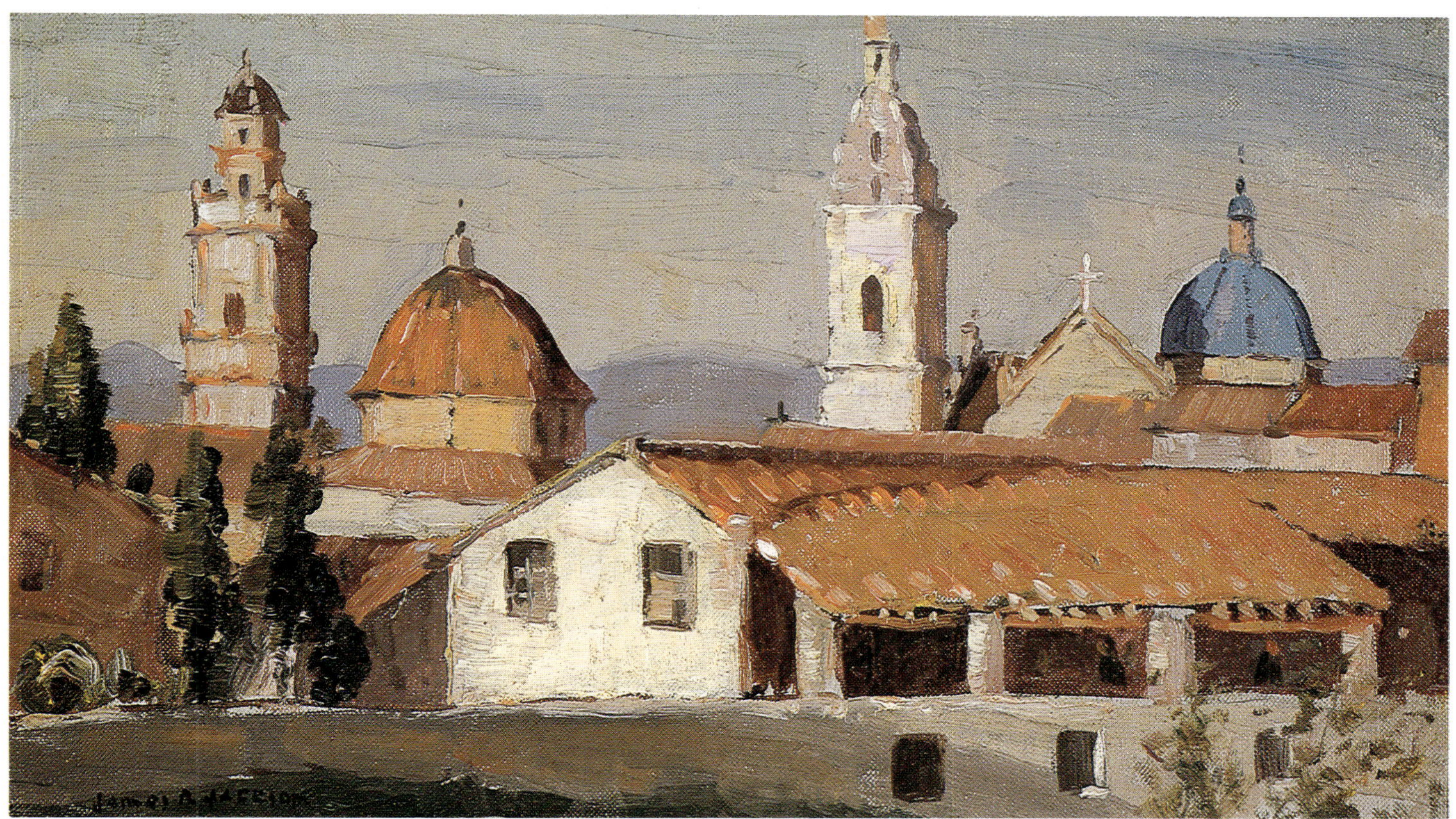

42   **OLD CITY, BALEARIC ISLAND** 1928 22 x 40 cm
Private Collection

in England would have been Jimmy's choice, as he preferred the continental atmosphere. He only exhibited one picture of London, and none of the English countryside, when he returned to Australia.

They returned to southern France and painted in the villages in the Pyrenees before crossing into Spain. They found Spain enchanting. The people were friendly and food and wine cheap. Jimmy and Dora fitted in well as their needs were simple and they were not unlike the locals in appearance. They stayed in very cheap accommodation; in small villages they found rooms in homes, usually eating the evening meal with their hosts.

The old towns, many with ruined fortifications reflecting aeons of history, supplied wonderful subjects with their colour, form, shadows and roof patterns. Many intimate, personal glimpses of courtyards and village life were captured on canvas. The women mostly wore long, dark-coloured dresses and did their washing near the local well or stream where, nearby, donkeys carried loads and goats grazed. Around Madrid and other inland cities the people were very poor, as was their diet — meat and fish were too expensive for many.

The two artists were always surrounded by people watching them paint and at times crowding in too closely. The children liked the look of Jimmy's pallet knife and also loved touching his paint and brushes. He found this very distracting while painting — so, at a comfortable distance, he drew a semicircle in the dirt, over which he asked them not to pass. His other tactic was to tell them that Dora, who frequently painted nearby, was far more interesting to watch as she was a woman, and ladies who painted out-of-doors in Spain were a rarity.

The country, with its ochres and blue skies, was a familiar palette and the Jacksons spent the latter part of the summer painting and exploring Spain in detail. Not fully understanding the political situation, Jimmy was arrested once for sketching in a prohibited area. He was taken by the police to the local station with his paintbox and canvas, where his painting was inspected by the senior officer. Fortunately, he did not have to spend the night in a cell as he was able to alter the drawings of the

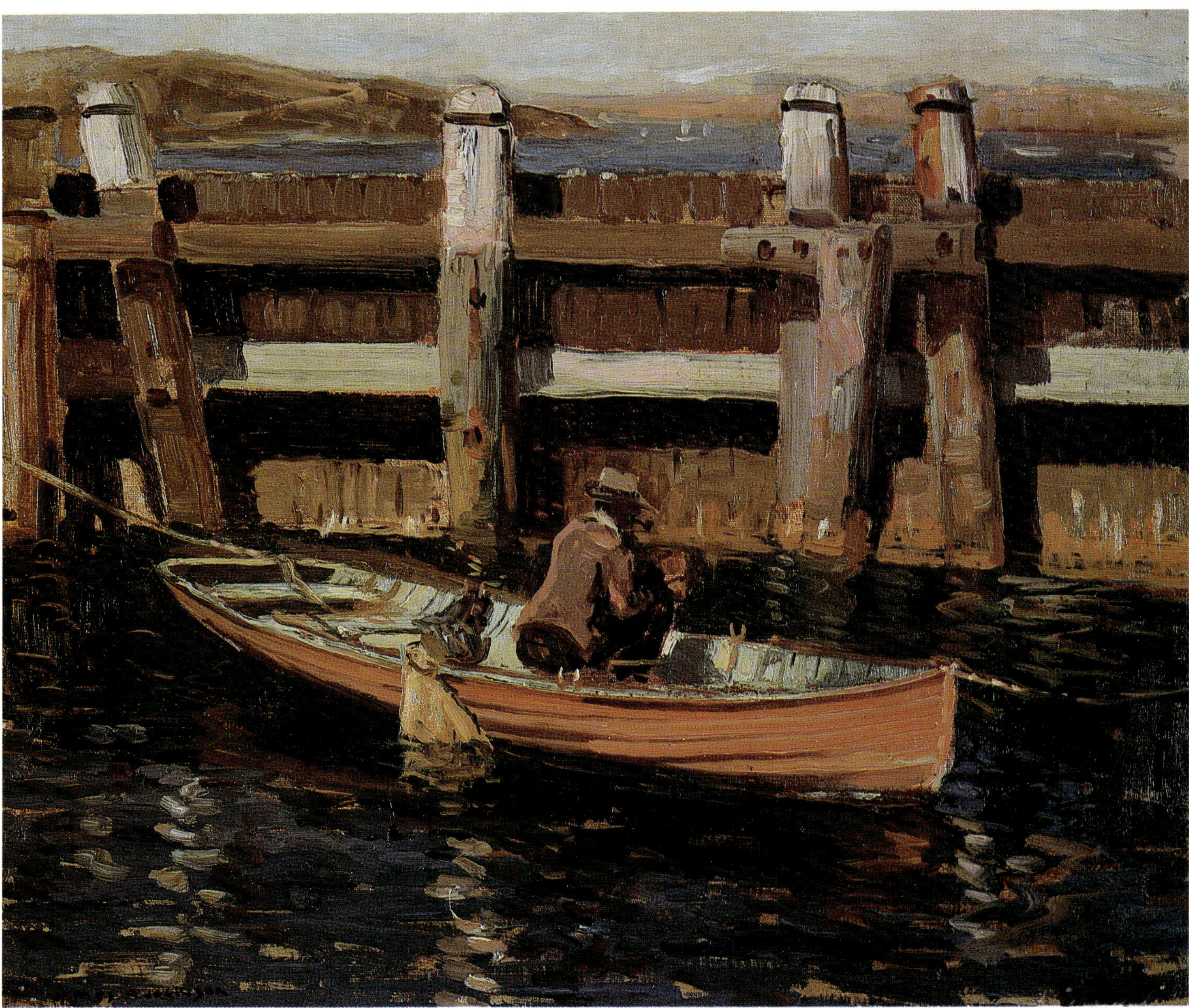

43   **FISHING, SYDNEY HARBOUR** 1928 42 x 51 cm
Private Collection

fortifications in the picture to the satisfaction of the constabulary. He recounted later, 'I was very scared when I was first arrested, but when they allowed me to alter the painting, I enjoyed giving them an art lesson'.

In the colder months, they painted in the south around Seville and Cadiz, then sailed from Valencia to winter on the warmer Balearic Islands. They loved these islands, especially the islands of Menorca and Ibiza. Here the people were still very poor but their diet was better as many were fishermen, and James could again enjoy fresh seafood.

The architecture of the churches was a wonderful mixture of spires and domes of various cultures. These, and numerous old forts, were built in golden-coloured stone, which poetically contrasted against the clear blue skies, while near their bases grew palms and cacti. It was here that they acquired their collection of ancient coral-encrusted pottery, as well as more recently made local amphoras and unusually designed painted plates.

During this trip, Jimmy painted on canvas as it was light to carry. His pictures were mostly paintbox size as he pinned the canvas to the inside of his paintbox lid and onto a sliding panel which fitted into the lid. He could carry two wet canvases at a time by this method and still have the reverse of the

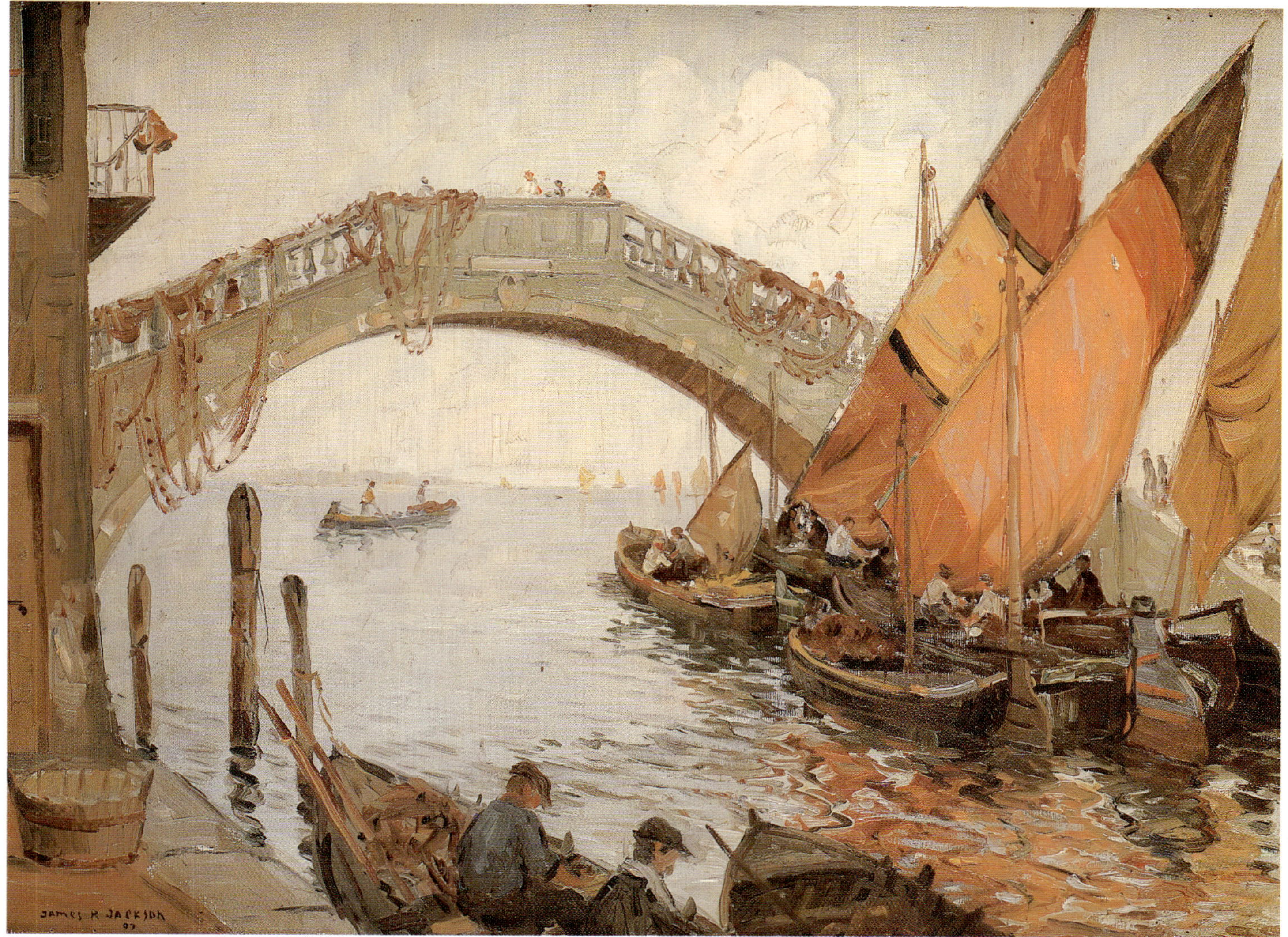

44   BRIDGE AT CHIOGGIA, VENICE 1907 Oil on canvas 49.5 x 69.5 cm
Felton Bequest 1928
Reproduced by permission of the National Gallery of Victoria, Melbourne

panel to use for a new canvas. When they were dry, he put them flat in his suitcase. Occasionally he would dry them in his room, but he found this was not such a good idea as the local people were very curious and sometimes touched the wet paint. He also painted large canvases which required stretchers; he was able to dry these more easily in his room by facing them, leaving a small gap, to another unpainted prepared stretcher, then tying the two securely. When dry, the pictures were removed from the stretcher and carried flat or rolled around a cylinder.

It was about this time that Jimmy started altering his signature by deleting the tops on his 'J's'. While in the Balearic Islands, he was represented by two pictures at the exhibition Oil Paintings, Water Colours and Etchings by English and Australian Artists, held in the Anthony Hordern Gallery, Sydney, in February 1928. These pictures were *Middle Harbour* and *To the Surf*. Other exhibiting Australian artists included Tom Roberts, Arthur Streeton, J. J. Hilder and Norman Lindsay.

Jimmy and Dora left Spain in March, with numerous packing cases full of pictures, Spanish pottery and old amphoras. Their return to Australia in April was greeted with much publicity, including numerous photographs. At interviews, Jimmy told of his impressions of European art and of village life. He described the cleanliness and simplicity of the white-washed houses, the village wells and the señoritas with their picturesque water jars. He also described how the Spanish housewife did not shake her carpets or clean her pots inside the house — this was all done in the street, where donkeys carrying water jars, goods and wood added to the congestion.

In the *Sydney Mail* article of June 6, he is quoted as saying: 'The arrival of an artist is looked upon as quite an event. As soon as I commenced to paint, a crowd would collect and watch me at work, sometimes for hours at a stretch and then decide that a man who worked so long without stopping must be in need of refreshments; whereupon some of them would disappear, to return shortly with wine and fruit, presented in a most courteous manner, but their welcome gifts were accompanied by a million questions.'

Jimmy at once started organising for a major exhibition of his European works. Only five weeks later, in May 1928, he mounted his French, Spanish and Italian Landscapes exhibition of thirty-seven paintings at the Macquarie Galleries, Sydney. He had extremely good press coverage, including photos of himself and several of the major works. His frequent introduction of human interest, brilliant lighting effects and varied colour schemes, and the fact that his style had broadened, were all commented on. These very colourful pictures still look freshly painted, and demonstrate his mastery of light effects, composition and brushwork. They exude happiness.

He followed this with an exhibition of forty paintings early in July at the New Gallery in Melbourne, where the National Gallery of Victoria purchased *The Bridge at Chioggia*. To mount two large one-man shows such a short time after his return from Europe was a major undertaking, especially with his commitment to the Royal Art Society's annual exhibition.

CHAPTER 8

The Depression Years

The small waterfront studio at Seaforth could not easily accommodate two artists. Dora, who had painted avidly in Europe, was now an accomplished exhibitor and was also thinking of having a family. They decided to build further up the hill and Dora set about organising the plans and the building.

The new house was a white-washed Provence-style home with green shuttered windows and pergolas. Dora's studio was in the attic while Jimmy's large separate studio with curtained, glass doors, opened directly onto an enclosed painting garden, where angophora gums shaded a fish pond. Naturally, this home was called 'The Studio'. It was completed well before the end of 1928 and I was born the following February. (Apparently Jimmy expected another 'James', so I was called 'Jacqueline', the French feminine form of Jacques.) From this studio, he painted the wonderful view over the Spit towards the Heads in a variety of seasons, moods and light effects.

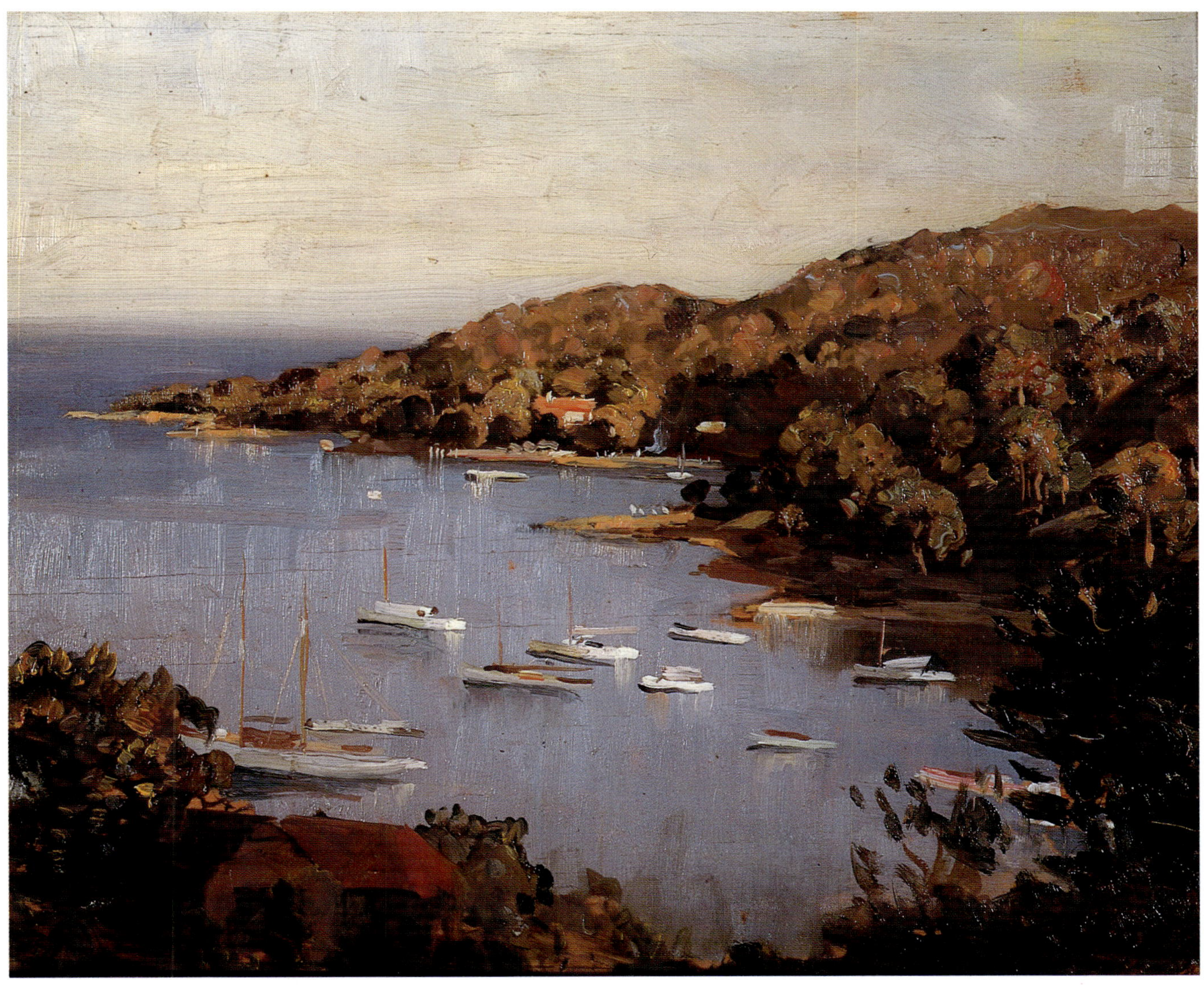

45   **AFTERNOON NEAR MANLY, N.S.W.** 1929 28 x 39 cm
Private Collection

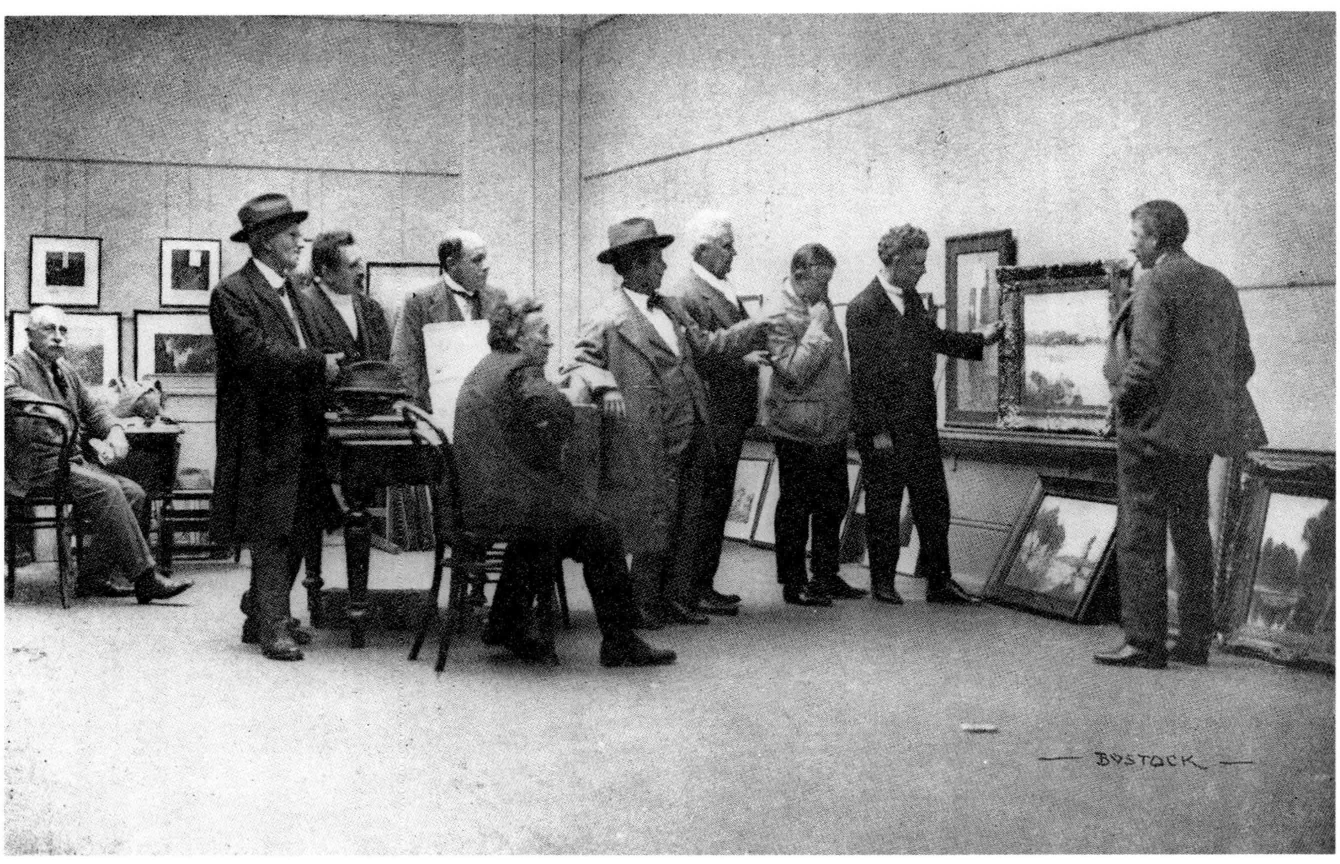

46   James and fellow artists at Royal Art Society. (James centre with hat)

James won a prize in the State Theatre's 'Australian Art Quest' competition in May 1929 with his *Pont Brescon Martigues*. There were some 1800 entries but only 300 were accepted, including five of his. Later, the Grosvenor Gallery mounted an exhibition of paintings of Sydney Harbour, in which three of his recent paintings were represented. These were *Autumn Afternoon*, *Evening Calm* and *An Evening Sky*. This was the beginning of his fascination with evening sky effects, with dazzling streaks of sunlight streaming down behind clouds. He had painted clouds before but now they became an integral, if not major, part of some of his pictures. The development of this theme, with impasto clouds, often with rain clouds moistening the landscape, resulted in darker skies with dramatic light effects in his landscapes for several decades.

Since his return from Europe, Jimmy's sales and economic position had been good. He employed models and painted large-scale full nudes in the studio, which he occasionally showed at later exhibitions. In November he was busy with the Royal Art Society's Fifty Years of Australian Art exhibition held at the Blaxland Galleries, in which he exhibited four varieties of his work. He also helped check the colour prints for the Society's publication associated with the exhibition, titled *Fifty Years of Australian Art*, in which he was represented. Then, following the stock market collapse, the Great Depression started and his sales began to dwindle.

Art sales have always been a sensitive indicator of the economy and by Christmas 1929 the worst was realised. Art sales zeroed. Jimmy remembered the hunger and hard times of the depression of his youth and the poverty in Europe. Food was his big consideration; as his only real ability to make an income lay in his art sales, which were now temporarily nil, he decided to live off the land. As they had recently acquired an old car for transport with the baby, they decided to let the house and go camping in the country, where they knew food was available and where Jimmy could paint. They were

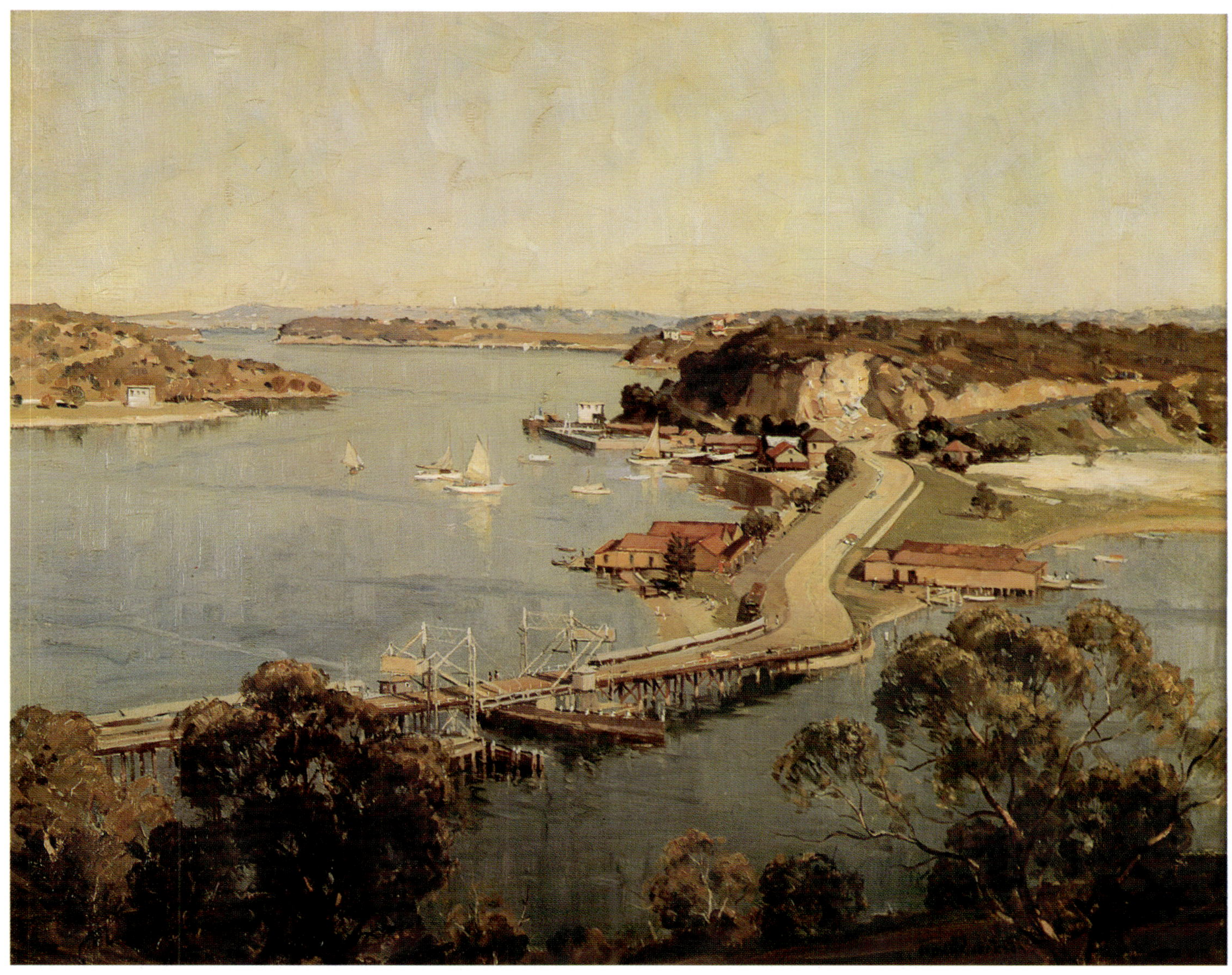

47   **THE OLD SPIT BRIDGE, MIDDLE HARBOUR, N.S.W.** 1930 71 x 92 cm
The View from James's Studio
Private Collection

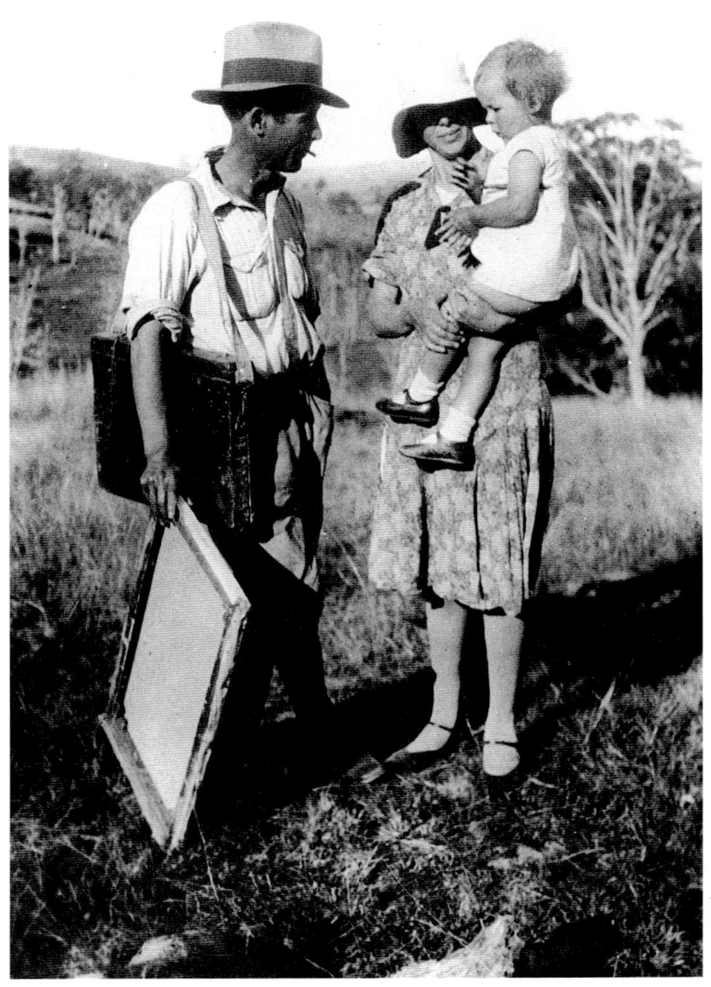

48 James with family camping at Peel River N.S.W. 1931

able to lock away the studio contents and their possessions in one of the rooms, and over the next four years intermittently let the rest of the house when they were lucky enough to find a paying tenant. They tried to come home for the winter months, to enable preparation for the Royal Art Society exhibition and to avoid the severe country winter cold and frosts.

They packed the old car with their tent, modest necessities and, of course, yards of canvas and paints. During the depression they literally lived off the smell of an oil rag. At first they returned to the Australian Capital Territory, where they again camped and painted before exploring the Lachlan River country on their way to Bathurst. Returning to 'The Studio' in the winter of 1930, Jimmy advertised that he was conducting 'Spring Out-Door Painting Classes'. Apparently he had few students, because from early summer they camped on the Peel River east of Tamworth.

Somehow in the new year, they managed to drive the old car to Gloucester via Nowendoc, over the steep narrow timber tracks which wind up and down in that mountainous wet-timbered area between Tamworth and Gloucester, New South Wales. They told of horrific 'roads' which were so narrow that there was no room to pass any traffic and too treacherous, slippery and steep to reverse on. Trucks, tied to trees with ropes, had to weight the near side so that they could scrape past on two wheels and the axle, while the other wheels hung over the edge.

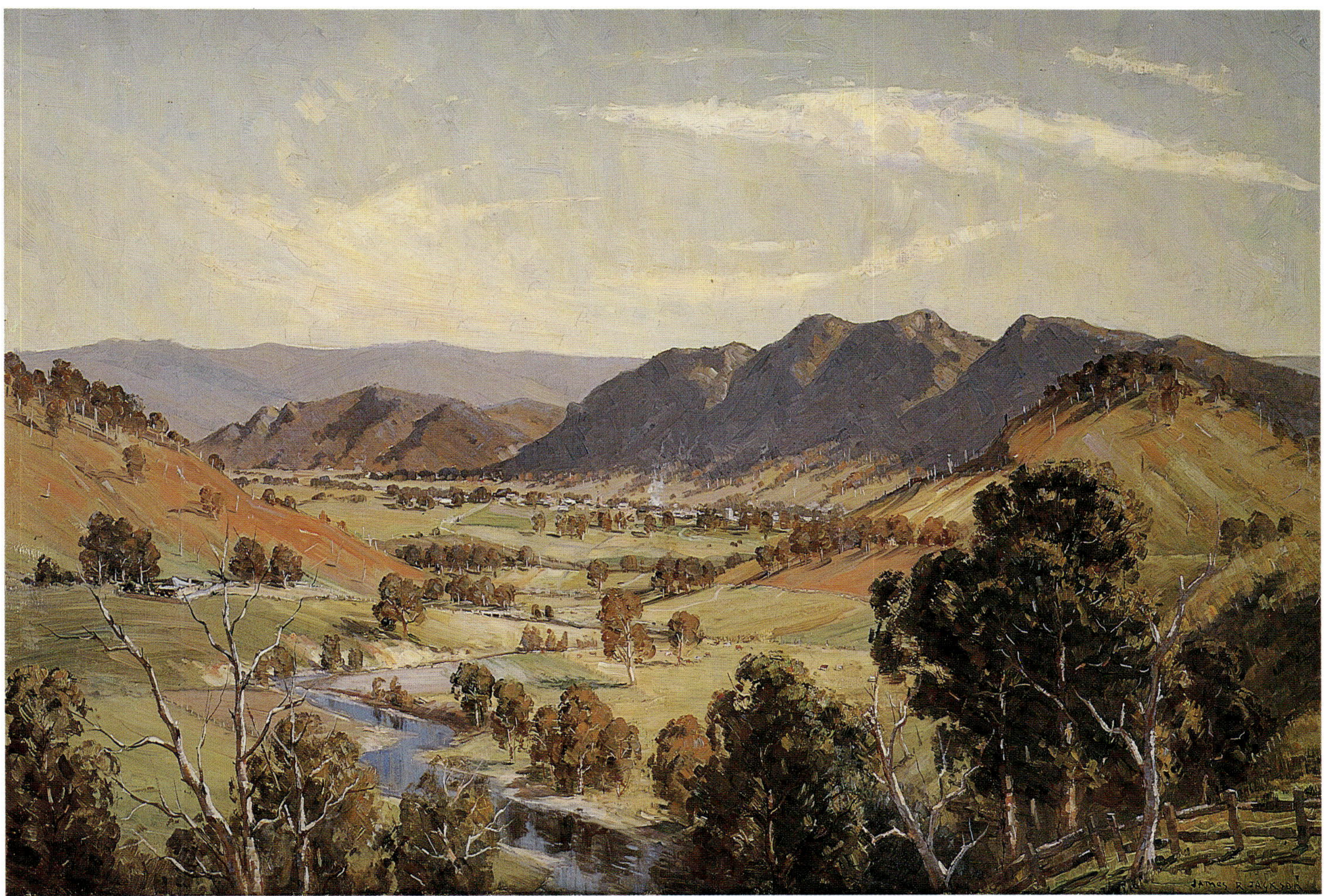

49   VALLEY OF THE MOGRANI, GLOUCESTER, N.S.W. 1931 64.8 x 95 cm
Reproduced by permission from the Collection of the Queensland Art Gallery, Brisbane

After these horrific experiences, the Jacksons camped for several months near Gloucester, which they loved, and stayed in the area until the end of June, while Jimmy painted large vistas of the Gloucester and Barrington scenery. Some of these were his best landscapes, and he exhibited them in the 1931 Royal Art Society exhibition. One, *The Valley of the Mograni, Gloucester N.S.W.*, is now in the Queensland Art Gallery.

They were befriended by all the country folk and many a small 'J.R.J.' was exchanged for provisions, milk and frying pans. Their address was 'c/o the local Post Office' and their camp consisted of the main tent and a fly stretched out like a verandah roof at the front. Visits by other artists, friends and family were frequent, while magpies and a wide variety of native fauna were daily callers. Of these, the most troublesome were the large river goannas, who were attracted by the smell of fat in the frying pans. So much so, that they made off with the pans, and apparently hid them where even Dora could not find them.

Jimmy put his fishing and hunting skills to great use and his catches were also traded for food, although Dora usually kept the trout. He disliked guns and rabbits were caught in string snares or by hitting with an accurately thrown stone. Harold B. Herbert, when opening Jimmy's 1940 Melbourne exhibition at the Sedon Galleries, commented: 'At Malmsbury once, he hit what we thought was a water rat at thirty yards — it was a platypus. He was full of contrition and nursed it back to health and strength on the river bank. It was uninjured. That's Jimmy — kind and agreeable! His sunny nature is revealed in his canvases.'

Jimmy did several drawings of the platypus before it returned to the river.

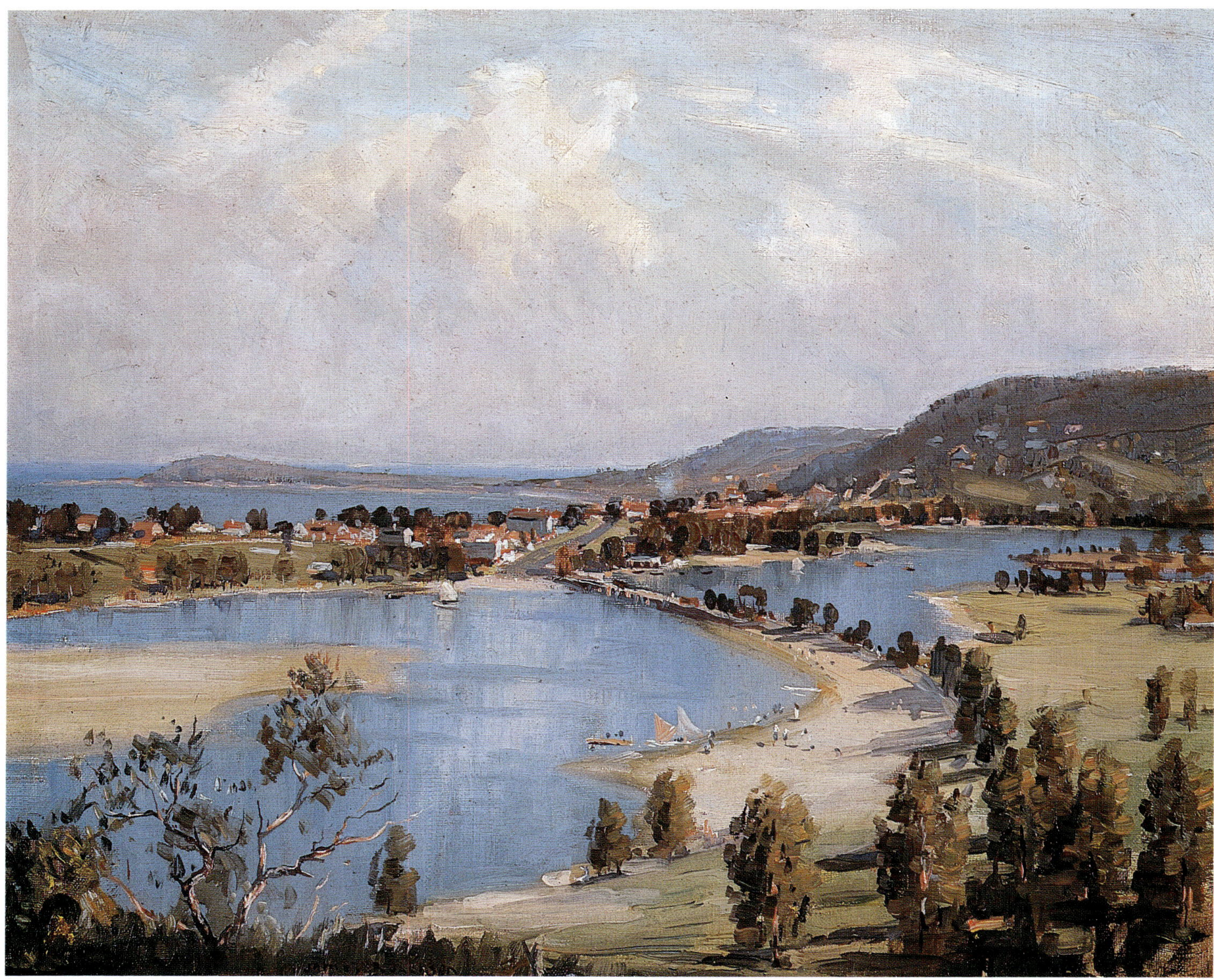

50   **NARRABEEN LAKE, N.S.W.** 1929 36 x 46 cm
Private Collection

Although money was very scarce, these early depression years were happy ones. Jimmy continued to buy quality art materials, and did some of his finest work on these country camping trips and around Sydney when he returned. Of the 1931 Royal Art Society exhibition, the *Sydney Morning Herald* art critic said on 31 August: 'Mr James R. Jackson shows two beautiful landscapes. One is *The Valley of the Mograni, Gloucester, N.S.W.* and the other *Northern Pasture Land, Barrington*. Both are important pictures and are in the front rank as examples of the highest type of Australian landscape art, thoroughly characteristic in subject and admirable in the quality of the painting. Mr Jackson's work is always interesting. *Narrabeen Lake* and *Evening Light on Middle Harbour* are two splendid pictures from his easel.'

The *Sydney Morning Herald* critic was sympathetic to artists in his August 1932 review of the Royal Art Society's exhibition: 'No class in the community has been hit harder by the depression than the artists. That is true whether their art is plastic and pictorial or musical or literary. Landscape painters, poets and musicians are all in the same boat. The market for their wares, that appeal to the imaginative and spiritual qualities of human beings, is terribly restricted when the resources of the average citizen have to be expended on such material necessities as food, clothing and shelter.' Further on the article says: 'James R. Jackson is a tower of strength to the society. There is beautiful draughtsmanship even in his landscapes.'

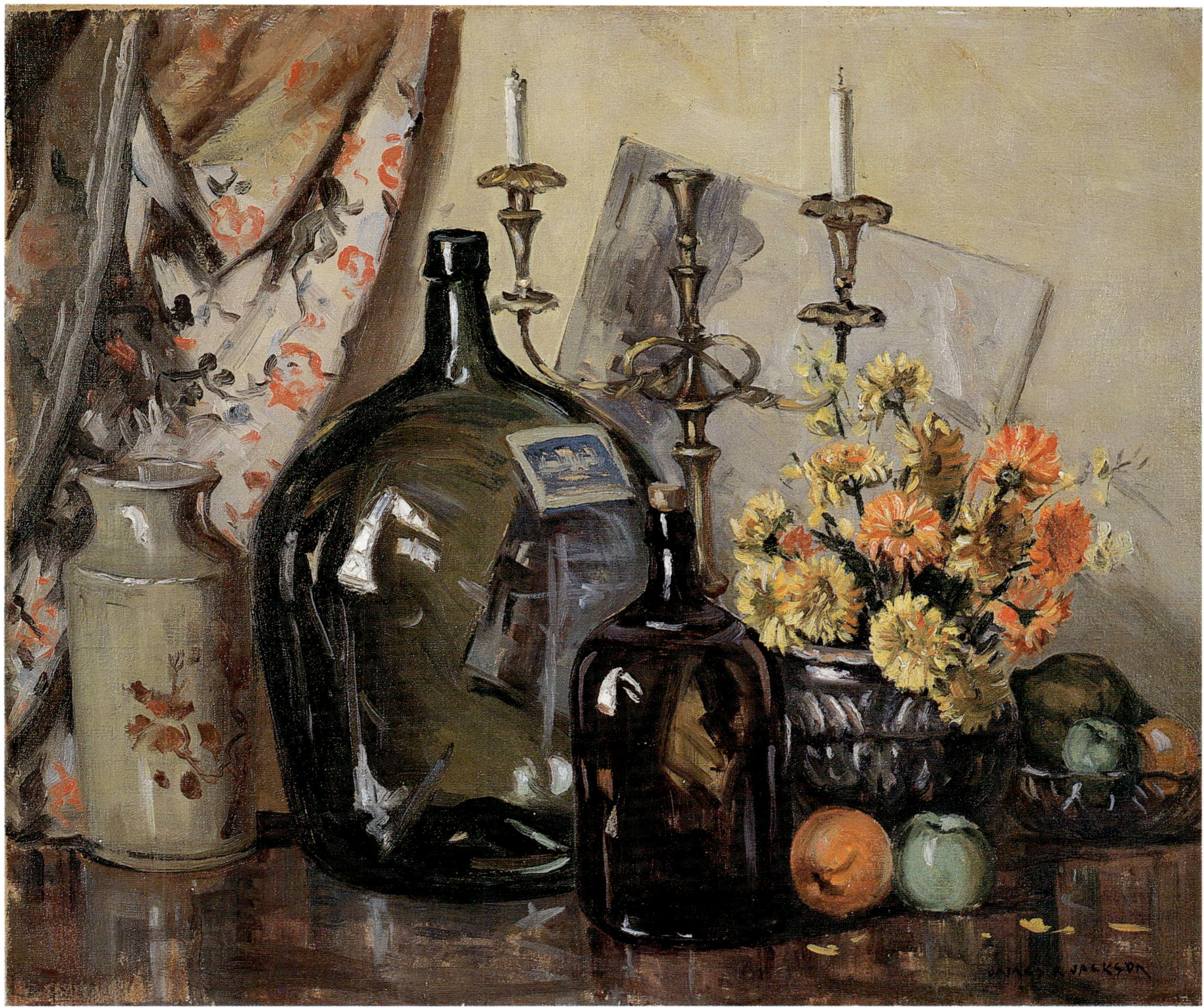

51   **STILL LIFE** 1933 50 x 60 cm
Private Collection

Artists tried to look after each other during the depression. In later years, Jimmy admitted that during the bad times, 'if one happened to be selling, an artist might sign the good work of a friend who was not, so enabling him to get a few quid'. The Jacksons were able to return to the Seaforth studio for a short while early in 1933 and in May of that year 'The Studio' was the subject of a major feature in the magazine *Australia Home Beautiful*. There were photographs by H. Cazneaux of Jimmy, his studio and the house. Jimmy's joy at being able to return to his studio is reflected in numerous large, beautifully executed canvases of the harbour, which he painted about this time.

Eventually, the car broke down and, not having the money for repairs, Jimmy was forced to leave it. This was not a problem for him as he never really liked using the car to go painting in — he felt he missed the scenery while driving. Actually he was a poor driver and was even worse at parking. He was very pleased when he once managed to get both the front and back of the car into the narrow garage.

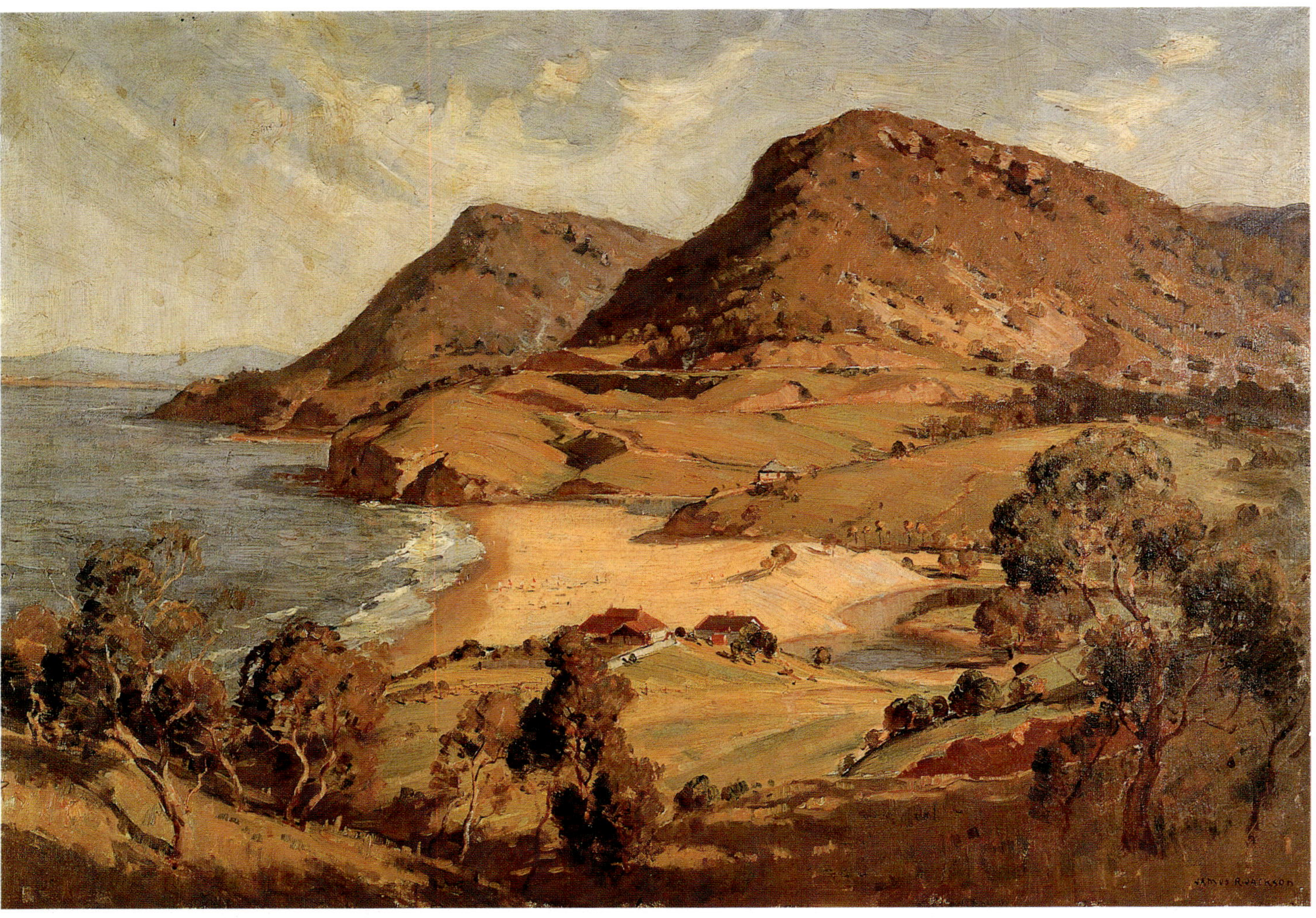

52 STANWELL PARK, N.S.W. 1934 64.5 x 94 cm
Private Collection

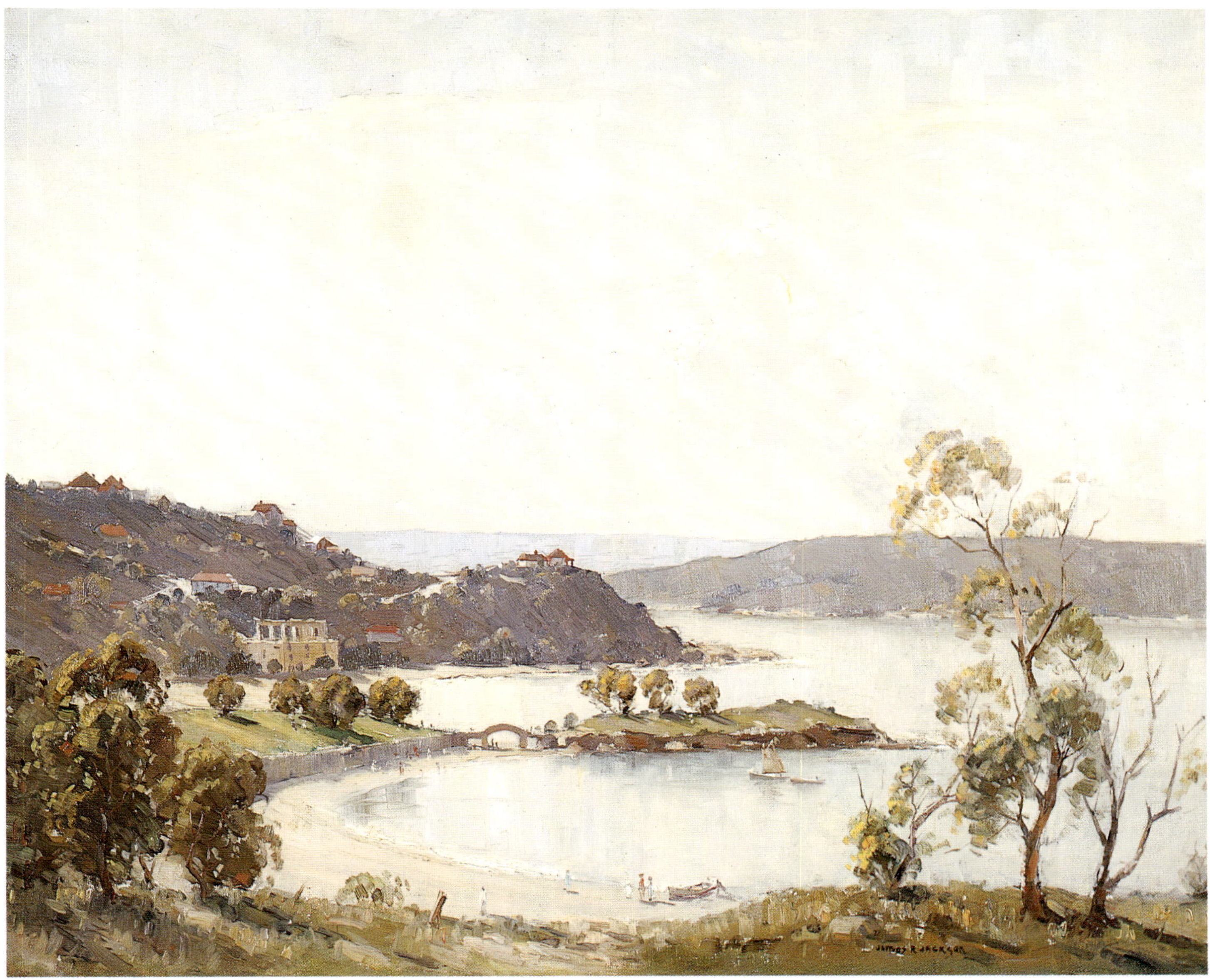

53   **BALMORAL, SYDNEY** 1934 65 x 85 cm
Private Collection

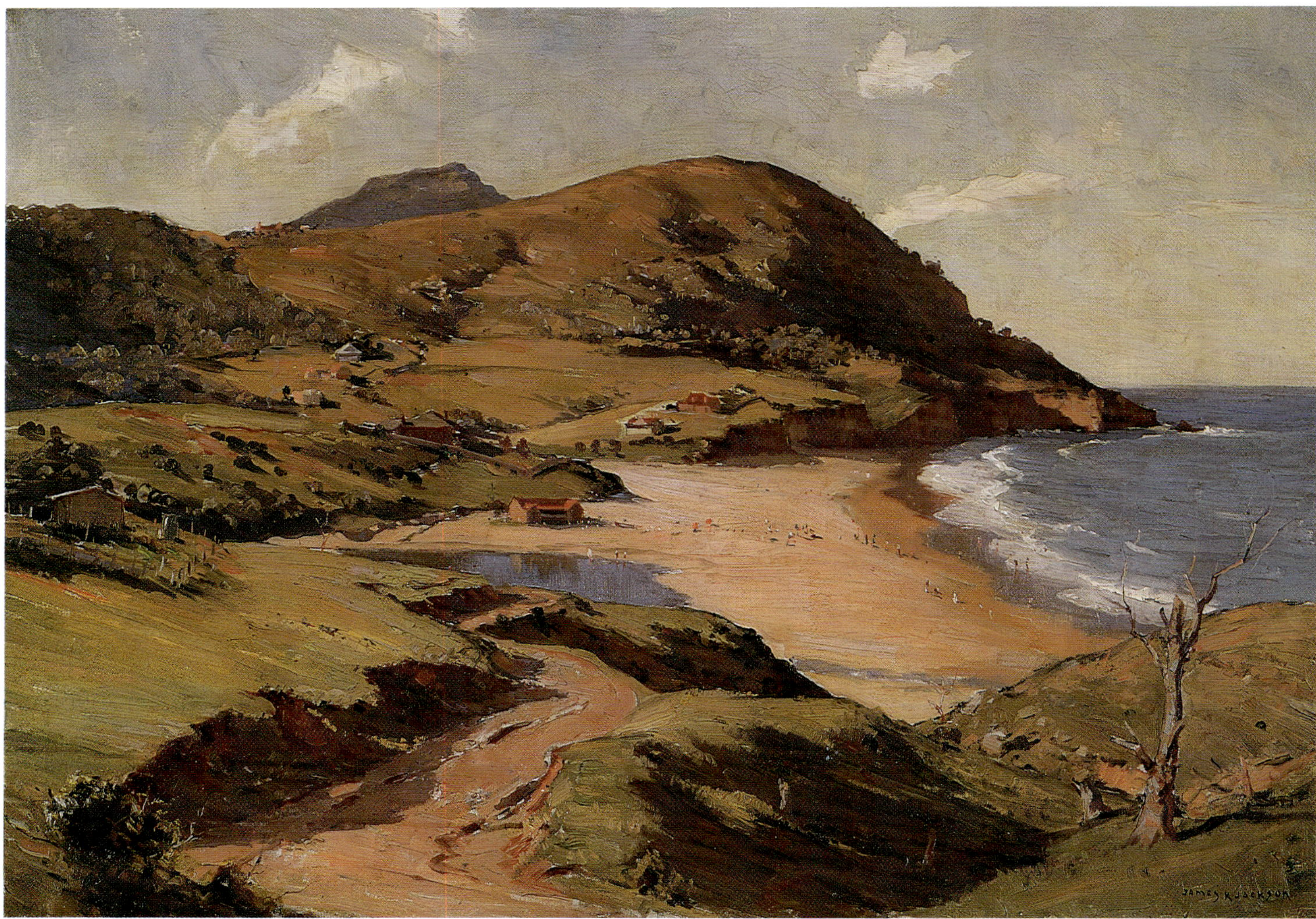

54 'THE OLD ROAD SOUTH COAST' 1934 Oil on canvas 66.5 x 96.3 cm
Purchased 1934
Art Gallery of New South Wales

During this period and in the later 1930s, several of Jimmy's major paintings were reproduced for sale in frames, and his *View of the Murrumbidgee River* appeared as a full-page colour item in the supplement to the *Sydney Mail Annual* in October 1933. He had never aspired to major positions on art committees, except the position of vice-president, as he was frequently away painting. However, since his return from Gloucester, he had been active on the committee of the newly built Manly Art Gallery. He continued this interest when he rented a small flat overlooking the beach at Manly.

In the Melbourne Centenary Art Exhibition of 1934, Jimmy was represented by five pictures. A few sales to kind patrons, including Howard Hinton, and to the Art Gallery of New South Wales, who bought his *The Old Road, South Coast*, a panorama of Stanwell Park, enabled him to return to 'The Studio'. However, money was still a problem as he spent a lot on art materials and sales were still very few, even though the Art Gallery of New South Wales bought his *Drying Sails* in 1935.

Jimmy became irritable, and at times depressed, and for several years he did not exhibit with his beloved Royal Art Society. He would say, 'No use painting, nobody wants them, may as well go fishing'. He took his frustrations out on Dora and on his paintings — he would have bonfires of his smaller and what he described as 'not up to scratch' works in his painting garden. I well remember the smell of those fires and of Dora's distress.

However, he would cheer up when he was able to buy a large roll of canvas. He would bring it home, discuss its quality, lovingly spread part of it out on the floor and describe the masterpieces which he was going to paint on it. Depending on the size of his stretchers, or his needs, he would cut out the required larger pieces. The smaller bits or paintbox sizes were often glued down onto ply. The glue

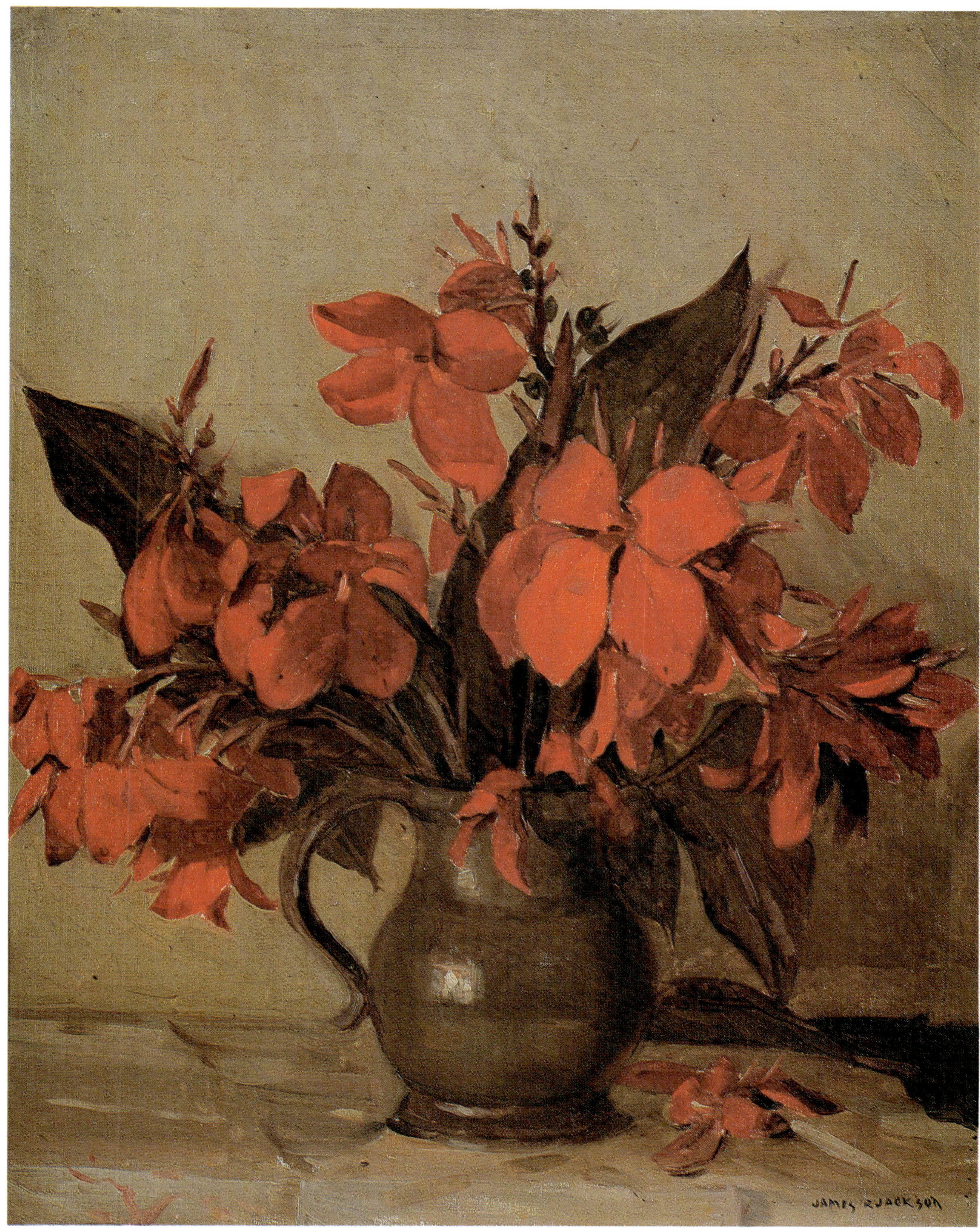

55   CANNA   1936 55 x 44.5 cm
Private Collection

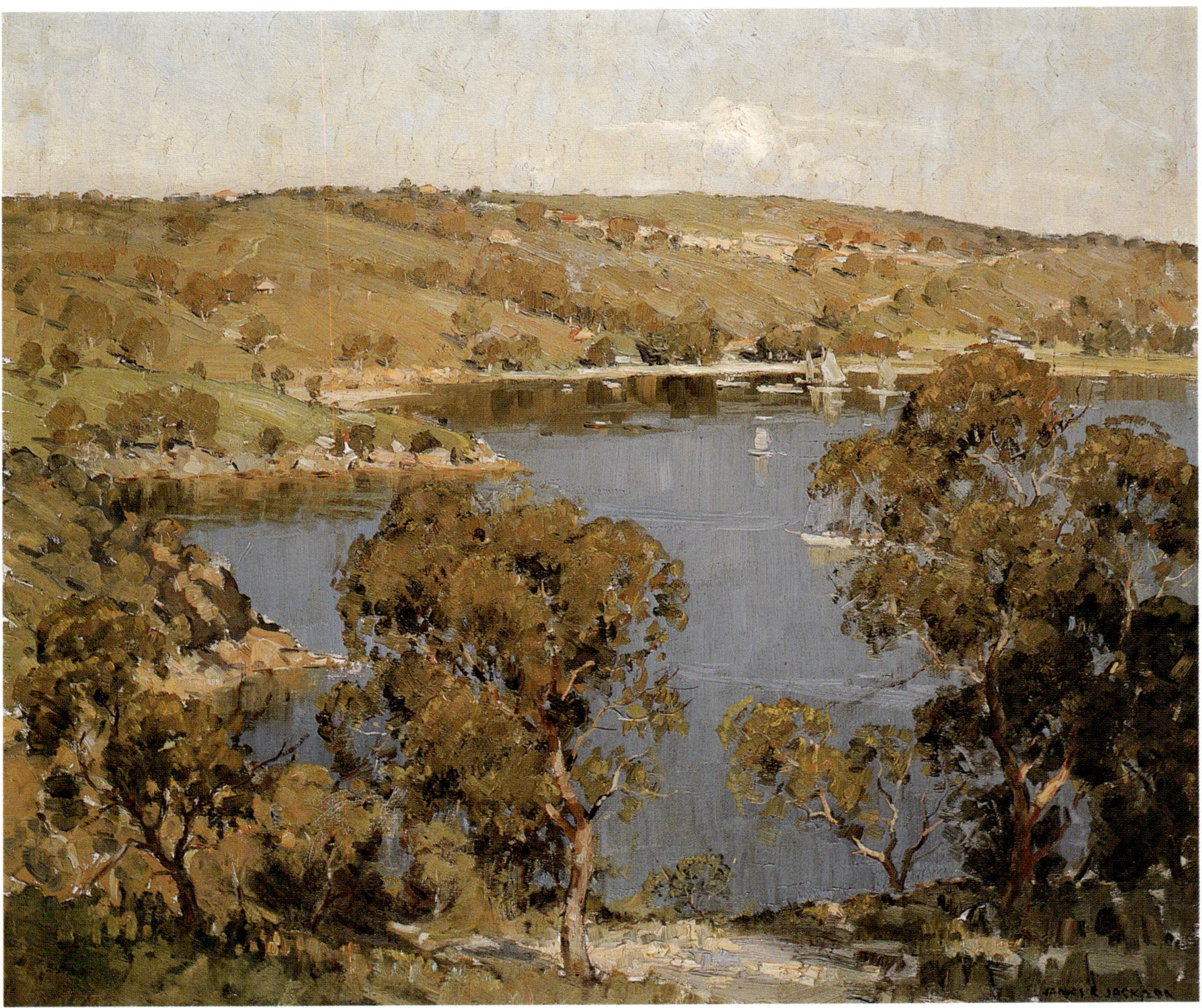

56   **HARBOUR FROM SEAFORTH** *c* 1933 Oil on canvas 61.3 x 71.3 cm
Felton Bequest 1936
Reproduced by permission of the National Gallery of Victoria, Melbourne

was some odious, tacky yellow substance which was heated over a double boiler on the stove and painted on when hot. The smell was worse than a forgotten piece of fish bait.

With the effects of the depression easing and the birth of a son called James, Jimmy prepared for a one-man exhibition — his first in eight years. His opening at Melbourne's Fine Art Gallery in May 1936 was very well reviewed. This was reflected by the headings in the *Sun*: 'Art With A Sparkle' and 'Brighter, Better Work By James Jackson'. His variety of subjects, which included nudes, flower studies, harbour pictures and landscapes, was appreciated and described by the art critic for the *Herald* as 'vigorous impressionism'; while the *Argus* critics commented on his design and fine colour, and also remarked that 'the result was a picture one would desire to live with'.

These pictures were his major works painted during the depression. The Felton Bequest of the National Gallery of Victoria bought his *Harbour from Seaforth*, a soft summery view of the harbour seen through well-balanced, partly shadowed trees. Although his pictures were very modestly priced, as he had dropped his prices, the effects of the depression were still present and his sales were not enough to cover expenses and framing. He was eventually forced to sell the house, rent a flat and establish a separate studio.

CHAPTER 9

The James Street Studio

James found the ideal studio on the corner of James Street, Mosman. It was handy to the Spit tram line and was already called 'The Studio' as it had been built for a photographer and was later used as a children's library. It had a door opening onto the street and was equipped with the basic necessities. From its window there were views of a lovely landscaped garden and Chinaman's Beach. It was here that he prepared for his important Sydney exhibition, held in June 1937 at David Jones Art Gallery.

This was his first one-man exhibition in Sydney since 1928. Included in his showing of sixty-four pictures were his recent southern Queensland landscapes. In the catalogue introduction, mention was made that he had been represented at the Paris International and British Colonial exhibitions, also that he had exhibited in other overseas exhibitions. The exhibition received excellent press coverage, with

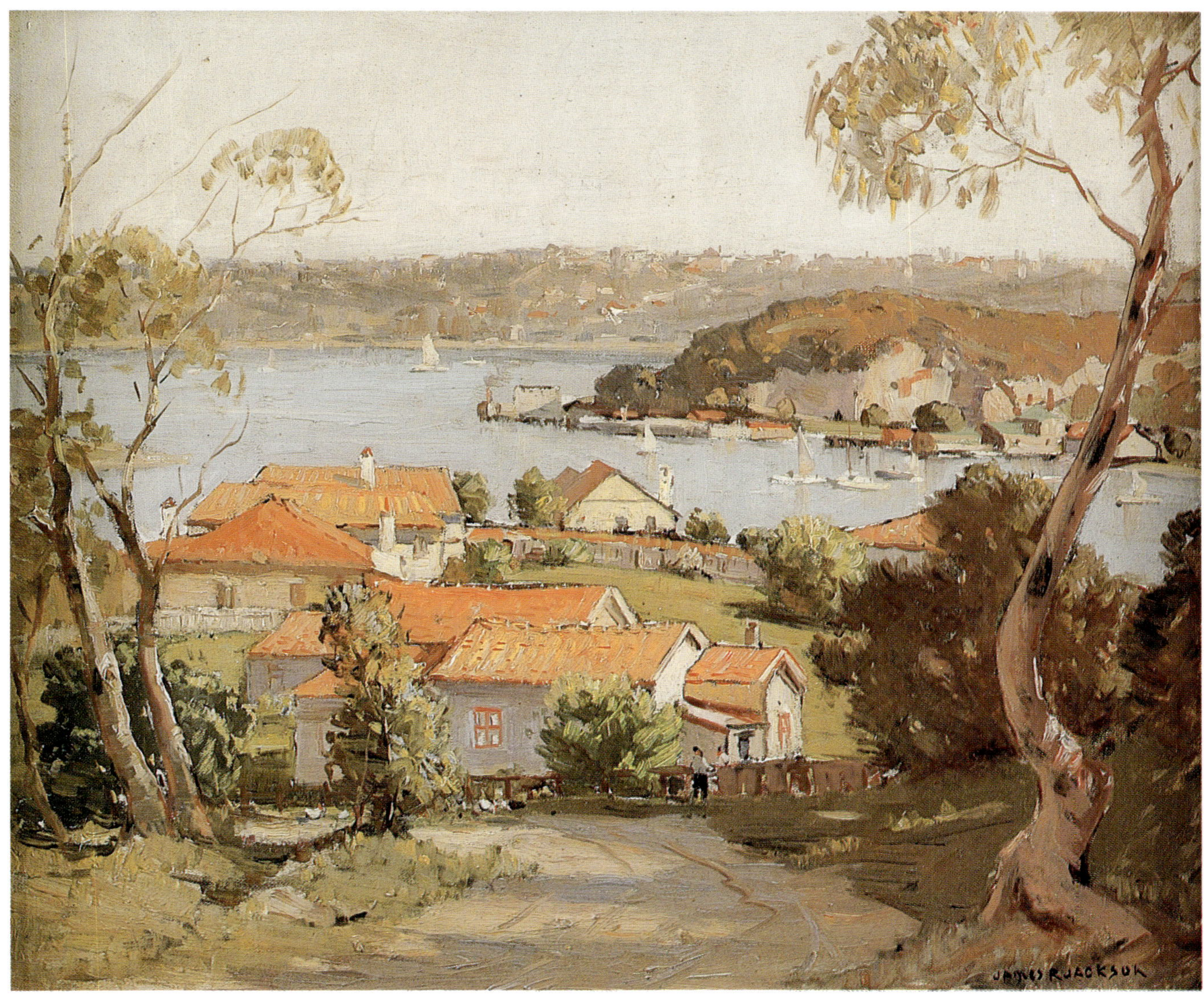

57   OLD ROAD TO MANLY, N.S.W. 1936 44.5 x 54.5 cm
Private Collection

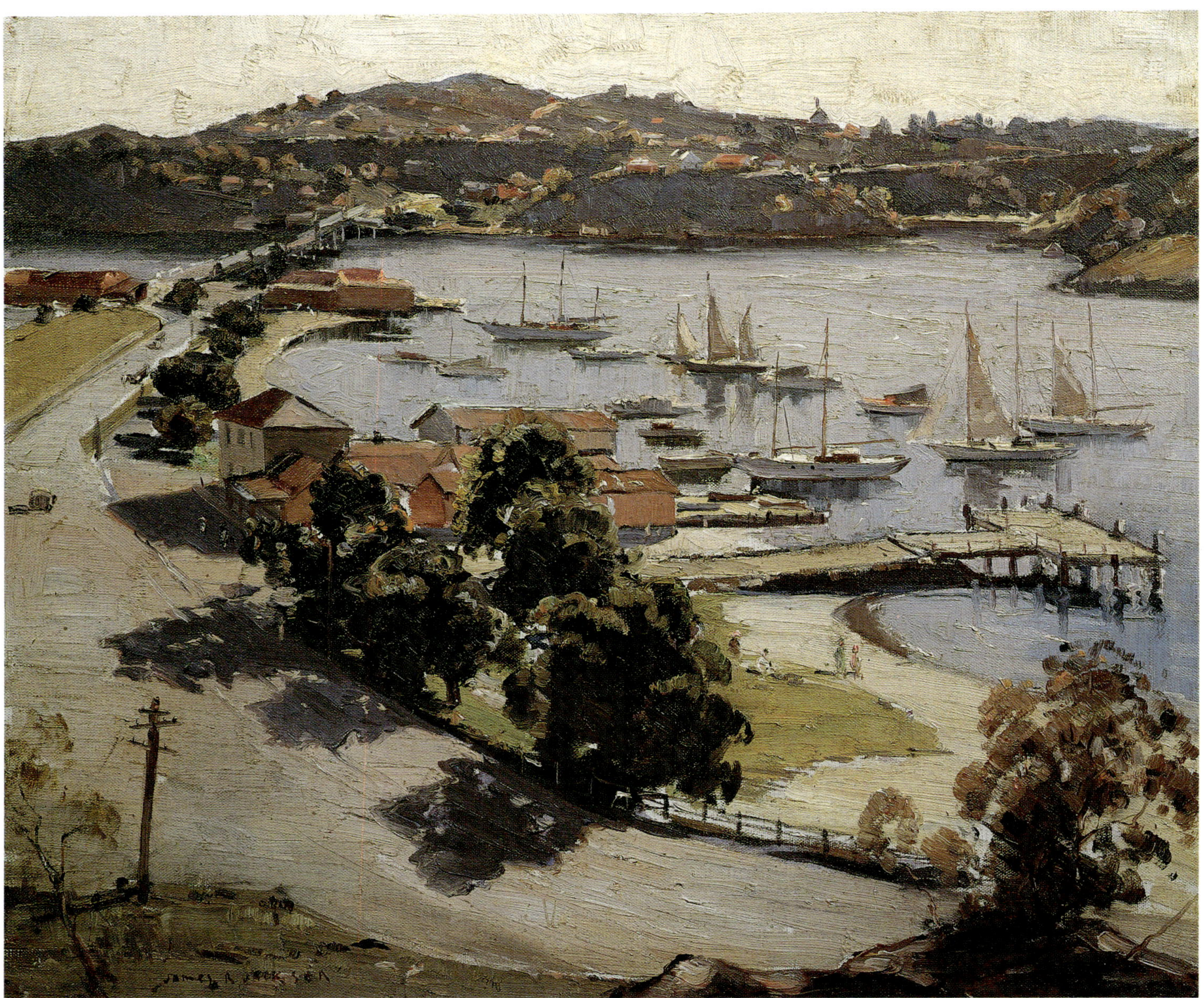

58   'DRYING SAILS', THE SPIT, N.S.W. 1935 Oil on canvas 46 x 54.7 cm
Purchased 1935   Art Gallery of New South Wales

photos of Jimmy alongside his pictures. It was opened by Mr B. J. Waterhouse, who was then President of the Board of Architects. He commented on Jimmy's ability to draw forms which 'have been richly and clearly expressed in easy strokes of pure colour'.

The review in the *Sydney Morning Herald* of 9 June said: 'For a number of years James R. Jackson has been recognised as an accomplished painter of Australian landscape. But he has never before done such fine work as now adorns the walls of David Jones George Street Gallery . . . One of the artist's happiest qualities is the way in which he makes a landscape sparkle with light'.

His catalogue records that his prices were still greatly reduced, with many of his harbour pictures being attainable for around 40 guineas; but the added marked crosses in pencil indicate that sales may have been sufficient to cover his expenses. Jimmy regularly attended this exhibition and was only too happy to tell of amusing and interesting incidents relating to all his pictures.

Earlier in 1937 *The Hills of Turon, NSW* was displayed at the Australian pavilion at the Paris International exhibition. In May of that year his picture *Drying Sails, The Spit* was reproduced in the catalogue of the Artists of the British Empire Overseas exhibition, held at the Royal Institute Galleries in London. This picture was also included in the 150 Years of Australian Art exhibition held at the Art Gallery of New South Wales.

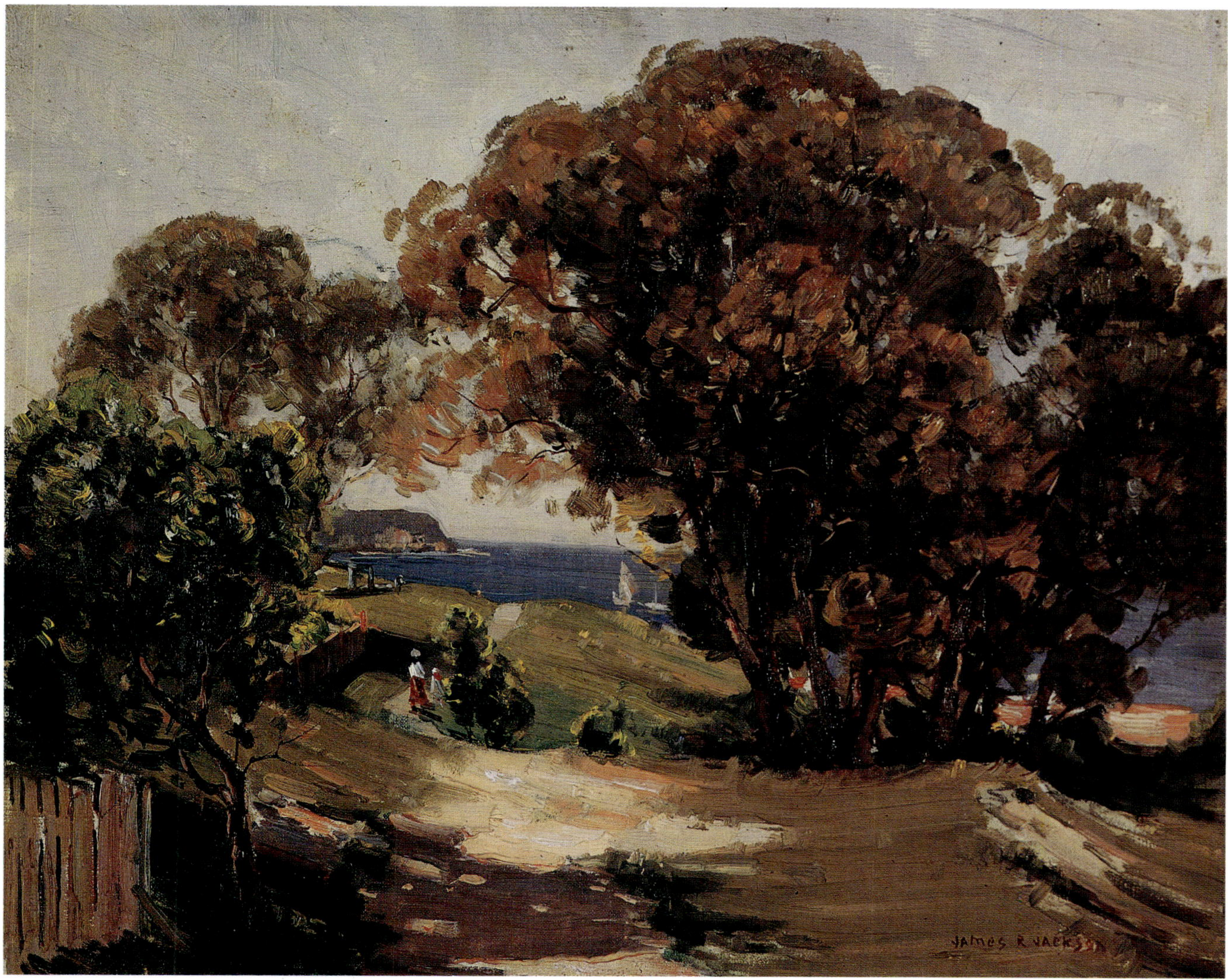

59 NORTH HARBOUR, SYDNEY 1936 Oil on canvas 40.3 x 50.7 cm
New England Regional Art Museum, Armidale, N.S.W.

The painting was purchased by the Art Gallery of New South Wales two years earlier in 1935 and was a view from above the quarry at the Spit. Painted almost into the light, it looks north and depicts an active foreground of trees, harbour, beach and sailing boats, with strong shadows and reflections. *Drying Sails, The Spit* has more recently been used as the cover illustration for a novel about the Mosman area.

For a few years before the Second World War, Jimmy rarely painted against the light but favoured a palette of full colour, as seen in the morning or afternoon with distinctive shadows captured by painting with the sun at his back.

His publicity at this time was very good and four of his pictures were illustrated in the *Home Annual* in October 1937. Of these *Pathway, North Harbour* is now in the New England Regional Art Museum, Armidale, New South Wales. The following year, his *Federal Territory, site of Farrer's wheat experiment* — painted from near the site on the river bank with a rhythmic background of mountains and sky — was illustrated. It was also reproduced in colour in the book *Australian Landscape*. During these late depression years, he was producing quality pictures in the mature Jackson style, with his delicate and discriminating use of detail. He still used high-grade canvas and oils and presented his harbour views in ornate frames, usually under glass. A simpler type of frame decorated his larger landscapes. Sales had only slightly improved and in Sydney he sold from his studio, exhibitions, and from private galleries such as Rubery Bennett's. In Victoria he exhibited with group exhibitions and privately through the Sedon Galleries.

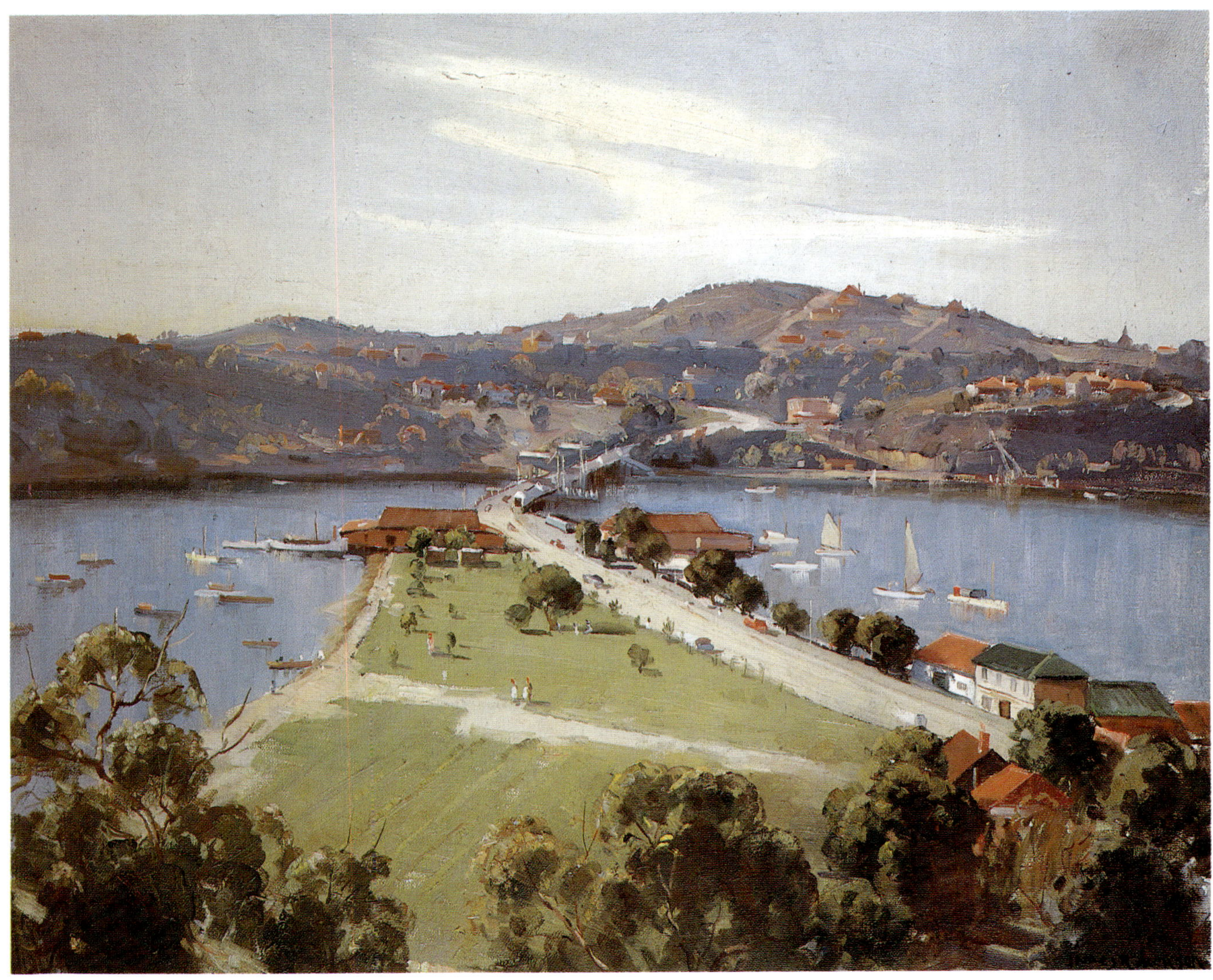

60   **THE SPIT, MIDDLE HARBOUR, SYDNEY** 1938 48 x 60 cm
Private Collection

Jimmy was appointed one of the foundation members of the Australian Academy of Art in 1937, and was very pleased with this recognition of his work and his standing as an artist. He exhibited in their annual exhibitions, held in various states, from 1938 until the Academy ceased to exist in 1946. The Academy was representative of artists from all states except Western Australia and the constitution adopted was broadly along the lines of that of the Royal British Academy. Although its formation was approved by the Federal Cabinet the previous year, there was opposition to its formation on the grounds that it was not truly representative of all the societies and that it had a preponderance of Society of Artists members. Its hoped-for royal charter never eventuated.

As a very young child, I frequently accompanied Jimmy on a day's painting around Sydney or on his framing visits to Parkers. Arriving at the Quay by the Cremorne ferry, he would visit several studios and galleries around lower George Street before I was able to satisfy my childish wonder of touching old Mr Parker's waxed handlebar moustache. Here he would seem to spend hours discussing frames, pictures and exchanging news. On a day's painting, we took a small lunch and a bottle of water and I amused myself by watching him paint or by building fairy houses out of white quartz pebbles; but I always had to be very quiet. When he had nearly finished, he would ask me to comment on the painting and offer suggestions. As I grew older he gave me a watercolour box and then a small oil paintbox. We continued our painting trips for many years.

During a hot dry summer early in the war, he took me painting to Gundagai. We travelled by train

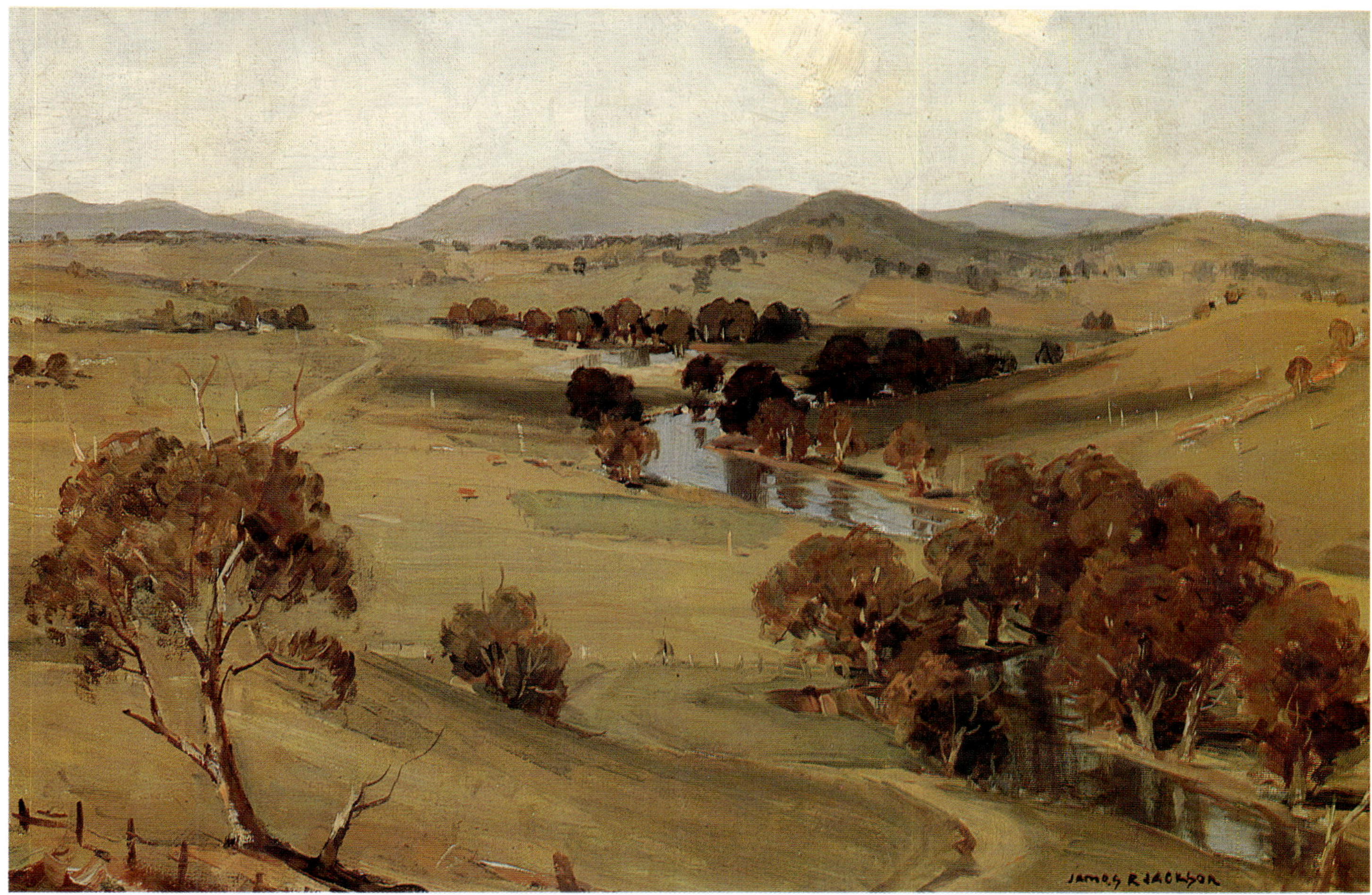

61 DUGONG NEAR YASS, N.S.W. 1937 36 x 55 cm
Private Collection

and stayed across the river at an old coach pub. Jimmy enjoyed walking back to town over the long rattling timber bridge in the cool of the evening. I remember his painting enthusiasm and his energy on this trip. Although nearly sixty, he never looked his age, neither did he believe it until years later when his remaining dark hair started to go grey. He was partially bald from his thirties. Jimmy's youthful appearance and manner partly enabled him to successfully alter his birth date and other records of his personal history. This created many discrepancies in the meagre available information about him (and also made my task of accurately tracing his early history more difficult).

On painting trips, he would climb steep hills carrying all his gear until he found the right view or felt inspired. He would look for a suitable place out of the wind so he could put up his umbrella, or preferably under a shady tree with no bull ants. Bull ants were the bane of his existence and he would frequently tell how many a masterpiece had been ruined by them: 'The little B's quietly climb up the inside of your pants. When above your knees, the leading ant says ''Bite now''. They do, and your lower body and legs turn into a stinging field and you can't get at them'.

Jimmy painted quickly and directly, rarely altering his work. He would set up his big canvases on the easel, and painted these standing where he had room to walk back to appraise them. Smaller works in the lid of his box were usually painted while seated on his stool — but at regular intervals he would walk back to view them from a distance. After composing the picture in his head, he roughed in the composition with pigmented turps, or occasionally in charcoal, then mixed his main palette colours. He applied these in broad masses, working down in tonal range. His initial paint was not thickly applied and this allowed his delicate addition of foliage, especially in trees against the harbour or the sky. Drawing and details of interest were impasted in colour contrasts added later as the picture developed.

Sometimes he would stop in the middle of painting to capture a transitory light effect or a passing sailing ship. If unable to paint them directly into his picture, he recorded these momentary glimpses in a vacant corner of his sky or on a spare panel in his box. If required later, they would then be transferred to a place in his composition.

Jimmy concentrated very hard while painting. So hard, in fact, that many a domestic cow, smelling and seeking his linseed oil, would come up behind him — the first he knew of its company was its salivary snort on the back of his neck. With his big canvases, he would have to return to the site several times as the light would change and alter the shadows. He used to say: 'One of the hardest effects to master in landscape painting is to capture the tonal relation of a bright sky over the gleam of long grass on the rise of a sunlit sheep hill'; and 'I only paint landscapes I love to paint and want to paint, otherwise it's useless'.

He hated being interrupted while he painted, but any onlooker who waited patiently in the background until he had packed his paintbox always received a good reception, especially if they offered a cup of tea. He made numerous friends and loved to talk in his high-pitched voice on many topics. He would philosophise or tell of his art travels, of how life used to be and the many changes he had experienced.

An afternoon painting session usually concluded with some fishing on a nearby river or wharf. After finding some bait, catching something appeared easy — but then he had years of experience in landing his dinner. He enjoyed his evening fish, and loved watching the changing colours of the sunset and water reflections. He would frequently advise and help other friendly fisher folk with their catches and many who were interested in art became his lifelong friends. At night he would tell bedtime stories which he never read but made up with great imagination. They were always happy stories, usually based upon bush animals or poor children finding comforts for their impoverished families. He never introduced broom-sticked witches or fairies — his stories were practical and usually finished with an entertaining moral.

As Jimmy had lived with the weather all his painting life, predicting it was no problem. In Sydney, a look at the sky and the feel of the wind in the morning told him precisely how the day would turn out and he chose his painting location accordingly. He never relied on published forecasts and the crackling radio annoyed him with its timed, often inaudible weather programme. As he knew every cove around the harbour, he would choose one sheltered from the wind, sometimes doing a morning and an evening sketch. Published rainfalls in country areas were referred to when selecting the locality for his next landscape trip as he liked dry, warm colours.

In July 1938 Jimmy mounted another one-man exhibition of fifty paintings at the Sedon Galleries, Melbourne. He included a few of his unsold works from the David Jones exhibition of the previous year. Most of the works had not been exhibited before; some were recent and others painted early in the depression. All were modestly priced but selling pictures in these post-depression years was still difficult. Two of his works were in the Art Gallery of New South Wales exhibition 150 Years of Australian Art: *Drying Sails*, lent by the Art Gallery, and *Old Road, French's Forest*.

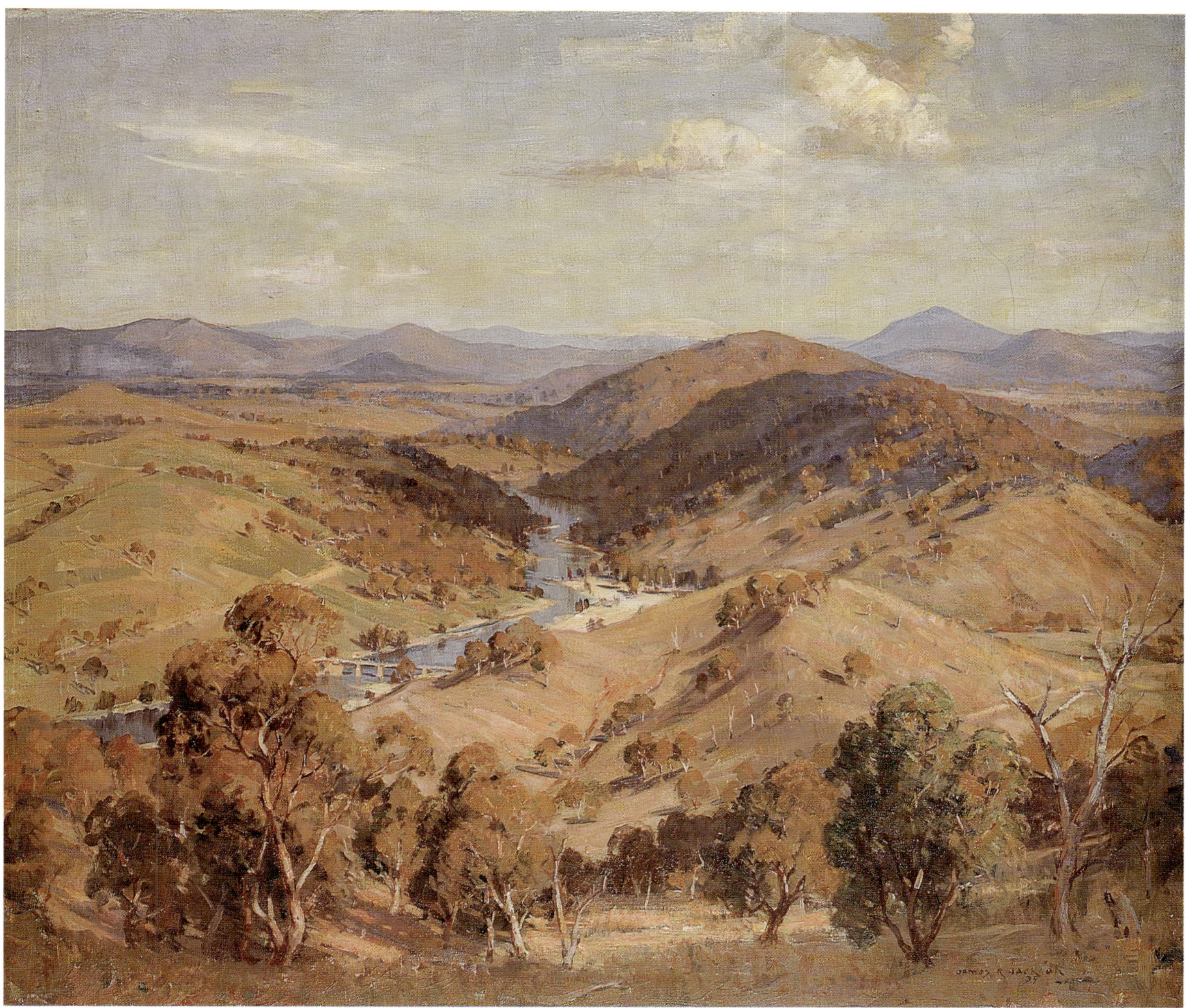

62   MURRUMBIDGEE CROSSING 1939 Oil on canvas 81.5 x 96.5 cm
Reproduced by permission of the Australian National Gallery, Canberra

Towards the end of this year, Dora decided to learn portraiture with W. B. McInnes in Melbourne, where we stayed for a year. Jimmy remained based in Sydney and during this period undertook long painting trips to the country. One was to the Australian Capital Territory, where he again painted the scenery along the Murrumbidgee River. His large canvas, *Murrumbidgee Crossing*, which hung in the dining room of the Lodge, Canberra, was painted during 1939.

Murrumbidgee Crossing is a magnificent panorama of typical Australian countryside and is one of his best landscapes. Its composition is unlike his much earlier *Valley of Tharwa*, as it is painted from a different location and follows the winding river with broad water expanses. Both pictures were painted in the shade of his large black umbrella, from near the tops of steep ridges, which he would have climbed many times to complete these canvases. Comparison of this 1939 picture to a similar composition painted at the beginning of the depression, shows his artistic development with the integrated use of sky and cloud patterns. His record of detail shows both clearing of the country and the growth of foreground trees. Towards the end of the year he stayed with friends in Sydney's northern beaches area, and from there painted powerful views of coastal scenery; of headlands rising towards the sea — their cliffs in warm part-shadow, complementing orange sands edged with shimmering violet transitions into the sea.

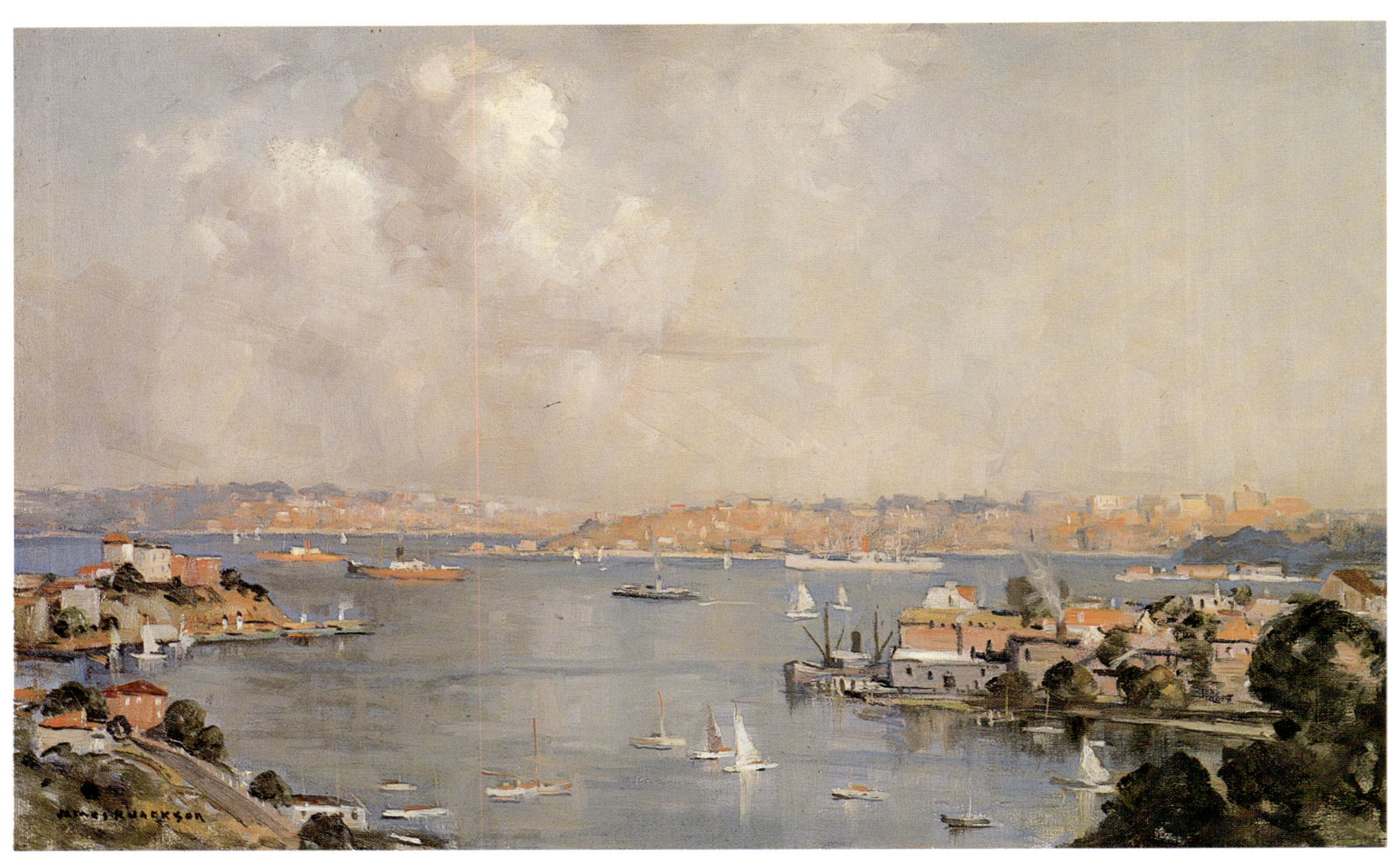

63   **SYDNEY HARBOUR FROM NORTH SYDNEY** 1939 47.5 x 76 cm
Latrobe Valley Arts Centre

CHAPTER 10

The 1940s

The Second World War was an unsettling time for everyone and it marked a turning point in Jimmy's life. His marriage collapsed and the effect of this, plus his wartime duties and changes in art styles, had a marked impact on his art and career.

At the onset of the war, Dora and the children returned to Sydney after a year in Melbourne and then moved house several times. Dora built a new home in Mosman which included a large studio for Jimmy. It was on an undeveloped steep bushy block with views out the Heads over Chinaman's Beach. Being a hard worker, she expected Jimmy to help her construct retaining rock walls for the bush garden, but he refused. Having lost his Seaforth studio, his interest in maintaining another house, with its attached mortgage, and in creating another large garden, had declined. He said he was an artist, not a gardener.

He used this new studio for only a short while, and from here prepared another one-man exhibition, which was held at the Sedon Galleries, Melbourne, in September 1940. It was opened by artist Harold B. Herbert, who also considered Jimmy to be one of Australia's outstanding landscape painters. This, and his subsequent exhibition held at Sedon's in September 1942, which contained his large *Sydney Harbour from Mosman Heights*, were perhaps his last totally representative exhibitions of his pre-war style.

Jimmy's exhibits in the 1940 Royal Art Society exhibition included his *Venetian Fishing Boats*, which the Art Gallery of New South Wales purchased. The following year, he included his *Mt. Blanc from Salonches*, which had been one of his major exhibits in his exhibition at the Macquarie Galleries. His *Hills of Sofala, N.S.W.* toured the USA and Canada with the Australian Art exhibition in the same year. Because of his war duties and unsettled home life he was not producing many works. In 1942 he won the George MacKay prize for a painting in the Manly Warringah Shire with his *Old Road, French's Forest*, which was finished some years earlier. At the annual Royal Art Society exhibitions he exhibited a few of his earlier paintings.

Jimmy joined the Camouflage Section for the Department of Defence around 1942. One of his postings was at Richmond Air Base, where he advised on colour for camouflage of aircraft, guns and netting. Never had he mixed such large quantities of paint, which was applied by spraying. He lived in one of the big dormitories, which he found either very hot or very cold and always crowded. Although he enjoyed the work, he was unaccustomed to the close living conditions, the regular hours and routine.

His new friends at the Department of Defence took him to Thomo's Two-up School. As this gambling establishment 'never existed' he could not draw the scene in his sketchbook, so he wrote colour notes and drew impressions in pencil on his shirt cuff. Later, with the help of these notes, he painted the scene from memory in his studio. Eventually, when he was over sixty, the Department of Defence found out how old he really was and discharged him.

During this early part of the war, Jimmy separated from Dora and returned to his old haunts at North Sydney. He used one of the larger rooms of a small stone house near Shore School as his studio, where

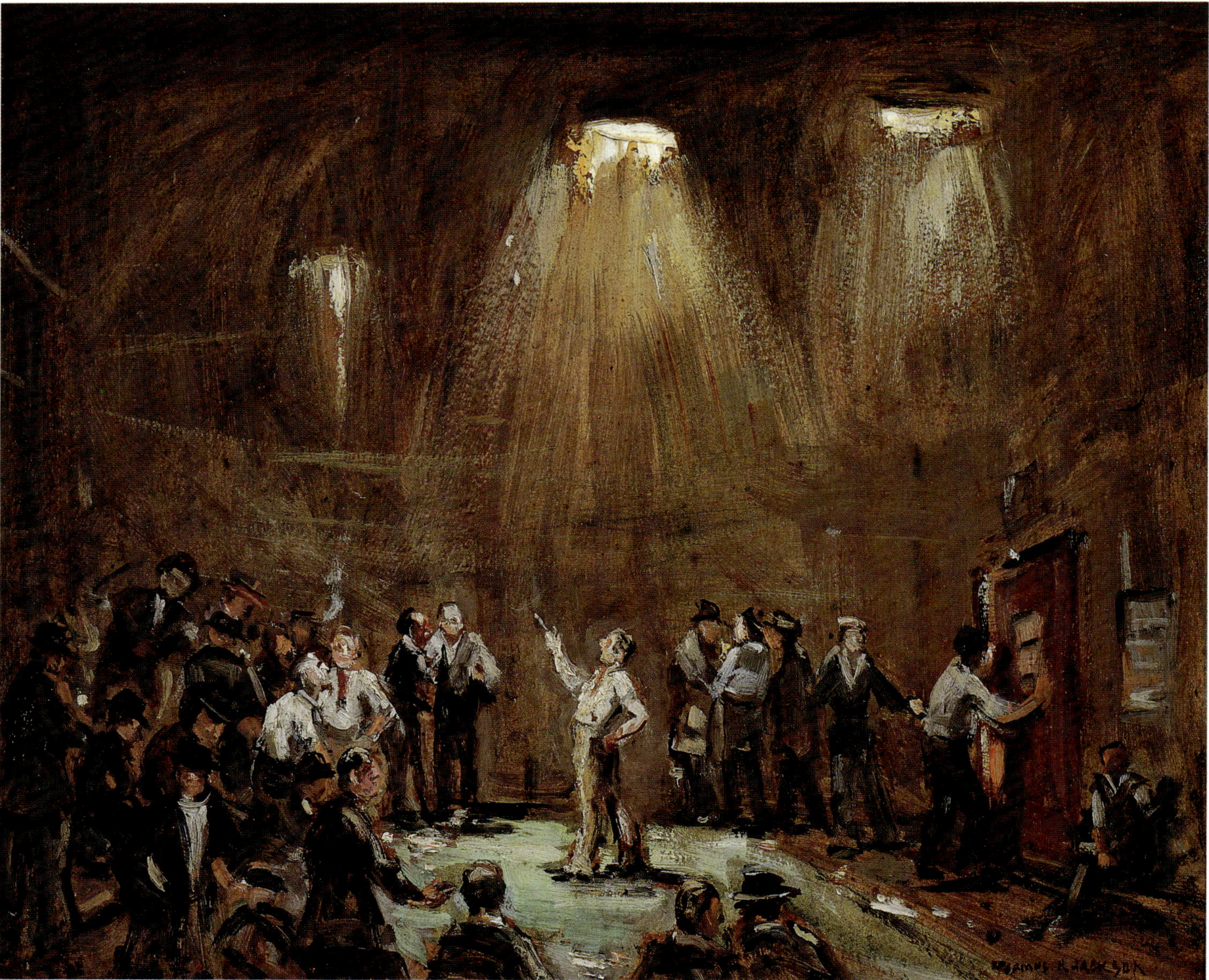

64 **THOMO'S TWO UP SCHOOL** 1942 39.5 x 50 cm
Private Collection

he remained, caring for himself, for nearly twenty years. The studio was very similar to those seen in old photographs of art studios in Paris taken just after the turn of the century. It was very simply equipped, with separate basic amenities, but full of atmosphere, canvas and paint.

In the summer of 1943–44 Jimmy was again free to paint but wartime restrictions on painting around the harbour were enforced, so he toured the north-west of New South Wales. Here he recorded the landscape of the Tamworth and Narrabri areas on large canvases. Several of these are painted from near the top of hills — to capture these views he walked up steep ridges on hot days carrying all of his equipment. These pictures combine his rhythmic designs of vast panoramas with typical non-productive cloud which streaks the inland summer sky. Returning from this trip, which helped to dim the memories of his personal upheaval, he painted in the Upper Hunter area, then changed his scene to the coast around Port Stephens.

During the 1940s, home interior decoration had changed and people were hanging fewer pictures and very few etchings. Pictures were not in great demand and art materials, especially good quality canvas, were very difficult to obtain. Safe transport for his large pictures was almost impossible to find. As a result, Jimmy's use and treatment of materials altered. He now frequently painted on prepared cardboard (paperboard) instead of canvas, so that his paint application on these smoother surfaces is

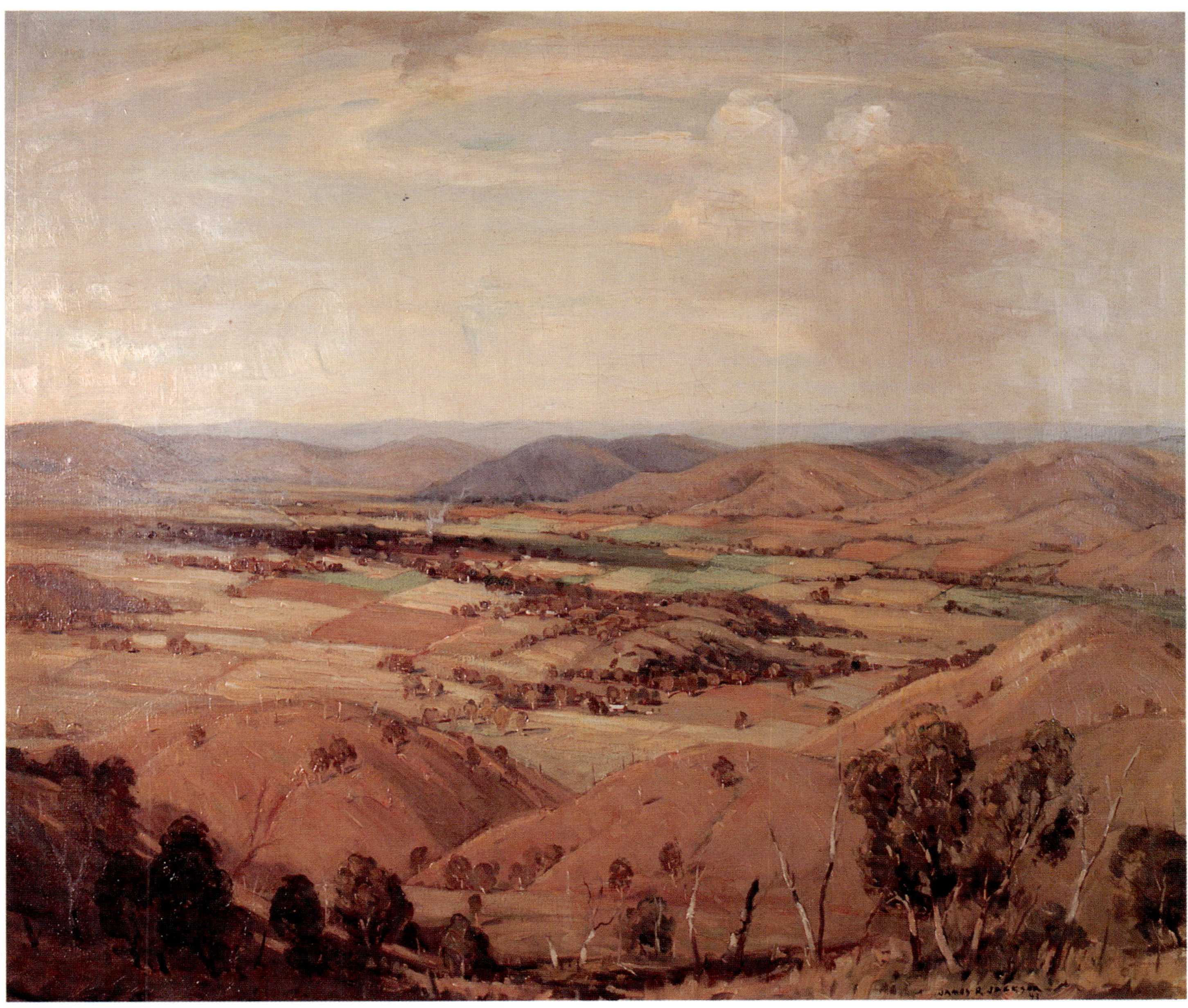

65   TAMWORTH LANDSCAPE, N.S.W. 1944 102 x 108 cm
Private Collection

usually not as generous. He would prepare the cardboard himself, sometimes with an off-white wash, but usually with a pink-coloured base. When he used canvas for his smaller works, he glued them down on cardboard or ply to save a stretcher, but he continued to use stretchers for his larger pictures.

His style had also altered: his paint was not as thick, his colours were lighter and the original, sketched-in composition outlines frequently remained, especially as outlines of buildings in his harbour pictures. In his landscapes, cattle and occasionally sheep, replaced figures as points of interest. But his fascination with light and mastery of painting clouds and sky effects remained unchanged.

The Art Gallery of New South Wales acquired his *The Viaduct Sodwalls* in 1945. This is representative of his landscape style of this period and shows his development of an atmospheric sky and its relationship to a dry pasture, with cattle watering at the river in the foreground. At the end of the war, he could again paint the harbour. *Little Boats, Middle Harbour*, a typical Jackson harbour painting, was purchased by the Art Gallery of New South Wales in 1946. This painting also demonstrates his materials at that time — a canvas glued down on paperboard.

Transport was still a difficulty and he had trouble finding enough accessible painting sites to fill the

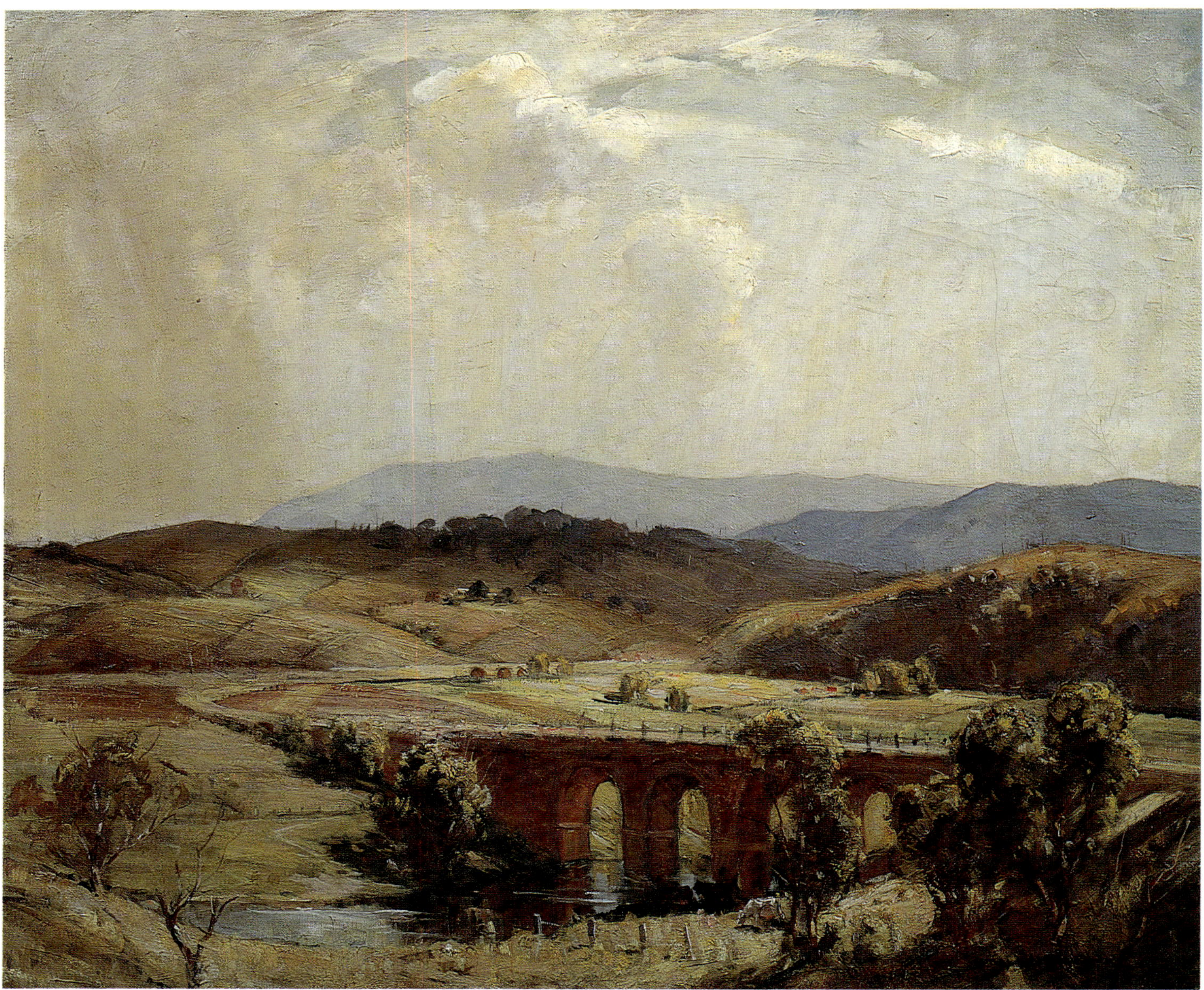

66 **'THE VIADUCT SODWALLS', N.S.W.** 1945 Oil on canvas 66 x 81.3 cm
Marshall Bequest Fund 1945
Art Gallery of New South Wales

void in his picture collection caused by the upheaval of the war years. He had always kept a reserve of paintings to show anyone who visited his studio. Most were for sale but his favourites remained with him for years, either hanging on the walls for him to enjoy or put away when any prospective buyer called. I asked him once why he did this and he replied, 'I don't want to part with them and the people always pressure you to sell them'. He never showed or sold a picture in his studio unframed. As he said, 'The frame dresses it up and I know what frame suits the picture'. Some of the frames in his early career and during the depression, when he could not afford good ones, are poor and the pictures would improve with reframing. I have seen some of his works reframed and improved, but unless done by a sympathetic framer, the new surrounding can detract from the effect of the picture.

With the easing of wartime transport difficulties, Jimmy was again able to travel interstate without major problems. Early 1946 found him painting in Victoria at Mount Macedon, then in the Dandenongs and in the Mount Gisborne areas. His landscapes varied from large panoramas with such wonderful titles as *Behold the Landscape*, painted near Mount Macedon, to intimate farm glimpses. He stayed with the Sedons in Melbourne for several months and from there painted over twenty canvases of the Mornington Peninsula.

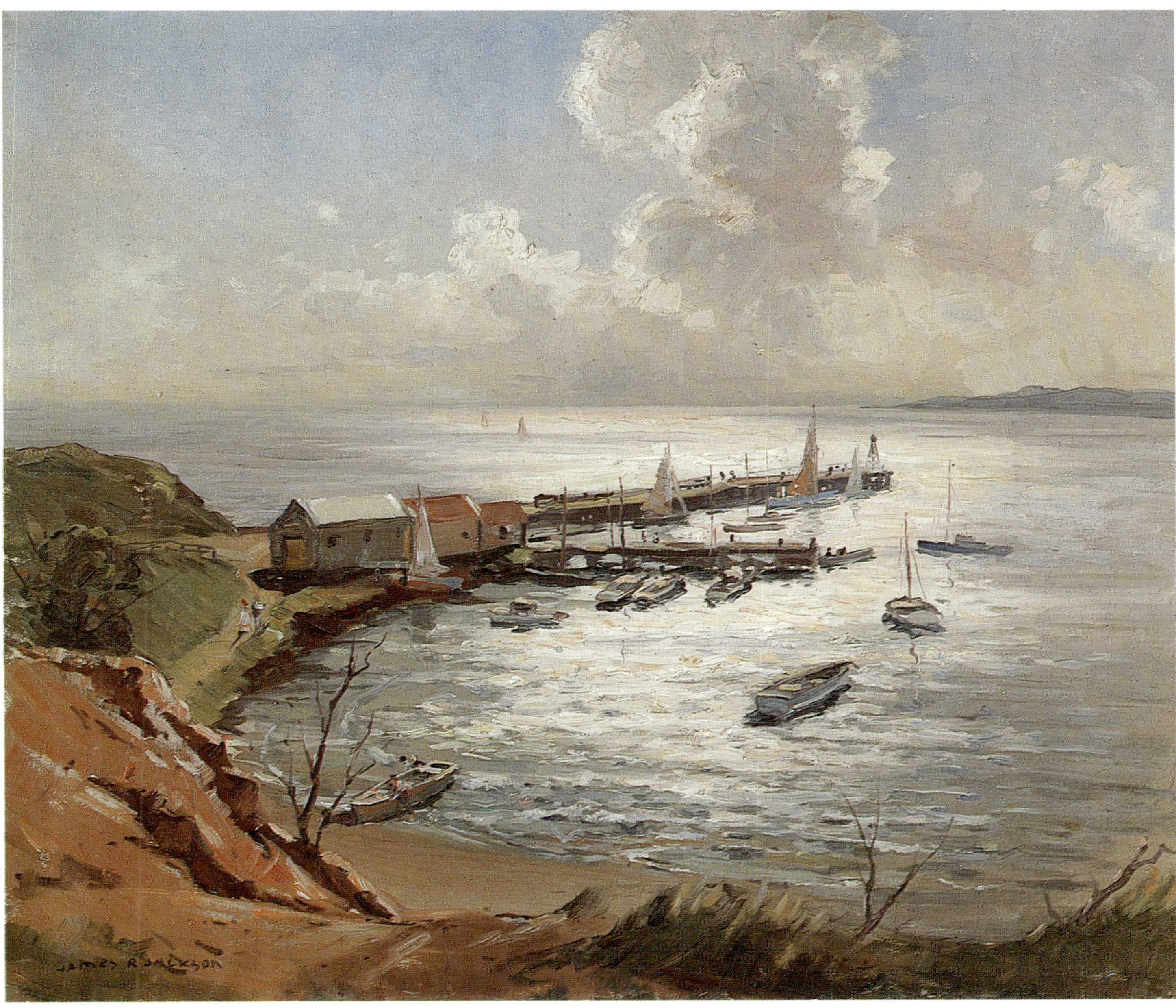

67   EVENING LIGHT, MORNINGTON PIER, VICTORIA 1946 50.7 x 61.1 cm
From the collection of the City of Hamilton Art Gallery, Victoria

In October that year, he held a large exhibition of fifty paintings at the Sedon Galleries in Elizabeth Street, Melbourne, and his sales were good. The majority of these pictures were his recent Victorian works, but he also included sixteen of Sydney Harbour and some New South Wales landscapes. To recover from the effort of mounting this exhibition, and the distress of his forthcoming divorce, he relaxed and went fishing at Paddy's Corner on the Thredbo River with a group of friends including the writer Frank Clune and Sir Hudson Fysh, the Chairman of Qantas.

In 1947 the Royal Art Society published *Australian Art Illustrated*, in which Jimmy was represented by two pictures: *Harbour Tranquility* and *The Story*. The latter was a large nude study which he had painted some years earlier, and depicts a lady reading and resting in a cane chair. *Harbour Tranquility* was a view looking down on the Spit. He was also represented in the Sedon Galleries March exhibition, Artists Past and Present. He was rarely in Sydney around this time as he made many country trips, either staying with friends or camping with fellow artists such as Harry Hanke. They camped on rivers near Gloucester in New South Wales and also painted the Snowy Mountain country around Old Talbingo. They always returned before exhibition time of the Royal Art Society.

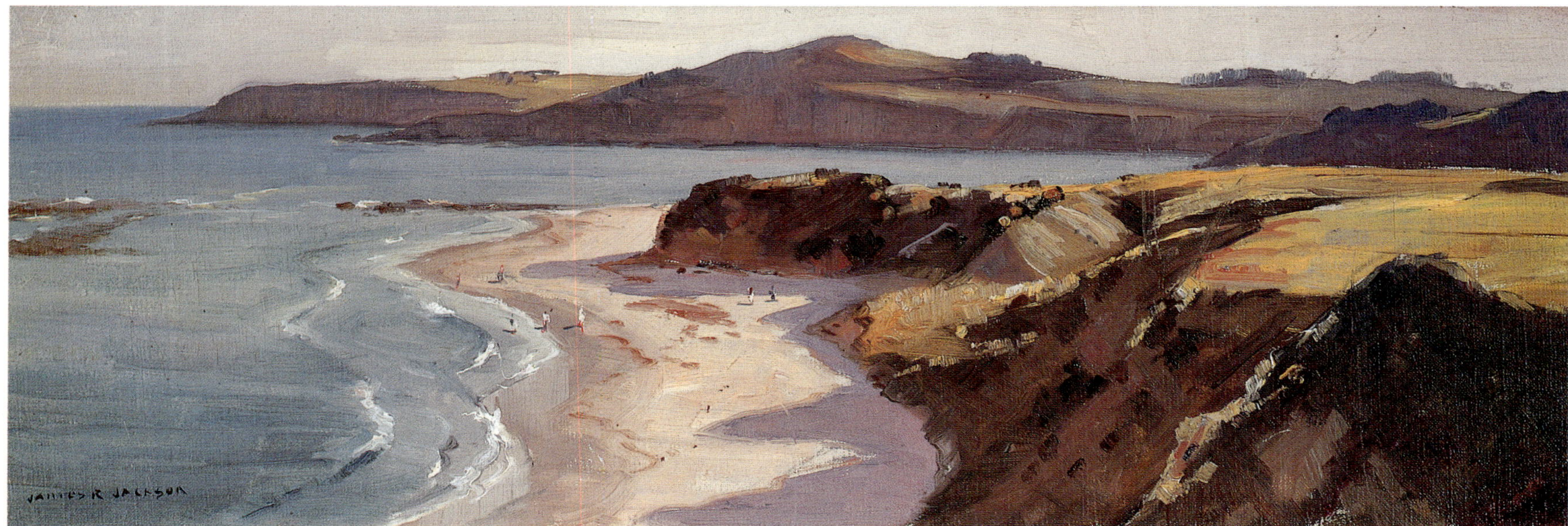

68   WESTERN PORT, VICTORIA 1946 22.2 x 68 cm
Private Collection

When Jimmy stayed with friends, he loved to sleep in a separate shed or a detached room as he always got up at the crack of dawn to capture the mood of the day or fish, and this allowed him the freedom to come and go without upsetting the household. As long as he could have his morning cup of tea see a film or to the theatre as he said 'nature offers more beauties and stories than Hollywood'. He enjoyed friendly visits or discussions over dinner and would sometimes listen to the radio. His fondness enjoyed friendly visits or discussions over dinner and would sometimes listen to the radio. His fondness of reading led him to admire the Chinese philosophy of life and their relationship with nature. He was always up-to-date with world news reported in the papers and often commented on the similarity of recent events to those which had occurred years before. In his spare time he was always busy drawing in his notebook, preparing his works for exhibitions or his fishing lines for fishing.

During the late 1940s, Jimmy started using auction houses to sell his pictures. At first he took in two or three a year to James R. Lawsons, Sydney, but later increased this number. Some were recently painted and others were older, unsold works. Although in his catalogue titles he tended to give the painting district, Jimmy was fairly secretive about his movements and his actual painting sites. This characteristic became more marked in his latter years.

Around the harbour he continued to mark his sites with excess palette paint as had many other artists. Jimmy usually used two palette knife wipes of harbour blue on the side of a nearby rock. It was always on the side because he said he did not want anyone sitting on wet paint — but the side was also more difficult to see. He would become upset if he found someone else's trademark extravagantly displayed and remark that 'some other blighter had cleaned his palette on top of the rock'. In reality he now regarded the harbour as his territory and this was acknowledged by many of his artist friends.

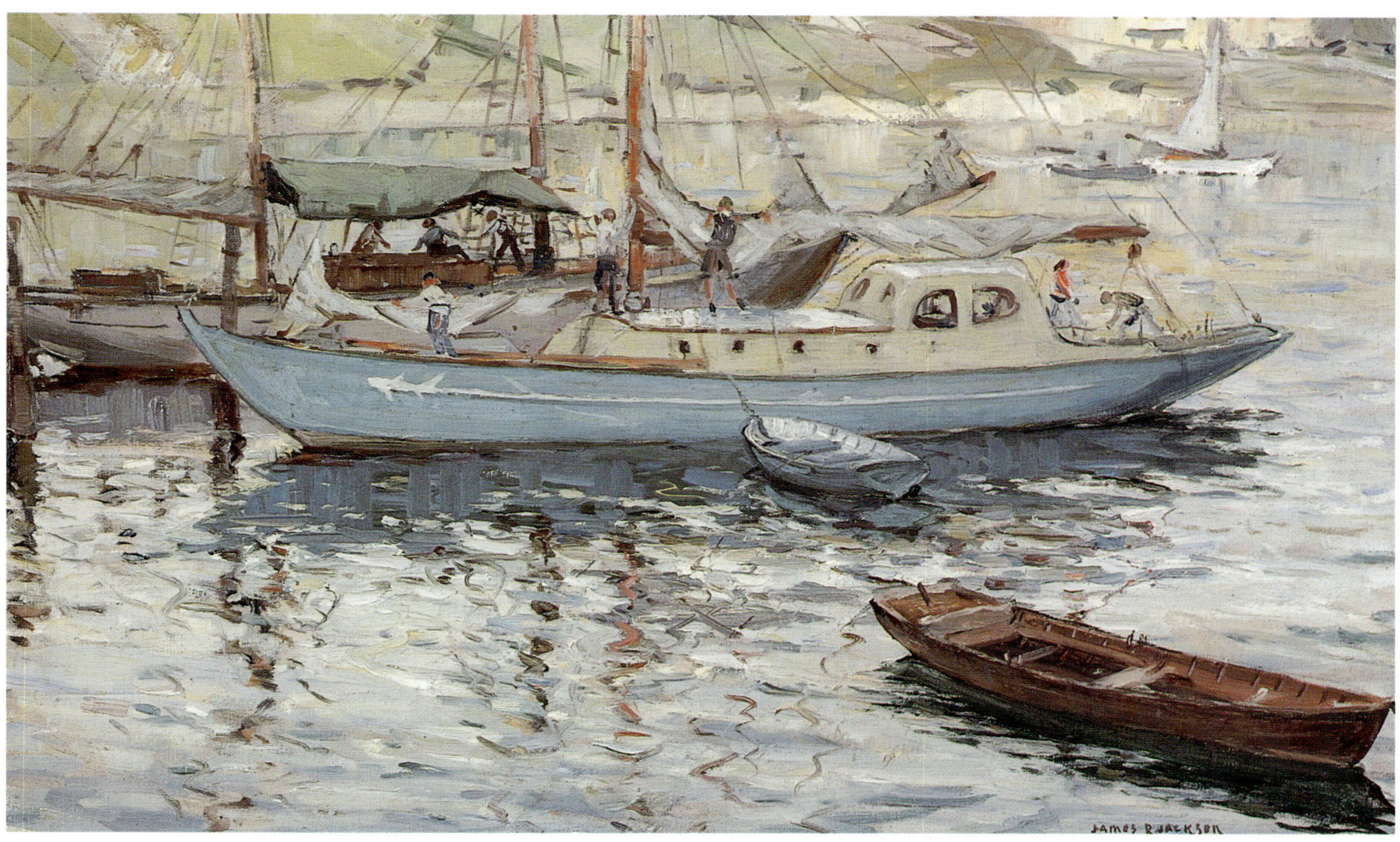

69 THE RETURN 1948 45.4 x 76.2 cm
Private Collection

Panel-shaped pictures of the harbour had previously featured in his works, especially his early ones, and they again became popular with him. In these, he reduced the big sky effects and concentrated on wider local interest. These pictures were painted on canvas laid down on board or on ply. In the 1950s he used the smooth prepared side of masonite, but he found this too heavy to carry and difficult to cut. At this time he experimented with painting on prepared thin cardboard for his smaller pictures, but as this tended to warp he soon reverted to his tried and tested materials. Unfortunately, in his later failing years, he painted on anything he could get his brush on and these included anything from very thin paper to corrugated board.

His sales at this time included *The Return*, to the Art Gallery of New South Wales, and a large picture for 200 guineas from the Sedon Galleries exhibition entitled Work of 12 Artists. This was held in February 1949 and artists represented included Frederick McCubbin, Tom Roberts and Hans Heysen. Jimmy's representation in another exhibition, Oil Paintings by Leading Past and Present Australian Artists, held at the Sedon Galleries in June 1950 included recent views of Broken Bay and Palm Beach.

Jimmy had always painted nocturnes and had exhibited them since 1911. In the postwar years, he

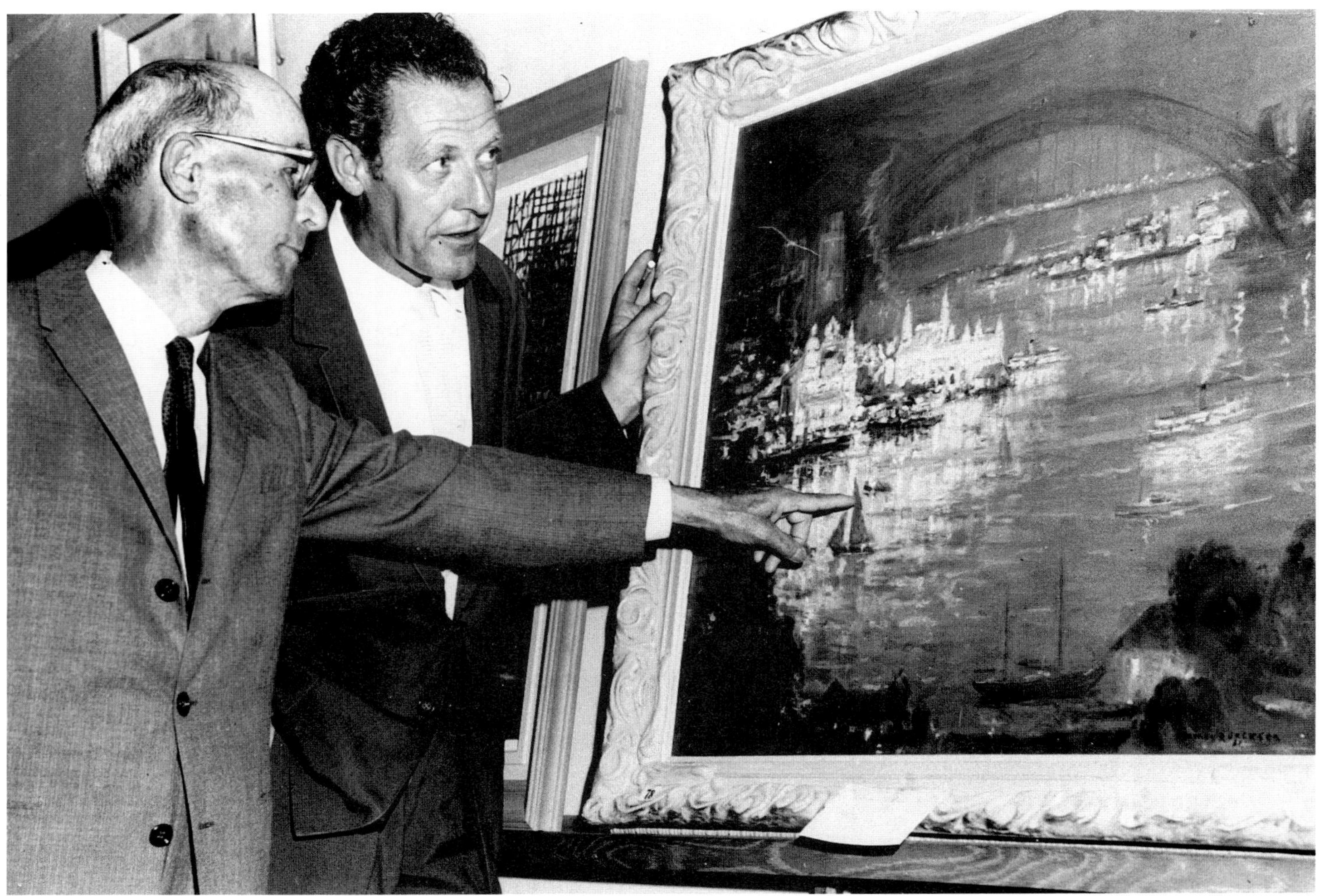

70   James showing his nocturne 'Luna Park' winner of W.D. & H.O. Wills Art Competition, 1961
      Credit: John Fairfax Group

started painting larger ones of the developing city with spectacular light effects. Night reflections from the buildings, the Sydney Harbour Bridge or Luna Park shimmered on the water. These were generally started outdoors at night and finished in his studio. The light for his palette was supplied by a candle in a kerosene tin with a hole cut in it. This gave a very mellow effect and helped him capture the soft night atmosphere. In 1949 he exhibited *Carnival*, a large night scene of Sydney Harbour. The original purchaser at the show's opening was offered more than twice as much as the catalogue price of 200 guineas a few hours later. In 1961 his nocturne *Luna Park* won the W. D. and H. O. Wills Art Competition. This nocturne of brilliant light reflections from the fun palace against the background of the Harbour Bridge, showed his ability to capture light effects, movement and colour — all under the gentle glow of night.

Bookkeeping and accounts were never one of Jimmy's fortes and with the loss of his record keeper, Dora, his increased sales and his advancing years, he found himself in a real mess with the Income Tax Department. Robert Young, the art restorer, told how Jimmy had to front up for a tax interview: 'He stood on one foot and then the other, not understanding why, after all his hard work he had to pay so much tax or how they assessed it. Finally, when asked how he had lived on so little, he replied in his light voice, "I didn't eat much that year." '

It took Jimmy some time to sort out his finances and during and after this period he lost all inclination to paint. In 1950, he visited his sisters in New Zealand; this was his last overseas trip and the New Zealand press gave him much publicity, claiming him as one of their long-lost sons.

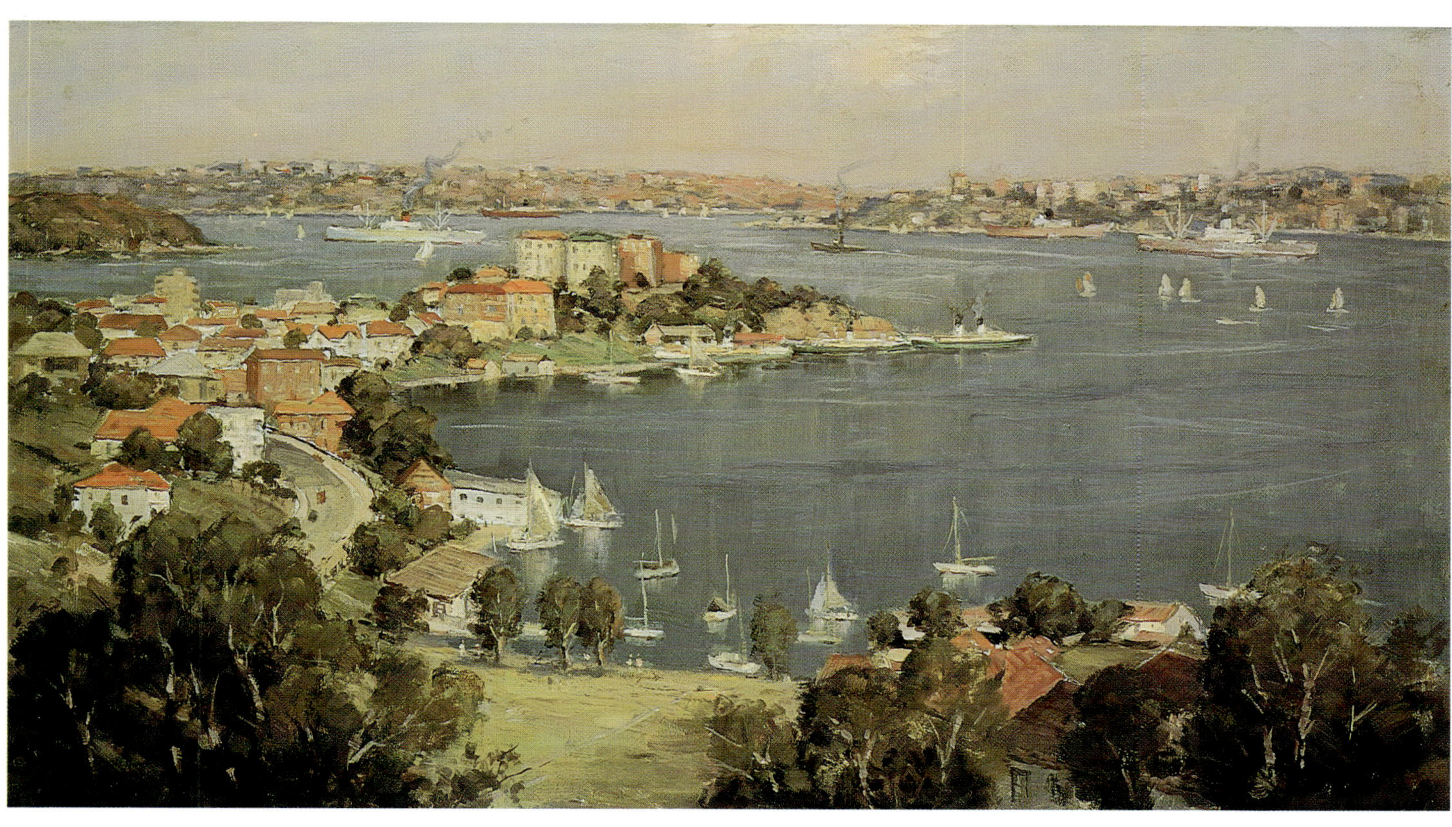

71 AUTUMN DAY, SYDNEY HARBOUR 1949 53.3 x 96.2 cm
Reproduced by permission, from the Collection of the Queensland Art Gallery, Brisbane

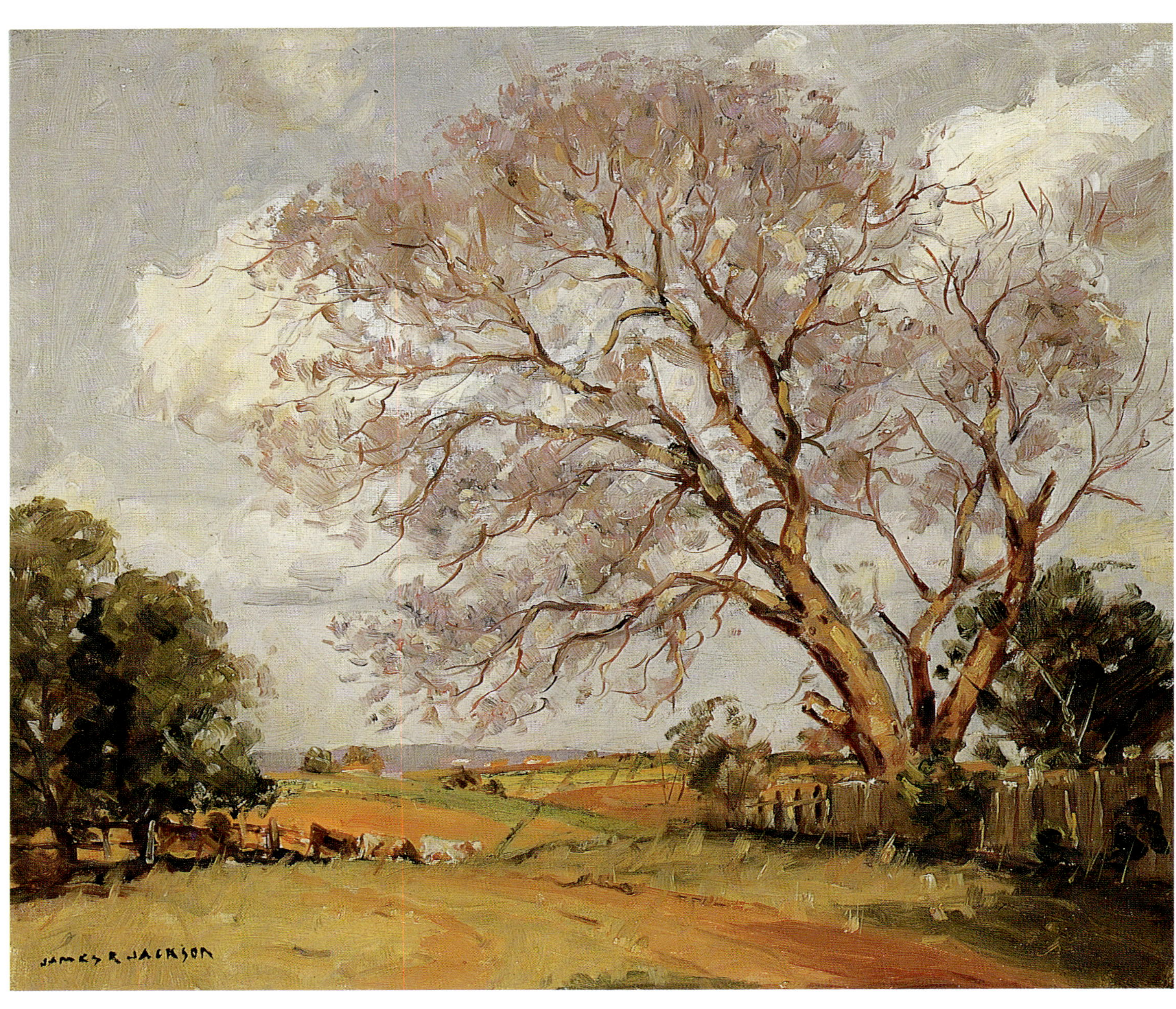

72 JACARANDA TREE 1949 44 x 55 cm
Private Collection

CHAPTER 11

The Later Years

*J*immy returned to the scenery of Bellingen, New South Wales, which he had discovered several years earlier, and painted these greener pastures with mastery. On his first visit he stayed at the hotel but was later hosted by Dr and Mrs Mervyn Elliott. Mrs Elliott would drive him miles to his painting place in the morning and return for him in the late afternoon. In this comfortable home environment he was able to paint large canvases with vigour and artistry. During the 1950s he frequently visited this northern area, painting at Dorrigo and also in the mountains around the upper reaches of the Macleay River. Nearby coastal scenery, including dairy farms, lush vegetation and the occasional flowering jacaranda tree feature in this fresh burst of energy.

Jimmy had not exhibited in the Wynne art prize since the early 1940s, but during the 1950s he sent in the occasional exhibit. These were not painted especially for the competition but were good pictures which he happened to have in his studio. He realised that with the changes in art styles, he now had little chance of winning, but he sent in to let the public see his work. He always maintained that other artists considered that he should have won the Wynne at least once in the 1930s, when he contributed larger prepared landscapes. Other competitions attracted him and he was pleased to be successful in many of them until the early 1960s. He won the Royal Agricultural Society Easter Show's Art Competition in 1960, the W. D. and H. O. Wills Art Competition in 1961 and the following year both the Manly Gallery and Grafton Art Prizes.

Gallery purchases by the Art Gallery of New South Wales of his *Sand Dunes, Botany* in 1952 and *Sunlight Sandhills* in 1953 also pleased him. These show his mastery of light effects combined with his composition skills. The difficulties of capturing the adjoining tonal similarities of the high-pitched sky in *Sunlight Sandhills* to the sunstruck, partially excavated dune, is managed by breaking the curve of the dune with some shrubby outline, soft shadow and rising cloud. Another painting of this period, *Brick pits, near Sydney*, is set in a purple-blue palette with ochre relief, and was given by him to the Royal Art Society as a Fellow's Painting. Although this may be called an industrial subject, the drawing and composition, combined with rising chimney-stack smoke and cloud effects, make it a very attractive picture.

The chairman of Royal Prince Alfred Hospital, Sir Herbert Schlink, entertained Jimmy for many weekends at his Pittwater home. During the evenings Jimmy had many long discussions with Sir Herbert and Lady Schlink, while in the daytime he painted water views glimpsed through the tall, spotted gums of the area, and canvases of Palm Beach. Jimmy travelled widely in these years. He painted in the Cowra district of New South Wales and then made his first visit to inland Queensland to Mount Isa. Here he delighted in the iron reds of the dry interior and his canvases were large and colourful.

In October 1954, Brisbane saw his first one-man exhibition of twenty-six paintings at the Moreton Galleries in Edward Street. These varied pictures did not include any of his recent Mount Isa trip, but were landscapes and views of Sydney Harbour and sold well. He continued to exhibit in Brisbane at these galleries, and held another one-man show there five years later.

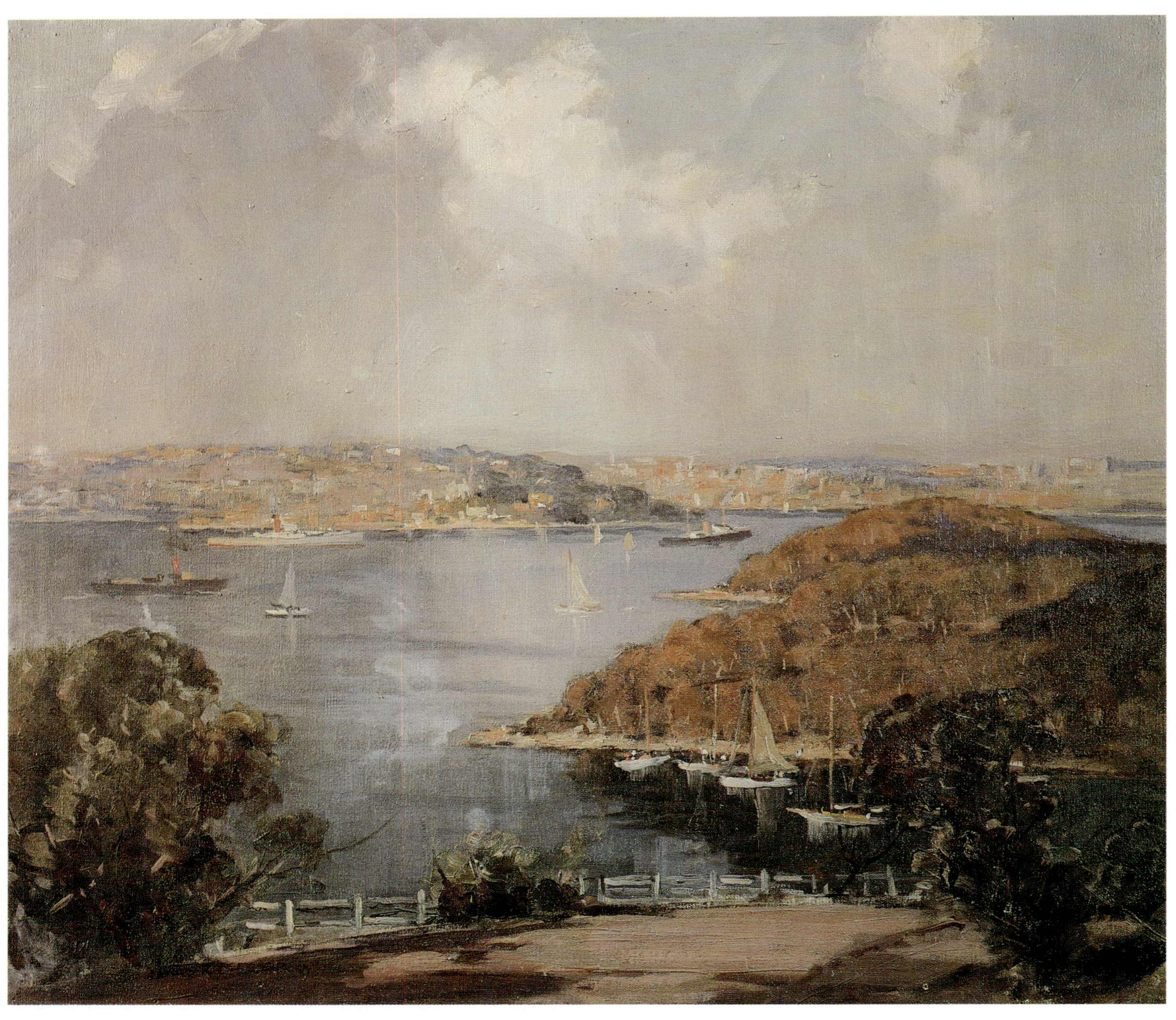

73   SYDNEY HARBOUR FROM GEORGES HEIGHTS 1952 51 x 61 cm
Private Collection

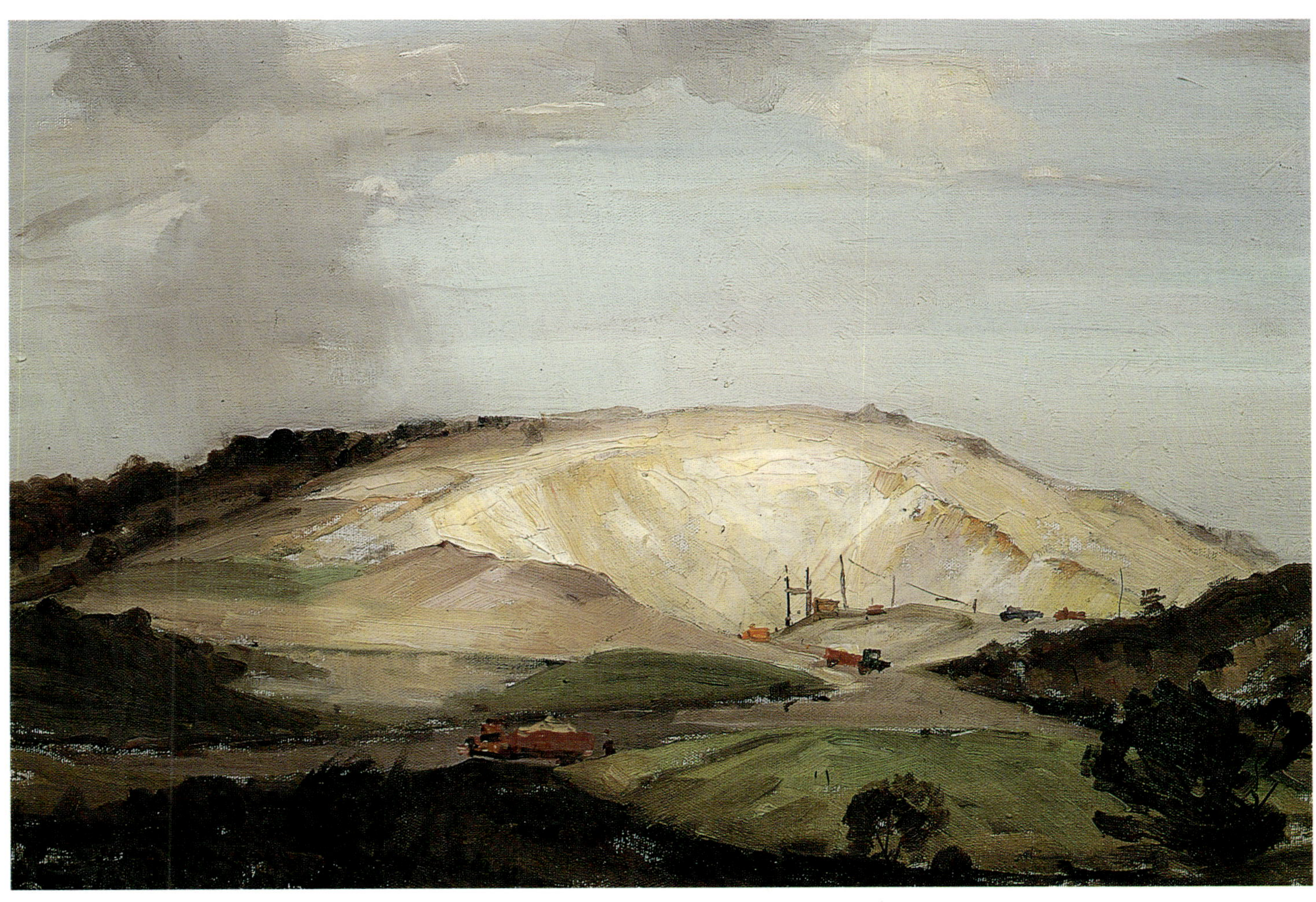

74   **'SUNLIGHT SANDHILLS'** 1953 Oil on canvas 40.3 x 60.3 cm
Purchased 1953
Art Gallery of New South Wales

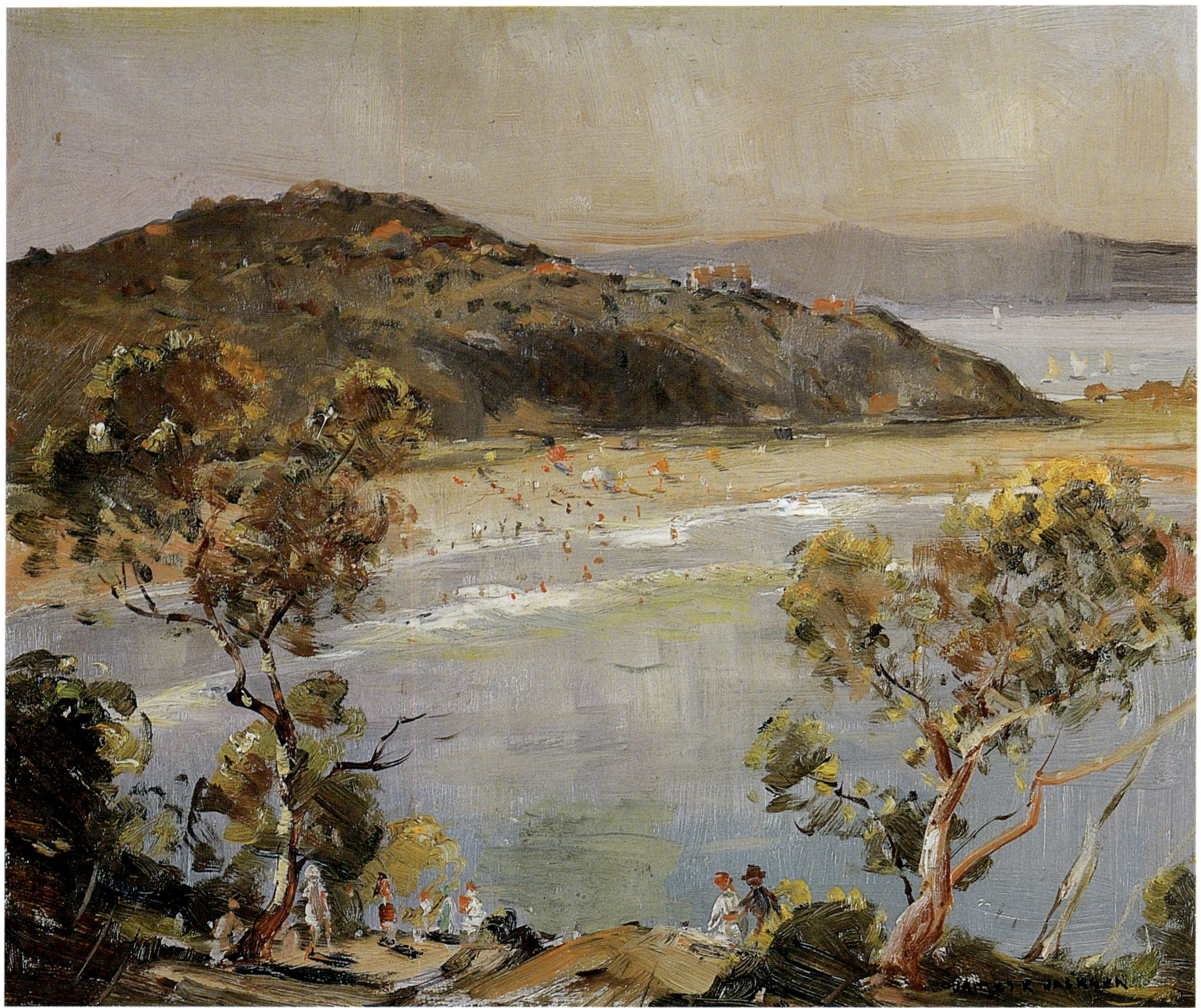

75   **PALM BEACH, N.S.W.** 1951 37 x 45 cm
Private Collection

Jimmy was offered many landscape commissions but would not take them unless he liked the scenery. He would say, 'I'll come out and have a look at your property and if I like it, I'll paint it, but if not, don't worry'. He said, 'The moment you take on a commission for the sake of money, it is invariably a failure'. He felt he was more successful when he enjoyed the subject and wanted to paint it. Sometimes in over-cleared country with wonderful views but no shelter, the station owner would erect a temporary shade shed for him to paint from, but usually he relied on his trusty old umbrella.

During this later part of his career, his mail contained numerous requests to contribute to fundraising art exhibitions for schools, groups or charities. He regarded most of these letters as 'a bother', as he had to be selective, to make sure that he would be represented with good quality artists. Also, to supply transport for one or two pictures at a usually, to him, inconvenient date was difficult. However, he did exhibit and sell many pieces in these exhibitions and also donated pictures to charities. Only rarely did he attend the official openings, as he never liked travelling at night and always went to bed early.

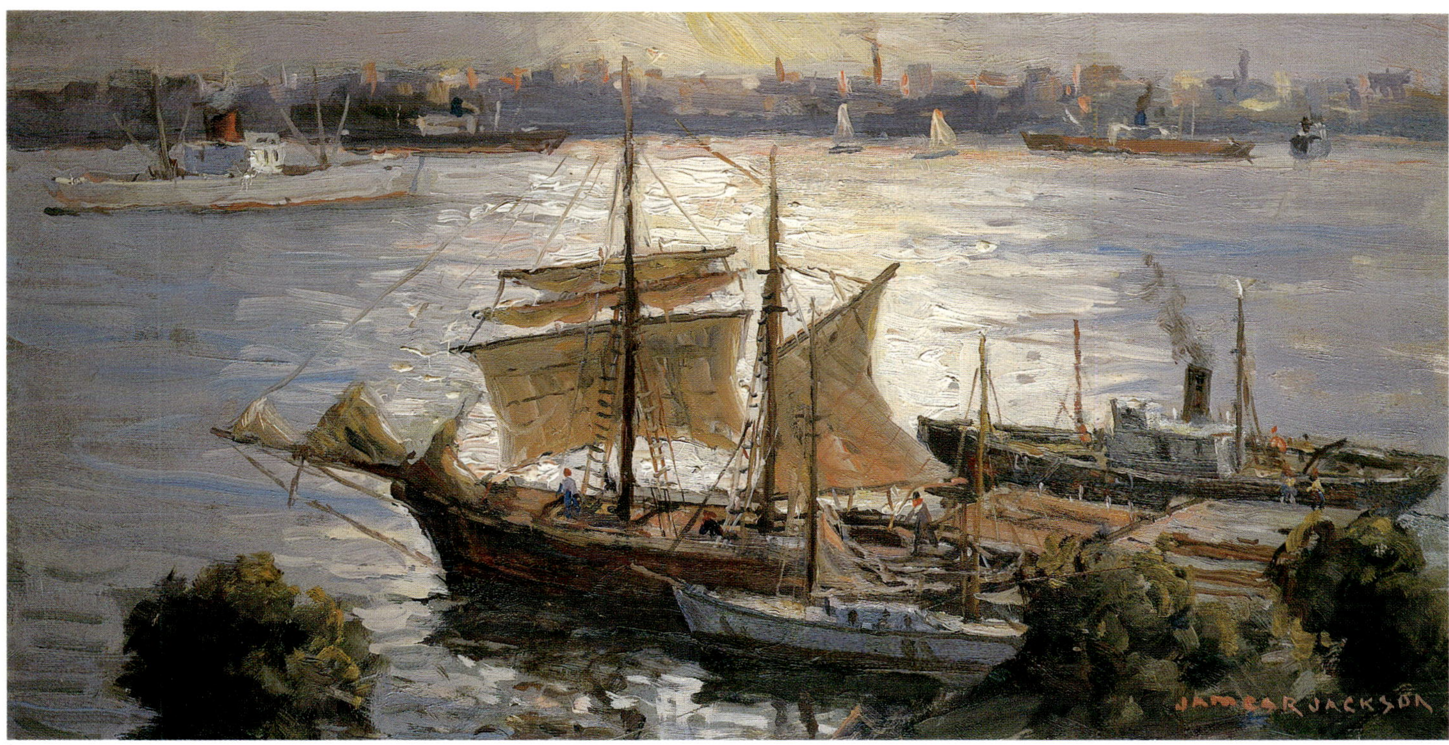

76 DRYING THE SAILS, SYDNEY HARBOUR 1954 26.5 x 57 cm
Private Collection

His last gallery purchase was in 1955 when the Marshall Bequest Fund acquired his *Pathway, Athol Gardens* from the Royal Art Society exhibition for the Art Gallery of New South Wales. He had painted this picture at the end of the war, and it is representative of his style during that stressful period. It was the last of his paintings acquired by the Art Gallery of New South Wales, who at present hold fifteen Jacksons. In the spring and into 1956, he toured and painted extensively in Victoria around Lake Eildon, the Mitta Valley and the south-east coast, then travelled up the Tambo River to Omeo. These recent pictures and some of the Dandenongs were exhibited in August at his major one-man exhibition held at the Sedon Galleries in Melbourne. His prices had increased and this was an interesting showing of forty-two major works. As well as his variety of Victorian and New South Wales landscapes, it included Sydney Harbour views, and three canvases of Melbourne's prominent landmarks, including one of St Pauls. This was the first time that he had actually exhibited paintings of Melbourne, although he had previously painted and shown the streets of Sydney and many European cities.

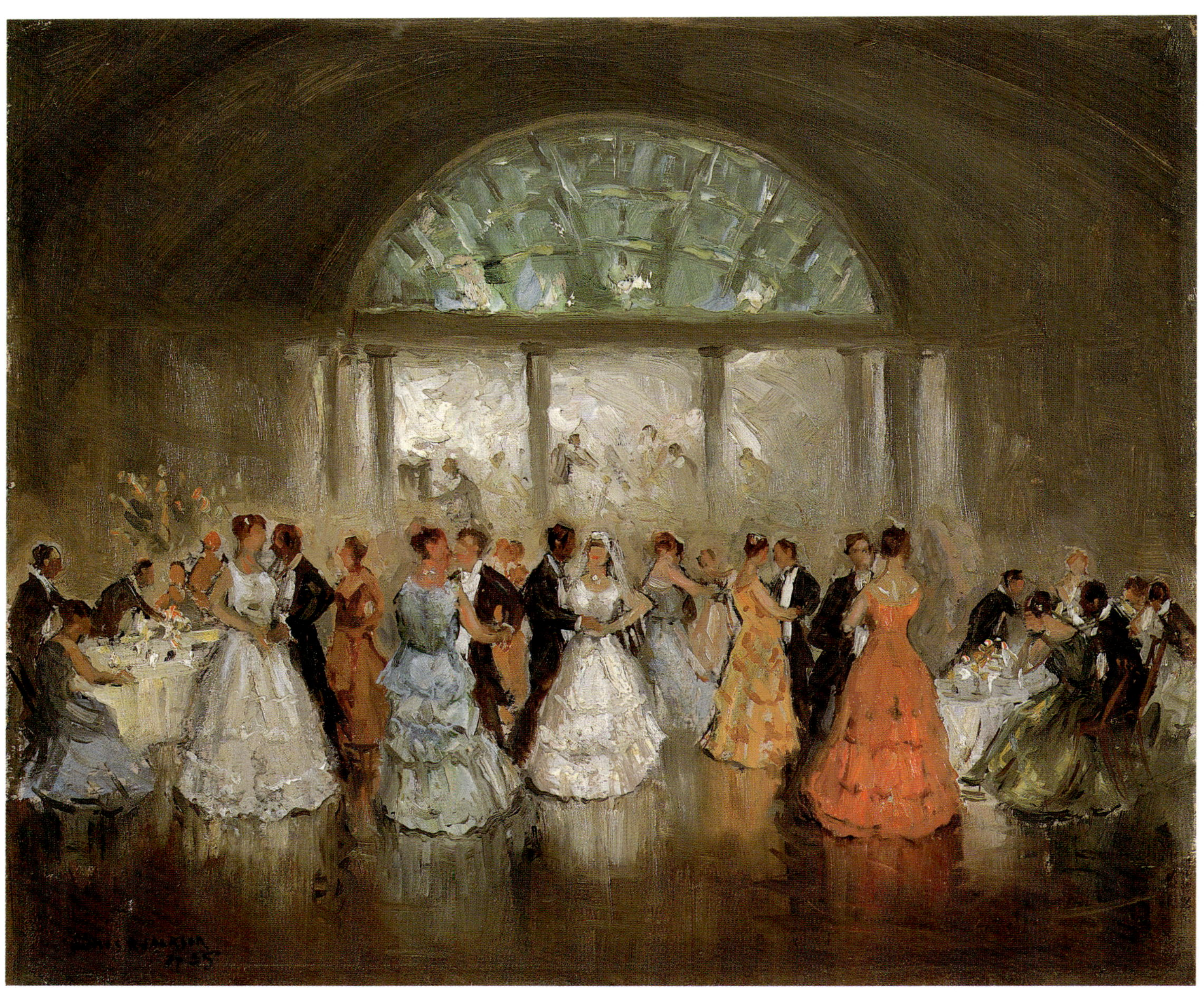

77   WEDDING RECEPTION AT THE WENTWORTH HOTEL, SYDNEY 1955 43 x 54 cm
Private Collection

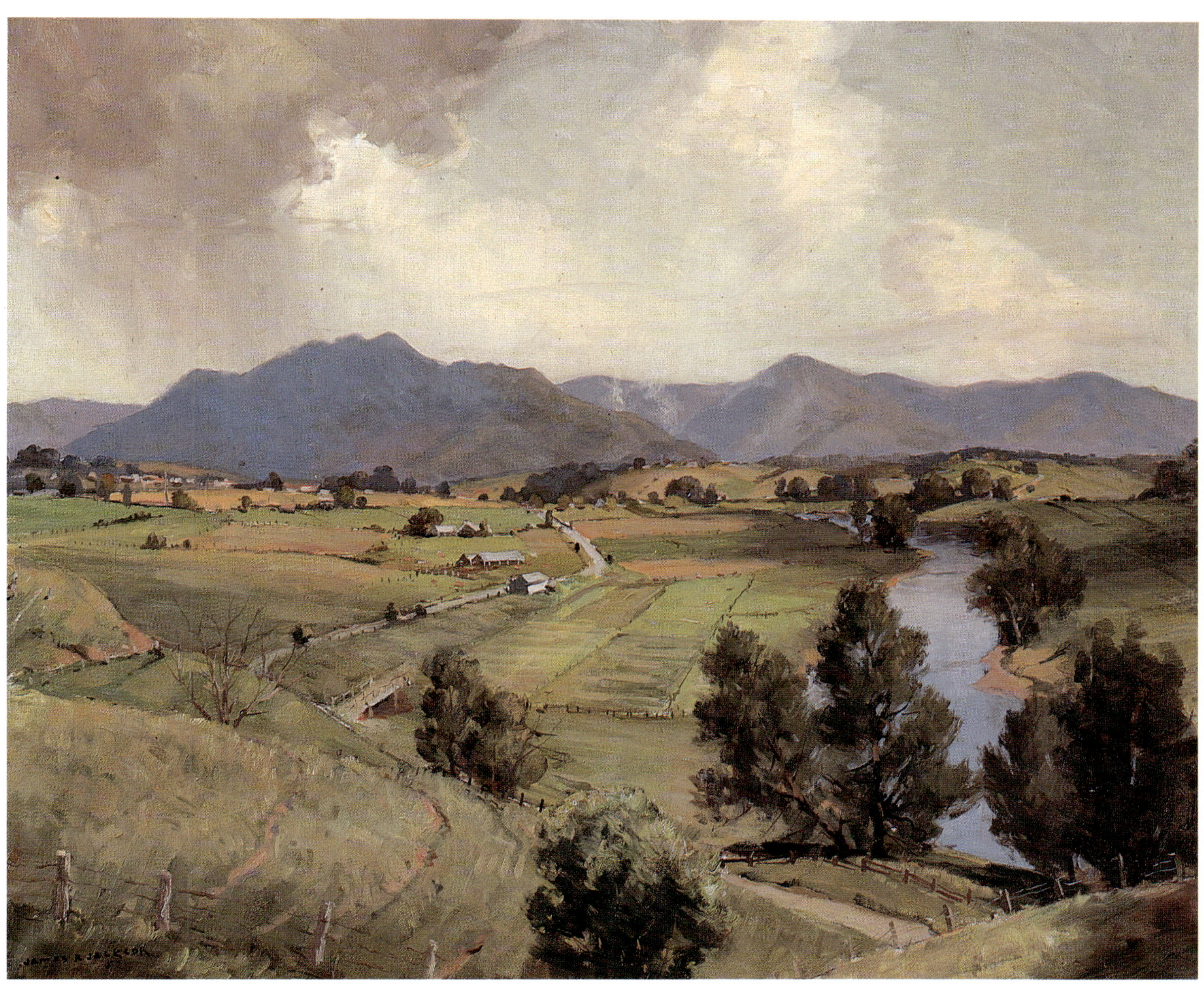

78   **BELLINGEN, N.S.W.**   1957 59 x 75 cm
Private Collection

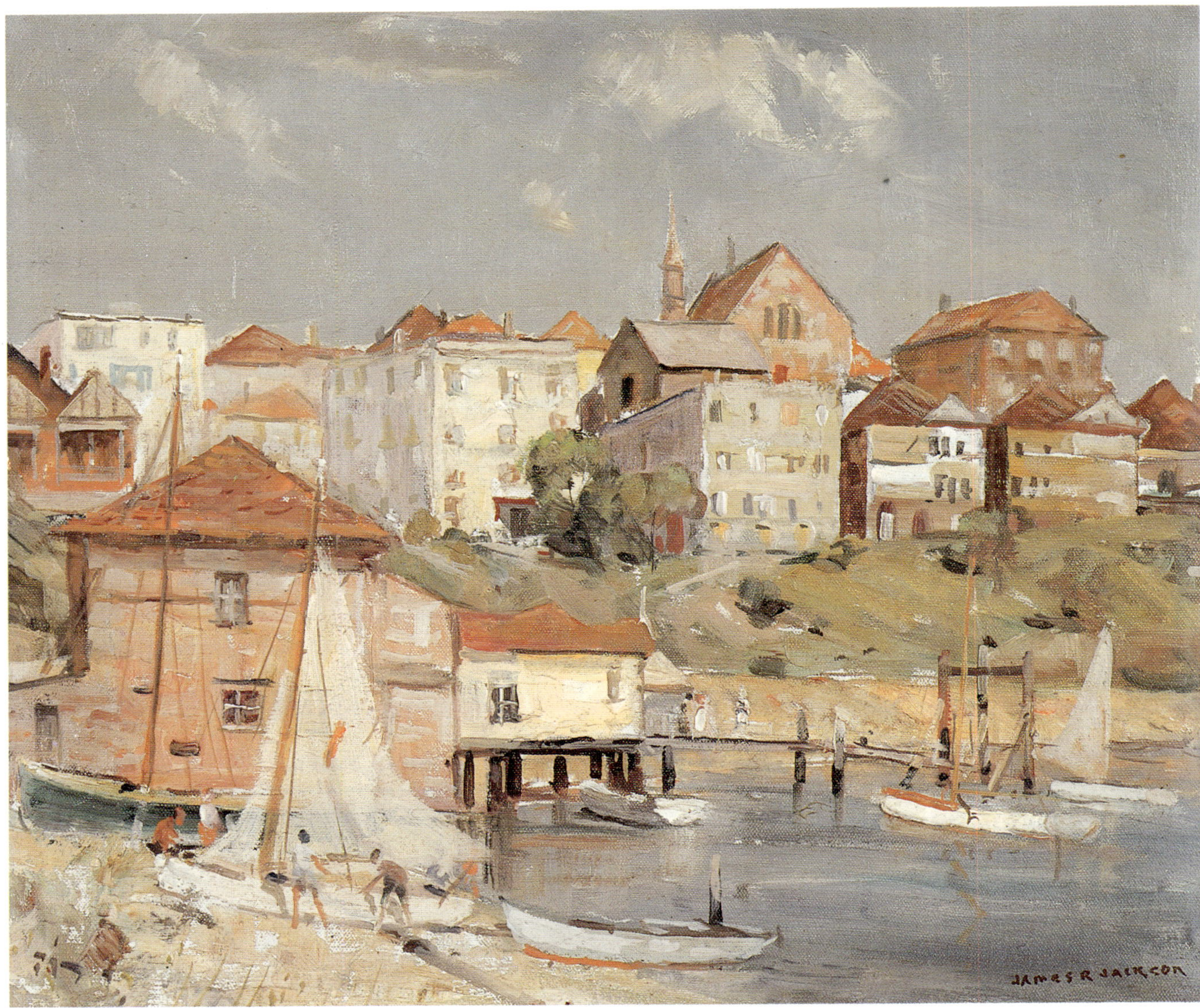

79   HOUSES, LAVENDER BAY, SYDNEY 1958 36 x 43 cm
Private Collection

When aged seventy-five, Jimmy had his first major illness, a heart attack from which he made a good recovery — but as he said, 'It scared the daylights out of me'. After this, he slowed down slightly, gave up smoking and admitted his age. Friends cared for him after his initial illness but then, being independent, he returned to his studio, continued to look after himself and soon started painting. This was at first locally, sometimes with artist friend Eric Langker, and then in the country. I drove him to many likely sites away from the bus routes for a day's painting, but he then still walked for miles to find a suitable subject. He rarely missed his evening's fishing and view of the sunset. If visited in his studio, he would become restless at sundown, walk to the top of the hill to see the colour changes, then down to Blues Point where he fished. His many postwar country camping trips with artists still continued, but camping was now replaced by room comfort. Henry Hanke recalled that when staying in hotels on these painting trips, Jimmy still got up at the crack of dawn, continued to dig for worms to catch trout, which he caught, and talked all night.

James continued to practise his drawing skills in his studio and outside. He still carried a small drawing book in his pocket and, if waiting for a bus, he often sketched nearby people, a street scene or any view. He missed the old buildings which he said 'had character' and was not enamoured with repetitious modern architecture. Neither did he like modern abstract art which showed no knowledge of fundamental drawing, tone or form. As for the modern macabre, splashed on in sombre colours with

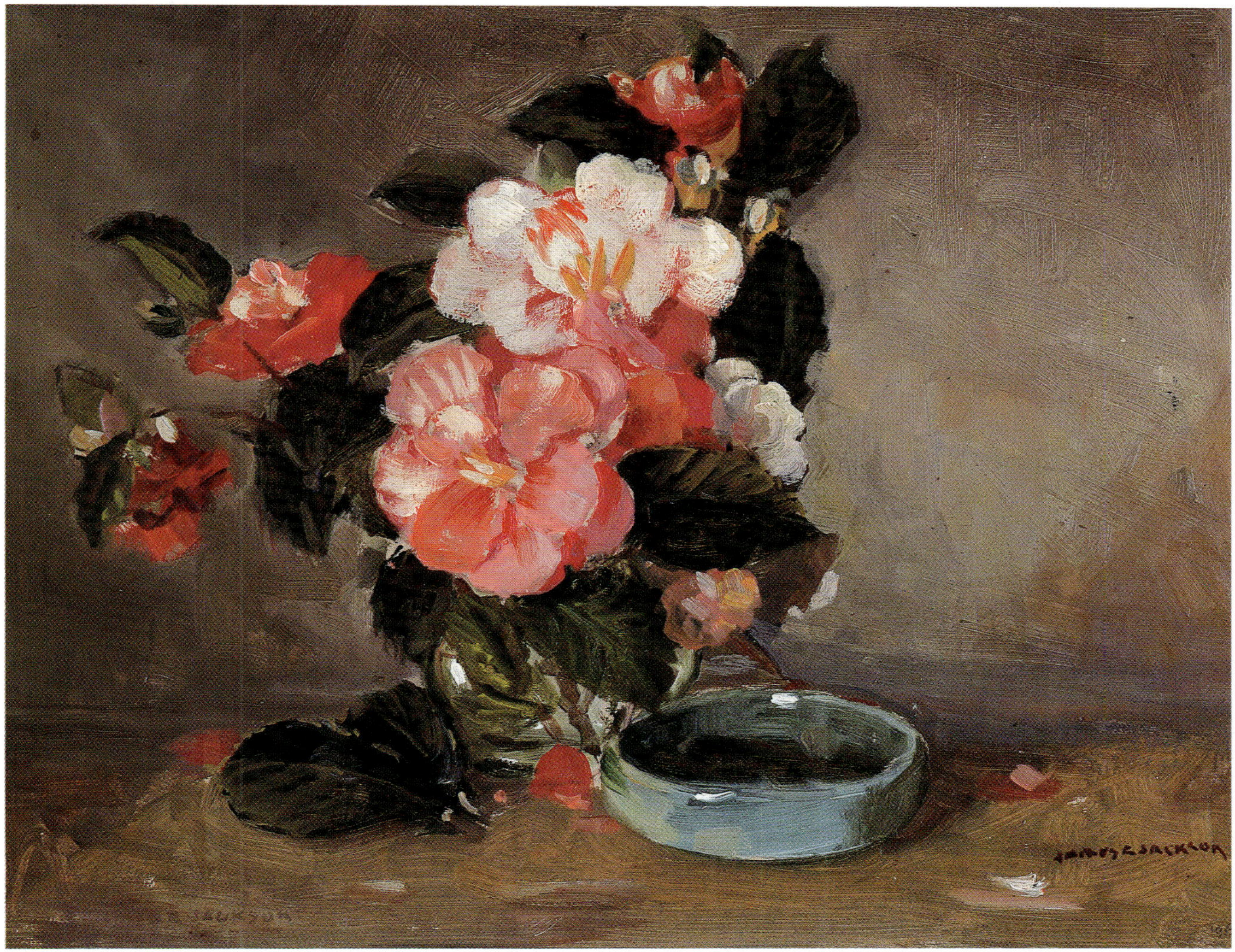

80　**CAMELLIAS**　1960 30 x 40.5 cm
Private Collection

red spurts of blood, he wondered why anyone would waste their paints, let alone hang them. However, he did like the new generation of artists such as Fred Williams, who could draw and who had good composition and colour sense.

When the old wooden Spit Bridge, described by some as the 'ugliest bridge in the world', was replaced by another in 1958, Jimmy rarely painted around the Spit. He loved this old bridge with its memories, its secret fishing places above the weed-covered pylons and its windy walkway. However, when old habits made him return, foreground trees partially concealed the new cement structure, which rarely featured in his new compositions. His views of the Spit painted after this time generally lack depth and quality of painting, being too sketchy, with too much emphasis on unusually large sailing boats in water showing little variation in colour. However, he maintained his interest in the land masses,

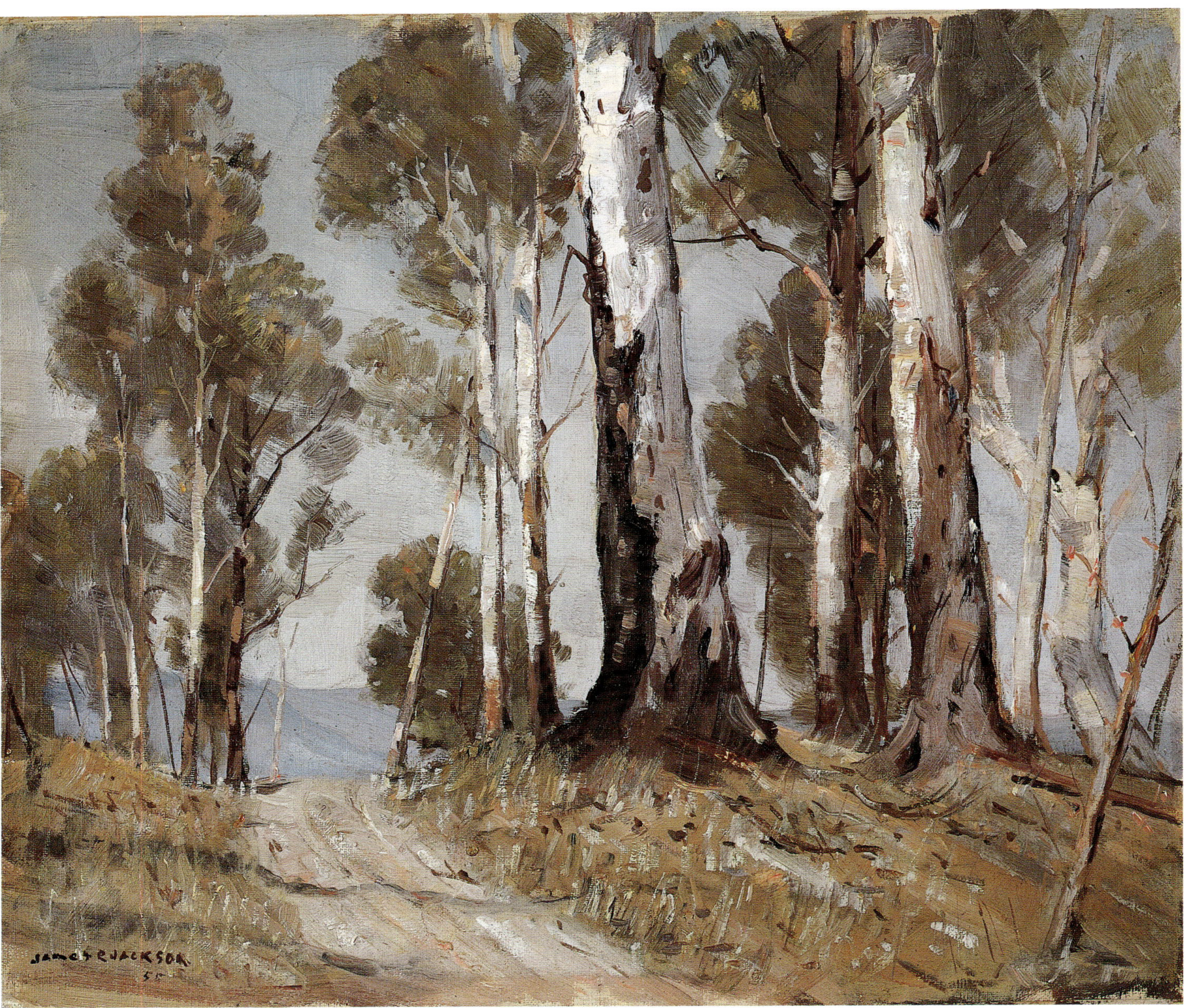

81   THE ROAD TO THE VALLEY 1955 36 x 43 cm
Private Collection

the quarry and the development of the park. At the turn of the century, he had painted a struggling sapling in the tidal sandy spit before it was developed. For years it was the only shade and point of interest in the reclaimed park, so in his pictures its growth is faithfully recorded over the decades. It is still there, now a mature Port Jackson fig surrounded by tall planted pines.

In 1958 his painting *Australian Bushland* was presented by the State Government to Her Majesty Queen Elizabeth, the Queen Mother, and is in her private collection. In this picture, a suggested pathway winds through sunlit gums and through breaks in shadowy stands of trees; a distant pasture and hill is seen. One of his landscapes was presented to the Malaysian Government by the Prime Minister, Mr Menzies, the following year. James again visited the inland. Having painted in the Rockhampton area, he flew to Central Australia and this trip is reflected in colourful ant hill pictures and in a series of monochrome drawings of Aborigines in the Tennant Creek area. In May 1959 he held a smaller one-man exhibition of twenty-five pictures at the Moreton Galleries, Brisbane. These pictures included many vistas of the far North Coast of New South Wales, as well as Sydney Harbour.

Although nearing eighty, he travelled extensively by himself in 1960 and 1961, painting around the Ovens River, Victoria, and along the Murray Valley. These are large open landscapes, some with

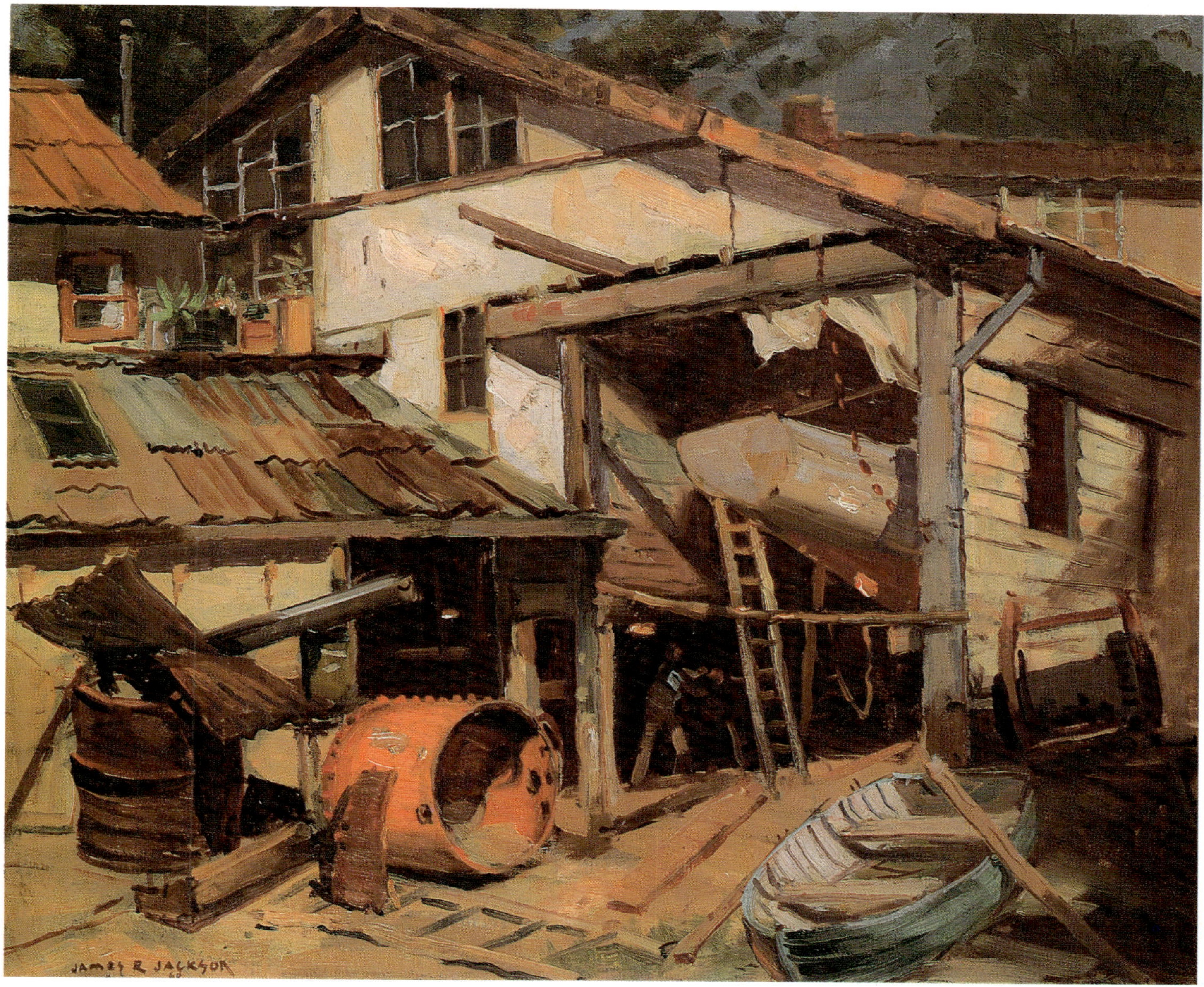

82 BOAT BUILDERS SHED 1960 46 x 56 cm
Private Collection

backgrounds of distant mountains, reflecting a dry inland with sheep and cattle watering at sandy rivers. In 1962 he won the Grafton Art Prize with his *Murray Valley*, and also the Manly Art Prize with his *Murray Valley at Jingellic*. In this, the ochre Jingellic hills near the source of the Murray River supplied a strong and harmonious background for his river reflections. Both pictures were painted on this trip and their style is reminiscent of his late 1930s period. They are evidence of his happiness with the country and his life.

Jimmy frequented art auctions around this time as he had become interested in his prices, especially those of the earlier works. He would often buy back his old works and reappraise them — and at times alter them. Pictures which he bought back were partly repainted and some, if not up to standard, were destroyed. Others he might cut down to alter the proportions. *Morning in the Studio*, which was painted in 1915, illustrated in *Art in Australia*, and purchased by the Australian National Gallery in the 1960s, is typical of this. Jimmy cut it down and slightly repainted the girl's hair. He resold these and recent works at his frequent exhibitions, presenting a mixture of his new and older styles. He also increased the number of pictures he sent to Lawsons Art Auctions.

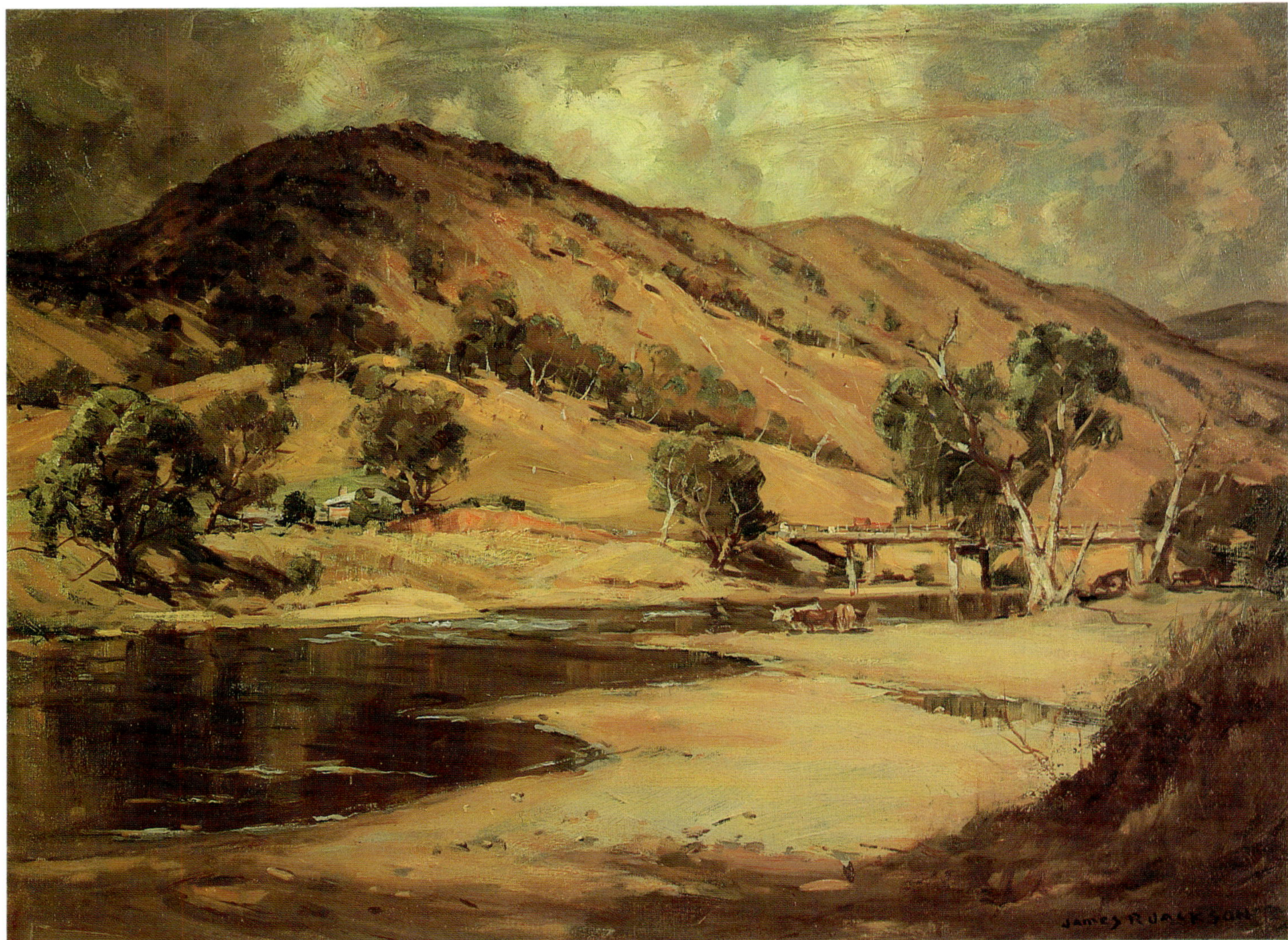

83   MURRAY VALLEY — NEAR JINGELLIC 1961 Oil on canvas 56 x 76.4 cm
From the Collection of the Manly Art Gallery and Museum, N.S.W.

There are many stories of Jimmy sending in wet pictures; fortunately the paint dried before they were displayed at viewings. On one occasion the auctioneer realised that Jimmy had forgotten to sign one of his recent harbour views but was unable to contact him before viewing day. Just an hour before the public entered, James raced in with his paintbox and signed it, hoping that no-one would finger the newly written signature.

There are a few stories about him in his failing years. When, for example, he found one of his old pictures at an auction viewing which he considered was 'not up to scratch', he returned with his box and tried to touch it up or repaint it. Luckily, the auctioneers at Lawsons, Christies or Joels did not appreciate wet paint on the viewing walls.

Colour prints of some of his works were now reproduced on Christmas cards. These pictures were nicely represented and depicted his recent landscapes with the interest in old sheds and boats. In the 1930s many of his major works, such as his large canvases of *Stanwell Park*, *Mosman Bay* and landscapes of the Australian Capital Territory were photographed in colour, framed and sold at various outlets. As he was never entirely happy with the accuracy of the colour prints, he had not permitted reproductions for many years as he considered prewar colour printing too variable. He wrote to me on one of his new Christmas cards, which had on its frontispiece a reproduction of his painting *Narrabeen Boatshed*, 'I will soon be leaving the old studio, hard luck, it's very difficult to find another'. In 1962 he moved his studio for the last time to a flat over a butcher's shop in an old building in Blues Point

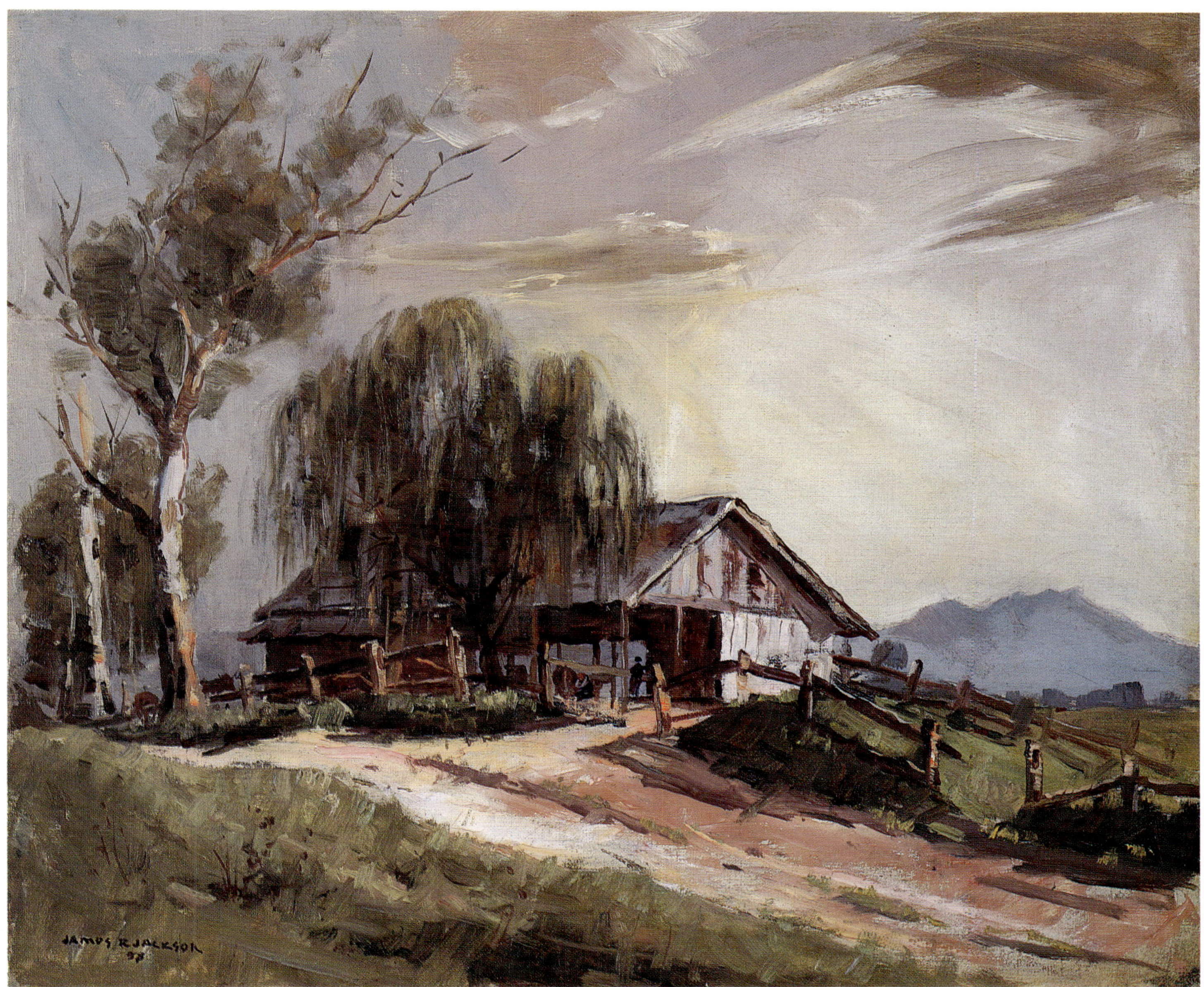

84   THE OLD COW SHED 1958 43 x 54 cm
Private Collection

Road, North Sydney. The noise of meat preparation early in the morning did not worry him as he was up as usual at daybreak.

Although he was not painting as much, his works were still being sought by corporations and banks to hang in their art collections and as gifts. As far back as 1929, the Royal Art Society profile mentioned that the late Lord Northcliffe and Sir Sam Fay purchased paintings by James R. Jackson for London collectors. His pictures were now spread worldwide in clubs and collections and Jimmy was represented in major art galleries and in most private art collections in Australia. Larger Australian collections in which his works were included are the Andrew, Cato, Ledger, Sheumack and Trout. In November 1963 the Art Gallery of New South Wales held an Exhibition to Mark the 175th Anniversary of the Founding of Australia, and he was represented by his 1920 *Morning, Middle Harbour*.

When he was eighty-four, the Royal Art Society made James an Honorary Life Vice-President. He was still, as he said, 'going strong', and he organised and held another one-man exhibition of thirty-six paintings in September 1966, at the Block Galleries in Melbourne. The foreword in the catalogue of this exhibition was written by Rubery Bennett, who commented that Jimmy's *Hills of Sofala* (NSW) had been recently purchased for the Texas National Art Gallery. Most of these exhibited works at the

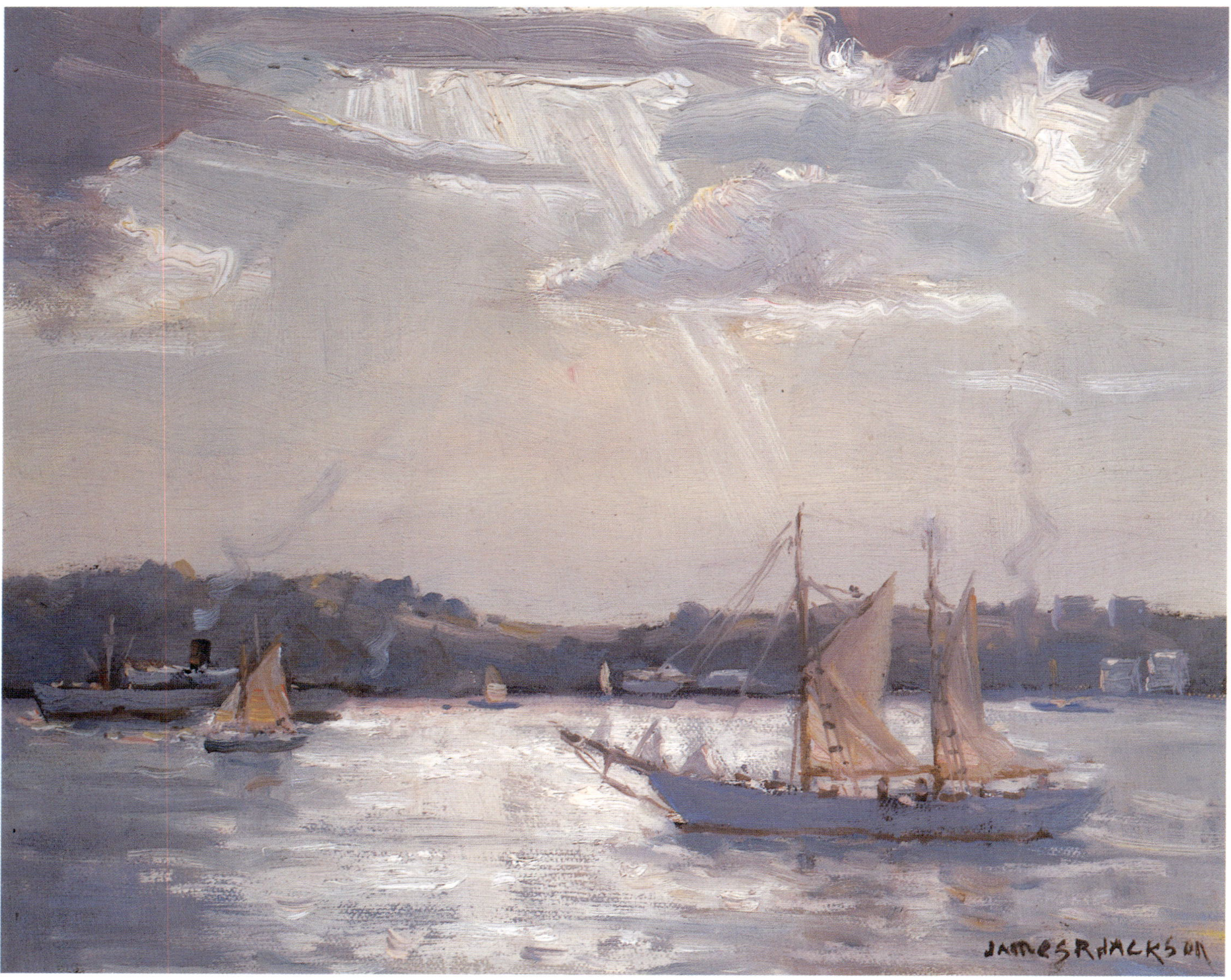

85   **EVENING SKY, BERRY'S BAY, SYDNEY** 1966 22 x 28 cm
Private Collection

Block Gallery were recent, but he also exhibited one of his very early portrait studies, *Halcyon Days*, which he had apparently recently acquired at auction. His prices had again markedly increased and he asked 500 guineas for *Peaceful Day*.

In reply to a Biography of Artist request by the New England Regional Art Museum in 1968, Jimmy wrote in a fairly steady hand, 'I try to paint things as they are, with my own outlook and expression'. After this, from his late eighties, he suffered several collapses, transient ischaemic attacks, which left minor effects on his fine coordination and his memory. He would not admit this and became very upset if it was suggested that he was not painting as well as usual, saying 'I'm painting better than ever'. So he continued to paint, and held his second last one-man exhibition (1968) at the Block Gallery, Melbourne. Most of these paintings which were all of paintbox size or smaller, depicted his recent trips. Some lacked his usual vitality and fine drawing skills and were not of his usual high standard but others were typically representative.

Visits and car trips with friends to the country were still enjoyed by him and he travelled well. When I took him to Narrabri in the north-west of New South Wales in 1969, he painted the beauties of the Namoi River and the Mount Kaputar mountain range with renewed vigour and was quite content to be left alone all day near his painting site. After again touring and painting the Bathurst and Bega areas,

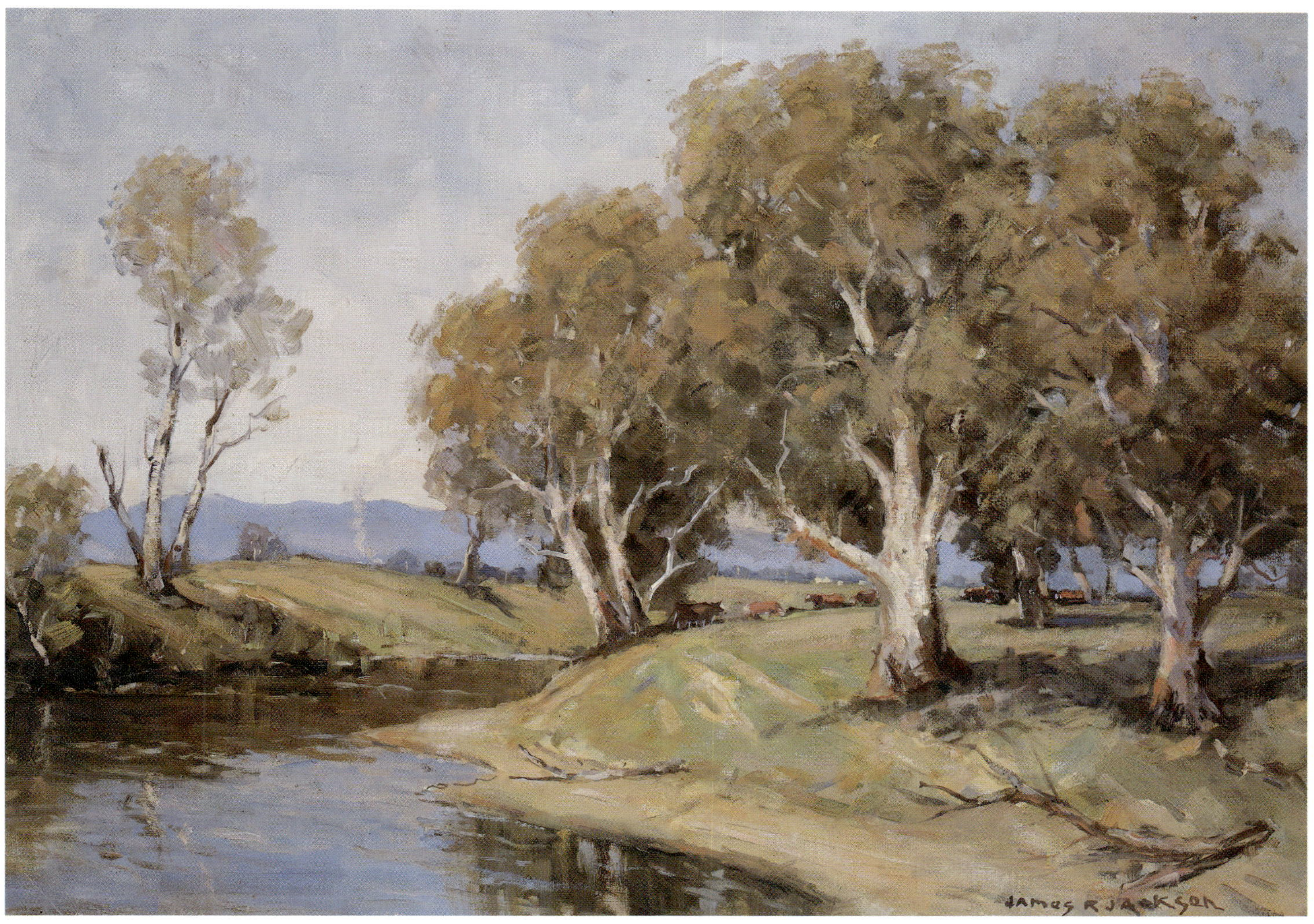

86   NAMOI RIVER, NARRABRI, N.S.W. 45 x 65.5 cm
Private Collection

he exhibited some of these pictures in July 1972 at his last one-man exhibition, held at the Block Galleries in Melbourne.

Mounting an art exhibition is hard physical work. Frames have to be selected, pictures tacked onto stretchers, nailed into frames and papered at the back. Eye hooks have to be screwed in, then joined by the hanging attachment. All have to be labelled, numbered, packed carefully and transported. The mental pressures of time restraint, cataloguing, pricing and hanging the exhibition are enormous, yet at the age of ninety, Jimmy was still exhibiting and doing so by himself. He had said some years earlier: 'You've got to analyse your work, and there's no other critic to tell you exactly what's wrong, so you have to be your own critic and creator at the same time, which is very difficult.'

At this age, he still painted the main harbour out-of-doors and produced many large canvases. These were painted from the north side, and looked to a distant city across striking light effects on the water, which he still loved to paint. Some show a return to his earlier painting qualities, and all demonstrate his continued fascination with light, harbour development and its activities. His background was now the highlighted, curved shells of the Opera House against the silhouette of a tall city. The unchanging bridge looked the same as it had when it was built forty years before. Jimmy reverted to his earlier custom of dating most of his pictures. In the early part of his career he dated nearly every canvas, but from the 1920s he was not consistent with his dating and his motivation for doing so at irregular intervals after that was uncertain.

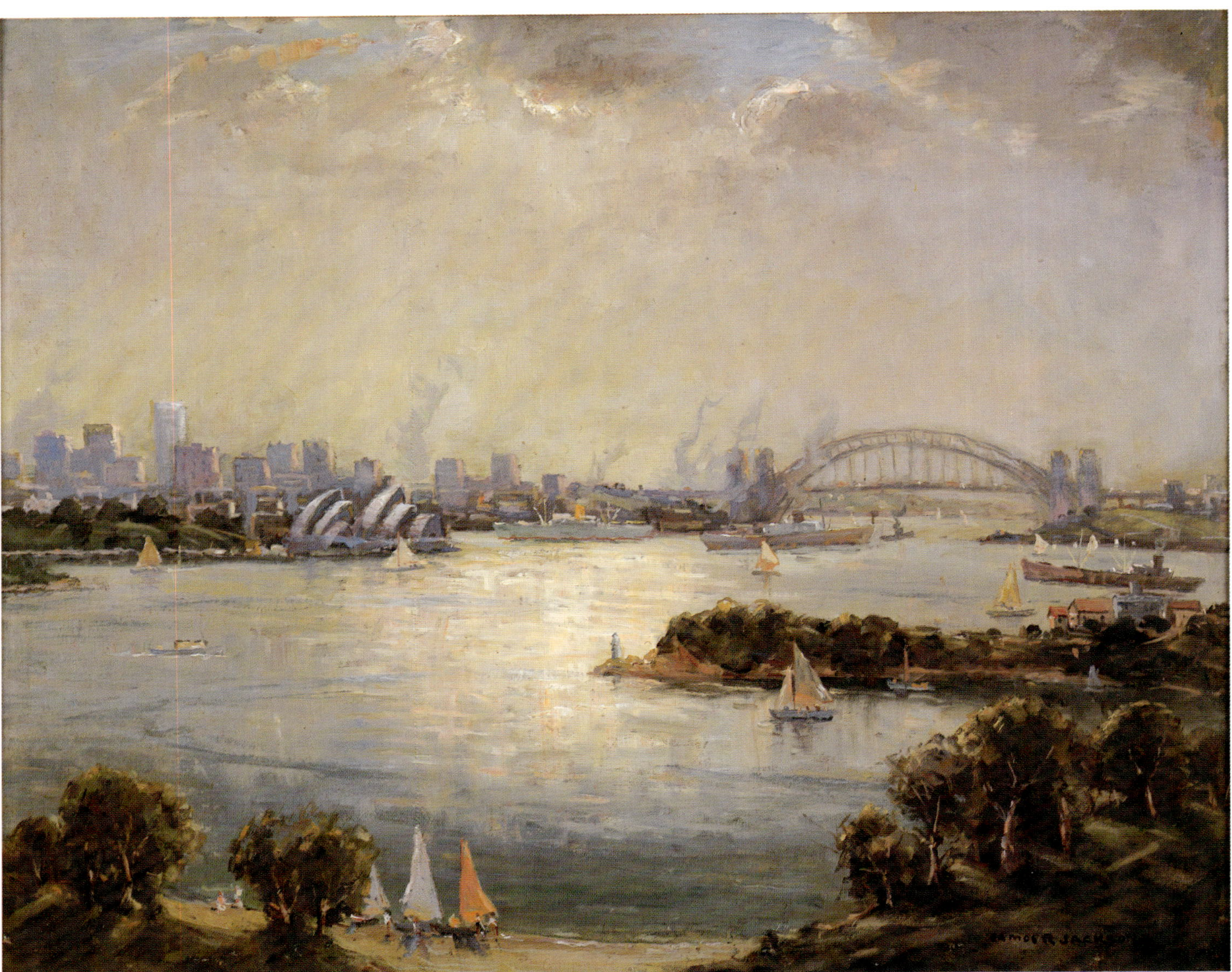

87   **SYDNEY HARBOUR** 1971 68 x 89 cm
Private Collection

In September 1973 Jimmy's right hand was injured in a traffic accident with a bus. His picture, taken in his studio, featured on the front page of the *Sydney Morning Herald* with the dramatic heading 'Painting days may be over'. At the interview James said, 'The bus knocked me flying off my feet and crushed my right hand up against the paintbox I was carrying'. At a following auction, the auctioneer commented on this and Jimmy's statement that 'If I can't paint, there's nothing left'. The price of a 'Jackson' increased with each reference.

For several years prior to his accident, Jimmy had exhibited only two or three pictures at the Royal Art Society's Annual exhibition, and of these, most were his older works. Although his hand recovered following the accident, his general health gradually deteriorated and his colour vision, especially for reds, began to fail. His eyesight until then had been good, but he now realised his limitations and 1974 was the last time that he exhibited with the Royal Art Society. He showed one of his favourite pictures which he kept in his studio and which was never for sale. This was *The Two Up School*, a figure study of men gambling at the notorious 'Thomo's', which he had painted during the war. It had hung on his studio wall ever since. Little Jimmy, as he was now affectionately called, was still to be seen carrying his box and sketching around North Sydney and fishing at Blues Point in the evenings. His pictures at this stage were very sketchy, and pink predominates in his foreground, headlands and sky.

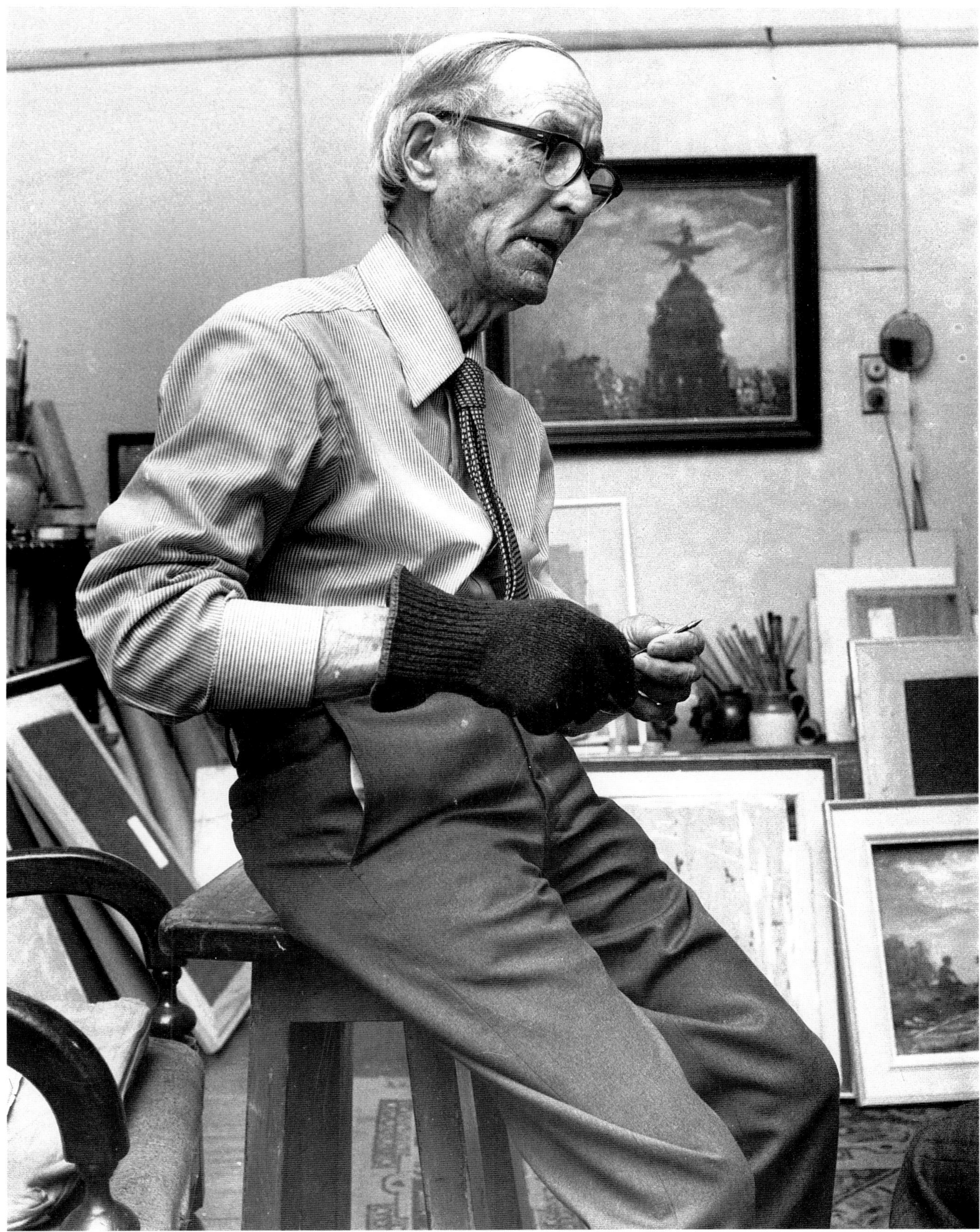

88   Photo of Jimmy 1973
Credit: Ian Macrae, John Fairfax Group

He still lived by himself at his studio, where he continued to refuse any domestic help or assistance. He said, 'People move things when they clean up, and I can't find them'. He continued to entertain his friends over a bottle of sherry at his studio, where many long talks were held. On other days he visited the homes of friends where he frequently stayed. Fred Jones, art collector and one of his old mates wrote: 'Jimmy Jackson was a delightful character and a great artist. He was a graciously humble gentleman able to open his heart and share his hospitality so easily. His interpretation of clouds and sunset effects was remarkable. He truly enjoyed an appreciation of beauty in sunlight and nature.'

Jimmy retained his independence and his happiness in painting until he suffered a stroke and died in 1975 on 9 September at the age of ninety-three years. As he had lived much longer than many of his contemporaries, we expected only a small funeral, but the chapel overflowed with his friends, colleagues and people interested in art who had come to farewell a gifted friend. It was pleasing to note their affection for him.

Jimmy once told me that his decision as a young man to become an artist and study overseas was very hard, but the most difficult thing was to keep working for perfection while enduring the hardships of his profession, knowing that there was no reward for a painter who fails. He travelled widely, experienced a very full and active life and succeeded in his chosen career. His life's journey is reflected in the variety of his paintings, which will be enjoyed by many generations. Art was his life.

List of plates

1   JAMES'S CREWING BOAT 1901 23 x 30 cm
Private Collection

2   THE SPIT, MIDDLE HARBOUR N.S.W. 1905
39.5 x 49.5 cm Private Collection

3   FISHING BOATS, VENICE 1907 44.5 x 54.5 cm
Private Collection

4   S. SIMEONE PICCOLO, VENICE 1907 60 x 49 cm
Private Collection

5   TOLEDO BRIDGE, SPAIN 1907 39.5 x 49 cm
Private Collection

6   PASSEO POLLENZA, SPAIN 1907 Oil on canvas on
cardboard 45.3 x 37.4 cm New England Regional Art
Museum, N.S.W.

7   CANAL BRESCON, MARTIGUES, FRANCE
1907 39.2 x 48.7 cm From the Collection of the Benalla
Art Gallery, Victoria

8   CHINAMAN'S BEACH, MIDDLE HARBOUR,
N.S.W. 1909 Oil on canvas 51 x 68.5 cm New England
Regional Art Museum, Armidale, N.S.W.

9   WATTAMOLLA BEACH NATIONAL PARK,
N.S.W. 1909 Oil on canvas 51 x 69 cm New England
Regional Art Museum, Armidale, N.S.W.

10   AUTUMN AFTERNOON, MIDDLE
HARBOUR, N.S.W. 1909 105 x 134 cm Private
Collection

11   BERRY'S BAY, SYDNEY HARBOUR 1910
60 x 60 cm Private Collection

12   CHARCOAL DRAWING OF HIS BROTHER
c 1910 29 x 26 cm Private Collection

13   SAILING c 1912 39 x 29 cm Private Collection

14   BRADLEYS HEAD, SYDNEY HARBOUR
c 1912 39 x 60 cm Private Collection

15   'OLEANDERS' 1914 Oil on canvas 151 x 113 cm
Purchased 1914 Art Gallery of New South Wales

16   'SPRING' 1915 Oil on plywood 40.7 x 30.5 cm
Dr & Mrs S. Gillies Bequest 1952 Art Gallery of
New South Wales

17   SAND DUNES 1915 30 x 40 cm Private Collection

18   THE DREAMER 1916 Oil on canvas 74.2 x 101 cm
Purchased 1916 Art Gallery of New South Wales

19   'THE HOLIDAY' 1916 Oil on cardboard
45.4 x 51.2 cm Purchased 1916 Art Gallery of
New South Wales

20   LADY WITH PARASOL 1914 Oil on plywood
39.4 x 29.5 cm Reproduced by permission of the
Australian National Gallery, Canberra

21   REFLECTIONS 1916 31 x 38.5 cm From the
collection of the Castlemaine Art Gallery, Victoria

22   DORA WITH PARASOL 1917 52 x 45 cm
Private Collection

23   James Painting at Taylor Bay, Sydney c 1918

24   MORNING IN THE STUDIO 1915 Oil on canvas
81.5 x 66.5 cm Reproduced by permission of the
Australian National Gallery, Canberra

25   DRYING SAILS, STOCKTON, N.S.W. c 1918
43.6 x 53.8 cm From the collection of the Benalla Art
Gallery, Victoria

26   AFTER THE REHEARSAL 1917 Oil on canvas
56.4 x 59 cm Art Gallery of South Australia, Adelaide

27   PICNIC AT TERRIGAL 1919 40 x 50.3 cm
Private Collection

28   FARM ON THE HILL 1919 30.5 x 40 cm
Private Collection

29   THE BATHERS 1920 60 x 60 cm Private Collection

30   DARLING HARBOUR, SYDNEY 1919
44 x 54 cm Private Collection

31   MORNING MIDDLE HARBOUR, SYDNEY 1920
Oil on canvas on cardboard 45.4 x 56 cm Purchased 1920
Art Gallery of New South Wales

32   A SYLVAN RETREAT 1921 112 x 102 cm
Private Collection

33   PATHWAY TO THE SEA 1917 19 x 25 cm From
the collection of the Tamworth Art Gallery,
New South Wales

34   ENTRANCE TO MIDDLE HARBOUR,
SYDNEY 1922 31 x 61 cm Private Collection

35   'DAWN' 1924 Oil on canvas 98.5 x 72.5 cm
Acquired 1924 Art Gallery of New South Wales

36   MIDDLE HARBOUR FROM MANLY
HEIGHTS, N.S.W. 1923 Oil on canvas 77 x 92.3 cm
From the collection of the Manly Art Gallery and Museum

37   SUMMER PASTORAL ACT 1925 61 x 64 cm
Private Collection

38   THE VALLEY OF THARWA, MURRUMBIDGEE
1925 Oil on canvas 63.5 x 81.8 cm Felton Bequest 1926
Reproduced by permission of the National Gallery of
Victoria, Melbourne

39   TAYLOR'S BAY, SYDNEY HARBOUR 1926
43 x 64 cm Private Collection

40   TORBOLE, LAKE GARDA, ITALY 1927
61 x 83 cm Private Collection

41   VENETIAN FISHING BOATS, ITALY 1927
Private Collection

42   OLD CITY, BALEARIC ISLAND 1928
22 x 40 cm Private Collection

43   FISHING, SYDNEY HARBOUR 1928 42 x 51 cm
Private Collection

44   BRIDGE AT CHIOGGIA, VENICE 1907 Oil on
canvas 49.5 x 69.5 cm Felton Bequest 1928
Reproduced by permission of the National Gallery of
Victoria, Melbourne

45   AFTERNOON NEAR MANLY, N.S.W. 1929
28 x 39 cm Private Collection

46   James and fellow artists at Royal Arts Society. (James
centre with hat)

47   THE OLD SPIT BRIDGE, MIDDLE HARBOUR,
N.S.W. 1930 71 x 92 cm The View from James's Studio
Private Collection

48   James with family camping at Peel River N.S.W.
1931

49   VALLEY OF THE MOGRANI, GLOUCESTER,
N.S.W. 1931 64.8 x 95 cm Reproduced by permission
from the Collection of the Queensland Art Gallery,
Brisbane

50   NARRABEEN LAKE, N.S.W. 1929 36 x 46 cm
Private Collection

51   STILL LIFE 1933 50 x 60 cm Private Collection

52   STANWELL PARK, N.S.W. 1934 64.5 x 94 cm
Private Collection

53   BALMORAL, SYDNEY 1934 65 x 85 cm
Private Collection

54   'THE OLD ROAD SOUTH COAST' 1934 Oil on
canvas 66.5 x 96.3 cm Purchased 1934
Art Gallery of New South Wales

55   CANNA   1936 55 x 44.5 cm Private Collection

56   HARBOUR FROM SEAFORTH c 1933 Oil on
canvas 61.3 x 71.3 cm Felton Bequest 1936
Reproduced by permission of the National Gallery of
Victoria, Melbourne

57   OLD ROAD TO MANLY, N.S.W. 1936
44.5 x 54.5 cm Private Collection

58   'DRYING SAILS', THE SPIT, N.S.W. 1935
Oil on canvas 46 x 54.7 cm Purchased 1935
Art Gallery of New South Wales

59   NORTH HARBOUR, SYDNEY 1936 Oil on
canvas 40.3 x 50.7 cm New England Regional Art
Museum, Armidale, N.S.W.

60   THE SPIT, MIDDLE HARBOUR, SYDNEY 1938
48 x 60 cm Private Collection

61   DUGONG NEAR YASS, N.S.W. 1937 36 x 55 cm
Private Collection

62   MURRUMBIDGEE CROSSING 1939 Oil on
canvas 81.5 x 96.5 cm Reproduced by permission of the
Australian National Gallery, Canberra

63   SYDNEY HARBOUR FROM NORTH SYDNEY
1939 47.5 x 76 cm Latrobe Valley Arts Centre

64   THOMO'S TWO UP SCHOOL 1942
39.5 x 50 cm Private Collection

65   TAMWORTH LANDSCAPE, N.S.W. 1944
102 x 108 cm Private Collection

66   'THE VIADUCT SODWALLS', N.S.W. 1945 Oil
on canvas 66 x 81.3 cm Marshall Bequest Fund 1945
Art Gallery of New South Wales

67   EVENING LIGHT, MORNINGTON PIER,
VICTORIA 1946 50.7 x 61.1 cm From the collection of
the City of Hamilton Art Gallery, Victoria

68   WESTERN PORT, VICTORIA 1946
22.2 x 68 cm Private Collection

69   THE RETURN 1948 45.4 x 76.2 cm
Private Collection

70   James showing his nocturne 'Luna Park' winner of
W.D. & H.O. Wills Art Competition, 1961
Credit: John Fairfax Group

71   AUTUMN DAY, SYDNEY HARBOUR 1949
53.3 x 96.2 cm Reproduced by permission, from the
Collection of the Queensland Art Gallery, Brisbane

72   JACARANDA TREE 1949 44 x 55 cm
Private Collection

73   SYDNEY HARBOUR FROM GEORGES
HEIGHTS 1952 51 x 61 cm Private Collection

74   'SUNLIGHT SANDHILLS' 1953 Oil on canvas
40.3 x 60.3 cm Purchased 1953 Art Gallery of
New South Wales

75   PALM BEACH, N.S.W. 1951 37 x 45 cm
Private Collection

76   DRYING THE SAILS, SYDNEY HARBOUR
1954 26.5 x 57 cm Private Collection

77   WEDDING RECEPTION AT THE
WENTWORTH HOTEL, SYDNEY 1955 43 x 54 cm
Private Collection

78   BELLINGEN, N.S.W. 1957 59 x 75 cm
Private Collection

79   HOUSES, LAVENDER BAY, SYDNEY 1958
36 x 43 cm Private Collection

80   CAMELLIAS 1960 30 x 40.5 cm Private Collection

81   THE ROAD TO THE VALLEY 1955 36 x 43 cm
Private Collection

82   BOAT BUILDERS SHED 1960 46 x 56 cm
Private Collection

83   MURRAY VALLEY — NEAR JINGELLIC 1961
Oil on canvas 56 x 76.4 cm From the Collection of the
Manly Art Gallery and Museum, N.S.W.

84   THE OLD COW SHED 1958 43 x 54 cm
Private Collection

85   EVENING SKY, BERRY'S BAY, SYDNEY 1966
22 x 28 cm Private Collection

86   NAMOI RIVER, NARRABRI, N.S.W.
45 x 65.5 cm Private Collection

87   SYDNEY HARBOUR 1971 68 x 89 cm
Private Collection

88   Photo of Jimmy 1973 Credit: Ian Macrae, John Fairfax
Group

Exhibitions

One-man Exhibitions

1921	February	Art Salon, Sydney
1922	May	Decorative Galleries, Melbourne
1925	June	Anthony Hordern Gallery, Sydney
1926	May	New Gallery, Melbourne
1928	May	Macquarie Galleries, Sydney
1928	July	New Gallery, Melbourne
1936	May	Fine Arts Gallery, Melbourne
1937	June	David Jones Gallery, Sydney
1938	July	Sedon Galleries, Melbourne
1940	September	Sedon Galleries, Melbourne
1942	September	Sedon Galleries, Melbourne
1946	October	Sedon Galleries, Melbourne
1954	October	Moreton Galleries, Brisbane
1956	August	Sedon Galleries, Melbourne
1959	May	Moreton Galleries, Brisbane
1966	September	The Block Gallery, Melbourne
1970	?	The Block Gallery, Melbourne
1972	August	The Block Gallery, Melbourne

Group Exhibitions

1908 Royal Art Society, Sydney (ongoing to 1974)
1916 Australian Artists War Fund
1916 Australian Art Association (ongoing to 1933)
1918 Art Gallery of New South Wales Loan Exhibition
1918 Australian Arts Club Exhibition, Melbourne
1919 Australian Arts Club Exhibition, Sydney
1921 Australian Artists, Gayfield Shaw's Art Salon, Sydney
1921 Colour Notes and Sketches, Gayfield Shaw's Art Salon, Sydney
1922 Bertram Stevens Memorial, Sydney
1923 Gift Exhibition, Farmers' Gallery, Sydney
1923 Exhibition of Australian Art in London
1924 Empire Exhibition, Wembley, England
1925 Loan Exhibition, National Gallery of Victoria
1928 Exhibition of Oil Paintings, Water Colours and Etchings by English and Australian Artists, Anthony Hordern Gallery, Sydney
1929 Paintings of Sydney Harbour, Grosvenor Gallery, Sydney

1929 Royal Art Society's 50 years of Australian Art, Blaxland Galleries, Sydney
1934 Centenary Art Exhibition, National Gallery of Victoria
1937 Artists of the British Empire Overseas Exhibition, The Royal Institute Galleries, London
1937 Exposition Internationale, Paris, France
1937 Australian Academy of Art (ongoing to 1946)
1938 150 Years of Australian Art, Art Gallery of New South Wales
1938 Group of 15 Independent Artists (ongoing to 1945)
1941 Australian Art Touring North America
1947 Artists Past and Present, Sedon Galleries, Melbourne
1949 Work of 12 Artists, Sedon Galleries, Melbourne
1950 Artists Past and Present, Sedon Galleries, Melbourne
1956 Artists Past and Present, Sedon Galleries, Melbourne
1963 An exhibition to mark the 175th anniversary of the Founding of Australia, Art Gallery of New South Wales
Numerous Prize and charity exhibitions

Exhibits in Art Prize Exhibitions

Wynne	1920s–1950s
Archibald	1921, 1922
Canberra	1913
State Theatre Art Quest, Sydney	1929
George MacKay, Manly Warringah	1942
Royal Agricultural Society of New South Wales	1960
W. D. & H. O. Wills	1961
Shire & District Art prizes, including Manly & Grafton	1962

List of Prizes won in Exhibitions in New South Wales

Manly	1924
State Theatre	1929
George MacKay	1942
Royal Agricultural Society of New South Wales	1960
W. D & H. O. Wills	1961
Manly	1962
Grafton	1962